T0256240

Tabletop Game Accessibility

This foundational resource on the topic of tabletop game accessibility provides actionable guidelines on how to make games accessible for people with disabilities. This book contextualises this practical guidance within a philosophical framework of how the relatively abled can ethically address accessibility issues within game design.

This book helps readers to build understanding and empathy across the various categories of accessibility. Chapters on each category introduce 'the science', outline the game mechanics and games that show exemplar problems, relate these to the real-world situations that every player may encounter, and then discuss how to create maximally accessible games with reference to the accessibility guidelines and specific games that show 'best-in-class' examples of solutions.

This book will be of great interest to all professional tabletop and board game designers as well as digital game designers and designers of other physical products.

Dr Michael James Heron is docent in games at the School of Computer Science and Engineering in Gothenburg, Sweden, and program administrator for the Game Design and Technology program. He is the author of the blog Meeples Like Us, the largest and best systematic analysis of board game accessibility currently available: https://www. meeplelikeus.co.uk/

Tabletop Game Accessibility

Meeple Centred Design

Michael James Heron

CRC Press
Taylor & Francis Group
Boca Raton London New York

CRC Press is an imprint of the
Taylor & Francis Group, an **informa** business

First edition published 2024
by CRC Press
2385 NW Executive Center Drive, Suite 320, Boca Raton FL 33431

and by CRC Press
4 Park Square, Milton Park, Abingdon, Oxon, OX14 4RN

CRC Press is an imprint of Taylor & Francis Group, LLC

© 2024 Michael James Heron

Reasonable efforts have been made to publish reliable data and information, but the author and publisher cannot assume responsibility for the validity of all materials or the consequences of their use. The authors and publishers have attempted to trace the copyright holders of all material reproduced in this publication and apologize to copyright holders if permission to publish in this form has not been obtained. If any copyright material has not been acknowledged please write and let us know so we may rectify in any future reprint.

Except as permitted under U.S. Copyright Law, no part of this book may be reprinted, reproduced, transmitted, or utilized in any form by any electronic, mechanical, or other means, now known or hereafter invented, including photocopying, microfilming, and recording, or in any information storage or retrieval system, without written permission from the publishers.

For permission to photocopy or use material electronically from this work, access www.copyright.com or contact the Copyright Clearance Center, Inc. (CCC), 222 Rosewood Drive, Danvers, MA 01923, 978-750-8400. For works that are not available on CCC please contact mpkbookspermissions@tandf.co.uk

Trademark notice: Product or corporate names may be trademarks or registered trademarks and are used only for identification and explanation without intent to infringe.

ISBN: 9781032541471 (hbk)
ISBN: 9781032541594 (pbk)
ISBN: 9781003415435 (ebk)

DOI: 10.1201/9781003415435

Typeset in Times
by KnowledgeWorks Global Ltd.

Dedication

This book is dedicated to Pauline Belford, my Mrs Meeple, without whom this book literally could not have been written. There is no part of this work on which she hasn't had an impact. She has been a constant encouragement and support. No other person has been so pivotal to the insights offered herein. She is not only my life partner but also my best friend. I am lucky to have her, and I probably don't say that often enough. I include it here so she can read it any time she likes.

Contents

Acknowledgements

Mafalda Samuelsson-Gamboa is one of my most trusted friends and co-conspirators. She is not only the person I probably argue with most consistently in my life but also the one with whom I'm happiest to find myself disagreeing. 'Friends take their thoughts for a walk, not to a battlefield' as she says. Our thoughts certainly reach their step-goal on a regular basis. I am constantly delighted to have her as a friend – she keeps me, and the work I do, honest.

Thanks to my parents for being forever supportive of this work and of me specifically. I don't know if this is the life my mother would have chosen for me, but she seems happy about it regardless.

I also offer my humble thanks to the many people who have provided access to their thoughts and insights on accessibility over the years. So much wisdom has come my way through conversation – both face-to-face and through social media. So much encouragement during the many hard-times. Thanks especially to Mike Crabb, Andy Robertson, Melissa Rogerson, Carla Sousa, Paul Wake, Sam Illingsworth, and Ian Hamilton. Special thanks too to the organisers at Tabletop Scotland, especially David Wright, for our collaborations over the years. Also to David Wright for being the man who found me a copy of Chinatown of my very own. You probably couldn't guess how much fun he's been responsible for.

Ertay Shasko (who runs the Sightless Fun blog), @RedMeepleRyan on Twitter, Will and Sarah Reed, White Cane Gamer, Jennifer Kretchmer, Erin Hawley, and Bryan Chandler are tireless advocates for accessibility in the board game space, and they all have outlets of their own I would direct you to for further information and inspiration. When I started Meeple Like Us, there was virtually no-one else talking about accessibility in a systematic manner. That's changed over the years, to the point it's difficult for me to keep up. I acknowledge again Andy Robertson for the work he's been doing with the Family Gaming Database to integrate accessibility into its remit.

The Tabletop Accessibility Guidelines (TTAG) were not an individual effort. Somewhere in the region of 50 people – many with embodied experience of disability – have contributed to the wiki that collated thoughts and submissions to this project. Many of them are unfortunately now only usernames on a website, but I draw special attention to Ian Hamilton (again), Chris Backe, Will Reed, Michael Kielstra, Juho Hitunen, White Cane Gamer, Louise Watch, Alysa Thomas, EntroGames, Erin Hawley, John duBois, John Brieger, and ADR. Each of them contributed to early candidate guidelines for TTAG and informed the work that followed with discussion, review, and critique. Their help has been invaluable.

Much of the work of Meeple Like Us was funded by Patreon support. I am immensely thankful to those that – literally – put their money where their mouth is. I especially wish to thank those who were most generous with their support. Daniel Singer, John Philpot, Michael Yoel, Rebecca Strang, Christopher Gebhardt, James Naylor, Helen Jeffries, Claus Hetzer, Joshua Zemke, Lisa Maynard, Ashleigh Crosby, Ilan Muskat, Mark Willis, Sabina Lawrie, Adrian Schmidt, Ben Taylor, Vivienne Dunstan, Aditi,

Adam Reineke, Lee Birnie, Jacob Martin, 'Unlimited', Mark Higgs, Erin Bray, Mike Smith, Mike LaFlamme, Jennifer Burkhart, Adelle Frank, Malaraa, Andrew Keddie, Pablo, Jonathan, Brian Garthwaite, Per Lysberg, and John Bain. Your support – whether past or ongoing – has been remarkable. You bought the games that informed this work.

I excluded David Gardner from this list because even in a subset of 'most generous supporters' he is an especial outlier. David has long been a friend of mine and had no need to buy my affection – he gets that for free whenever he likes. I know for a fact that he has supported this work far, far in excess of his actual interest in the topic of board games.

Thanks to the proof readers of this work – Pauline (of course) but also Greg Bataard and Cátia Casimiro. Cátia too deserves a shout-out for approaching me at a board game convention to pitch a research collaboration that was so interesting I said 'yes' immediately. I hope you hear more from both of us as time goes by.

I offer thanks to those game companies that have generously provided review copies for this work. Asmodee Nordics and Asmodee more generally have been supportive of this project for a long time. Czech Games Edition and Hub Games too have offered review copies with startling enthusiasm. There are too many to individually name here, but I will especially shout out Janice Wren and Bez Shahriari for being indie game publishers who took accessibility seriously even when there were so many other calls on their time.

Thanks to those of my students who have indulged my fascination with this topic and even occasionally worked with me on exploring it. Hayley Reid and William Guillermo Munoz especially stand out here, but there have been so many others both at my own university and at other institutes.

Sincere thanks to Taylor & Francis editor Will Bateman, who gave much support and guidance through the construction of this book. Thank you, you rock.

Finally, phew, I want to thank the hundreds of thousands of people who have visited Meeple Like Us over the years. All it took some days to energise me was a burst of interest in an article I thought had gone unnoticed. I have corresponded via email with a lot of you, and many offered their own thoughts and insights into the work through comments and critique. I hope you've found the work as useful to yourselves as I found your corrections and reviews were to me.

I have undoubtedly missed many people in this list – it takes a village to write a book like this, and I'm an old man with only dim recollection of the past. If it's any consolation, I will remember your omission in the depths of some sleepless night and the fact of it will haunt me until the morning comes.

1

Introduction

There's an awkward truth at the heart of all investigations into game accessibility – tabletop or otherwise. It's that **inaccessibility** is where **fun** comes from. It is this fact that makes this topic what it is – simultaneously fascinating and impossible, alternately frustrating and transformational. And in this book, we're going to spend a couple of hundred pages wrestling with the implications.

That wresting is what's going to make it fun!

Before we get too deep into the weeds here though, let's wind this back to a different, more fundamental topic – why should you listen to a word I have to say about game accessibility?

Since 2016, I have been working on an informal research project I have termed **Meeple Centred Design**. We have User Centred Design as a usability principle, Player Centred Design for games, and Machine Centred Design for robots. Meeple Centred Design follows that template. Meeple (singular: Merson) are the ubiquitous stylised human-shaped board game pieces that you find in literally hundreds of board games. The word itself is a contraction of 'my people'. So, this book is about design centred on 'my people', which is to say, geeks and nerds who are into board games.

I'm a funny guy, you see. I say that to you in advance because I find people often don't notice unless I tell them.

The project began simply enough. I had been getting ever deeper into the wonderful variety of tabletop games that have been released over the past few decades. As I saw my board game pile become a board game shelf, and that board game shelf expand into board game bookcases, I felt a need to try and connect what was happening in my home to what I do in my job. And what I do in my job are 'games' and 'accessibility'. Well, I had the games ....

Back in 2011, I received my PhD from the University of Dundee. My thesis was focused on 'technology to assist an aging workforce'. Funded by IBM, it was about finding ways to lower the barrier of participation for older workers in society. Broadly, it was a PhD about accessibility – identifying obstacles that stood between someone and a goal they wanted to achieve and then eliminating or minimising those obstacles.

Don't worry, I'm going somewhere with this.

My work identified – or perhaps, corroborated – three issues associated with older adults working with new technology. Unless they grew up using that technology, I found that:

1. Most older adults whom I worked with didn't know that they could change the behaviour of a computer through configuration.

DOI: 10.1201/9781003415435-1

2. If they did know they **could** change behaviour, they often don't know **what** specific behaviour and **how** to change it.
3. If they did know what behaviour and how to change it, they often didn't because they worried they wouldn't be able to change it back.

What this means is a whole raft of accessibility solutions built into our everyday computer operating system went unused – whole decades of state-of-the-art usability improvements that never saw the light of day. That wasn't because the solutions didn't work but because the **people** didn't engage with them.

You can probably already see that this is a problem that has little to do with games. But I looked to games for the solution.

In 2001, Microsoft published a game called **Black and White**. Developed by Lionhead Studios, it was an evolution of the 'god sim' genre pioneered in 1989 by Peter Molyneux's **Populous**. **Black and White** expanded upon the formula by giving you – the god in training – a supernatural animal that you could teach through a system of positive and negative reinforcement. Pet it, and it would be more likely to do the thing that you just saw it do. Punish it, and it would be less likely to do that thing in the future. By observing your grand beast, you could gradually mould its behaviour so that it could be left to perform tasks autonomously. If you liked that it would occasionally stock up the village storeroom, you'd give it a little 'good girl!' pat. If you preferred to put the (literal) fear of God into your worshipers, then you'd scratch behind its ear as it chowed down on a mouthful of villagers.

And so, I found the solution – or at least, **a solution** – to the problem within the innovations of gaming. I built a replica system for a computer that stalked the user's behaviour across everything they did. If someone had difficulties double clicking, then your 'operating system animal' would change the double-click threshold and then present its change for judgement. If you liked what it did, it would be more likely to intervene in the future. If you didn't, it would be less likely. But it would keep checking and checking to see if the intervention was still needed until you eventually compelled it into silence or approval. Over time, this permitted for the user and operating system to come to an agreeable balance between usability and intervention. If you care about the details, you can check out the papers I published on the topic. You'll find them linked in the bibliography at the end of this chapter. You probably shouldn't though – this is back story, nothing more.

So, in **my** mind I had taken a fascinating game system and turned it into an accessibility aid. Over time, I've come to realise what I did was basically reinvent Microsoft's loathsome Clippy and give him power over the whole of your computer. 'Hi, it looks like you are having problems finding your mouse cursor!'

My point here though is that even when my work wasn't about games, I found a way to bring games into it. My entire professional life has been to create a trajectory that meant I worked with games, **and** accessibility, for a living. Any opportunity I had to explore the intersection of my professional interest (accessibility) and my personal hobby (gaming), I took. And thus we find ourselves here with this book, many years later.

As my board game collection expanded, my thoughts turned to the accessibility of these many boxes that had started to oust ever greater numbers of my books from my shelves. And I thought, as so many academics do, 'there's a paper here I think'.

I honestly thought I'd do an analysis of three or four games, write a paper that says 'This is an interesting problem domain for accessibility and someone – not me – should definitely look into it at some point'. I'd move on to other things. I expected to be done with this topic in a month ….

… and again we find ourselves years later and I'm still digging into this fascinating puzzle with all my fingers and my toes. It's fair to say, when this began, that I didn't really discover a new research interest. I found a new research **obsession.** It was all I spoke about, professionally, for years. I still talk about it as often, and as widely, as I can. There are few ways a student – one of my own or one somewhere else in the world that has just stumbled upon the work – can get my attention quicker than asking 'Can I talk to you about board game accessibility?'

As I started looking into these games, I began documenting the project on a website – Meeple Like Us (https://meeplelikeus.co.uk). I considered it little more than an ongoing log of research notes that others might find passingly interesting. Every time I analysed a game, I would write a review (to sharpen my own critical skills) and what I termed an **accessibility teardown.** The latter document was the meat of the work – I would systematically evaluate each game through various analytical perspectives and outline the accessibility issues and innovations that I had detected. Each game would be graded in each category, and those data points would represent a flag embedded as part of a growing exploration of the accessibility landscape. It was never really intended for 'other people'.

Over time though, other people made their way to the site. It became a regular recommendation for others when they encountered people seeking accessible games.

It's fair to say it is the largest and best systematic analysis of board game accessibility in the entire world. It's fair to say it only because it's pretty much the only one.

Or rather it's the only one that investigates so many different accessibility factors across so many different games. In the wake of Meeple Like Us, other sites with more specialist foci have emerged. In many cases, I will happily concede they offer much better insight than I have been able to provide. We'll come back to that later. When Meeple Like Us was launched though, there was no site like it. Discussions around the board game accessibility were scattered and often only incidental. Video game accessibility was in the ascendency as a topic, but board games had nothing equivalent in terms of critical mass.

All of this is a long-winded way to say – I hope you can trust me with my insights on the topic because they have been long-fought and hard won.

The Inaccessibility of Fun

That brings us back to the point I made at the start of this chapter. One of those insights is what makes this work so fascinating, so endlessly interesting, and so impossibly complex. It is this - there is a hard, unbreakable link between fun and inaccessibility. The first cannot exist without the second. This is, as far as I am aware, a unique problem in accessibility work.

That's … **challenging** when trying to improve the accessibility of games and it's going to take a whole book to unpack the implications. Good job we've got this one!

Let's simplify the problem a little because we have a lot of ground to cover and informal gaming discourse has made the terrain treacherous.

First of all, we'll begin with a definition. I've already outlined inaccessibility as 'an obstacle that stands between someone and a goal they want to perform'. From the perspective of the work I do, that obstacle can be almost anything. It can be linked to a physical difficulty – 'I cannot see this information', 'I cannot manipulate this token', and 'I cannot hear this signal'. It can also be linked to a sociological barrier – 'I do not see this as being a hobby for me' or 'I do not feel represented in the games I play'. It can also be economic – 'I cannot afford to buy this game'. It can be emotional … after all, we all know what it's like to play with a bad loser or an obnoxious winner. And it can be intersectional, made up of multiple different kinds of obstacle that come together in ways that create new, compound, difficulties.

This is **inaccessibility**, for the purposes of this book. And it's our job here as designers, publishers, analysts, and players to reduce that inaccessibility so that those goals becomes **accessible**. Or at least we work to ensure the inaccessibilities become impactful to fewer groups of people.

There is though another definition of accessibility that comes up in game discourse, and it makes it difficult for gamers to have a meaningful conversation because it muddies the ground. This is a kind of accessibility that is better described as 'approachability' or perhaps 'learnability'. Here there are no real obstacles – or rather, the obstacles are designed to be worn away over time through mastery of gameplay systems. We might consider here video games like **Dark Souls**, or **Cuphead**, or **Celeste**. These titles are intentionally highly difficult, designed to be punishing, with the mastery of gameplay being the solution to that difficulty. Thus, **Dark Souls** is often described as 'inaccessible' independent of the frame of definition we use for this book. The solutions proposed to this perceived inaccessibility are things like difficulty modes, which are often instantly dismissed as being fundamentally antithetical to the design of the games. This rejection is not without merit – **Dark Souls** would not be what it is unless it cleaved as tightly as it does to the 'mastery through persistence' model of design. I would agree with those that say **Bloodborne** would not be **Bloodborne** if there were an 'easy mode'. **Celeste** is both counter-example and supporting evidence. **Celeste** comes with many tremendously useful features for improving the accessibility (as **we** term it) of play. But the experience of play is radically different when they are employed.

This introduces an important wrinkle in our discussion … accessibility (in the sense **we** use it) may sometimes seem to come at the expense of the intended experience of the game. We can't have, as our goal, that 'a game must be fully accessible'. We will inevitably destroy that which we love in the process. **Scrabble** without the need for linguistic dexterity would not be **Scrabble**. **Snooker** without precise positioning would not be **Snooker**. We have to be careful with the surgery we perform on a design – precise with our incisions – because we are cutting around delicate tissue.

I'm going to do something ill-advised here to illustrate my point. I'm going to describe the game of **football** (or **soccer**, for those that have decided to use the name **football** to describe a sport in which you mostly *carry* a ball). It's ill-advised because I'm not a sports guy. I barely understand football. But it's an accessible (see what I did there?) frame of reference for most.

Imagine the genesis of the game, somewhere in eleventy BC. Let's imagine its inventor, Ugg. Ugg has had a great idea – it would be fun to kick a stone through a pair of other stones. Ugg places two stones to form a makeshift goal a couple of feet away, lines up a kick, and launches another stone, the 'ball', towards the target. Goooooaaaalll!

Ugg is flushed with success. Or … actually, no. Ugg is indifferent because that wasn't fun. It wasn't fun at all.

Ugg ponders the problem and decides on a solution – make the task more difficult. The goal is moved 30 feet away. And now Ugg has to manoeuvre the 'ball' along the ground. Kicking it from where it lies often results in a miss. Ugg kicks the ball from foot to foot to get closer to the goal before launching it on target!

Gooaa … ll. I guess?

Still not fun, so Ugg grabs a passing friend. Argh. Of the Lanarkshire Arghs.

'Stand in goal', Ugg says. 'And try to stop the stone from going past you'.

'What's a goal?', asks Argh.

They try again, and Ugg finds that it's a lot more fun! Ugg launches the stone, Argh tries to block. It sails past! GOOALL! Ugg looks like a champion! Argh looks like a chump! Ugg **could not be happier** with how the game went.

'That was great!', says Ugg.

'That was rubbish!', says Argh.

Argh has a much, much more difficult task than Ugg. Trying to stop a fast-moving stone from flying into a large goal is way harder than kicking the same stone into the goal. It's just not fair. So Argh recruits ten friends to help with the defence of the goal. Now Ugg has to manoeuvre the ball past ten defenders before he can score. Ugg makes the attempt. Ten defenders rush towards the lone striker ….

… later, when Ugg regains consciousness, a bleary eye is turned accusingly to Argh.

'That was great!', says Argh.

'That was rubbish!', says Ugg. Perhaps slurring the words a little because cave dwellers didn't have a great handle on what concussion was.

Argh installs a second goal behind Ugg. Ugg grabs ten friends. Argh protests. Each tries to bring in another person to adjudicate disputes, but they can't agree on whose friend should be allowed to make rulings. They employ a trader from another village instead. Ugg finds out the game is a lot easier if he starts biting people instead of kicking the stone, and so the adjudicator starts to punish players for violence. A culture starts to emerge where the rules and the rules **about** the rules grow, shift, and change in line with the experience people have of play. Observers gather around as the game evolves. At a certain point, with a certain layering of rules, procedures, and **interpretation** of rules and procedures … suddenly everyone is having **fun.** It's fun for the people playing. It's fun for the people watching. Ugg and Argh come together, proudly announcing to the crowd 'We have invented the game of **stone-kick**!'. Everyone cheers.

What we can see here in this little fable is the gradual introduction of **inaccessibility**. The accessible version of the game is 'launch a stone at a target', but it's not fun. It lacks challenge. It lacks opportunity for demonstrating mastery. There's no flush of success, no pain in failure. Every feature that is brought in to make the game more fun is an intentionally constructed inaccessibility. Football doesn't occur naturally in the world; it has to be invented. Every inaccessibility it contains was put there as part of its design.

All games are constructed from **intentional** inaccessibilities. To design them out of the experience is to destroy the fun.

The goal in any game is not to accomplish a simple task as easily as possible. It's to accomplish a set task in a way that is obscure and awkward but not so obscure and awkward that it is unpleasant to perform. We need to take a holistic view of this topic – a game is a balance between 'the things we need to do' and 'the things that stop us doing them'. All of those 'things that stop us doing them' are put there by a game designer.

But ….

Not all of those things were **intentionally** put there. This is where we find the flex in the dilemma. Our goal, from the perspective of making accessible games, is to identify the **unintentional** inaccessibilities and excise them from the design.

One of the additional issues that serves to separate game accessibility from accessibility as a general pursuit is the tricky concept of *verisimilitude* or to borrow Stephen Colbert's term, 'truthiness'. Some things just feel more authentic than others. Part of the process of building an emotional connection with a game comes from the ease with which you can just immerse yourself into play. That sometimes comes from sublimating the real as it becomes the virtual.

Hands up – how many of you have garages, attics, and/or bedroom cupboards full of plastic musical instruments you once bought to play **Guitar Hero** or **Rock Band**?

No, put your hand down. I can't see you.

There's a reason you bought those peripherals. It's easier to feel like Jimi Hendrix[1] when you are flailing away at a pretend guitar than it is when you're tapping buttons on a controller. Pulling the trigger on a gamepad to fire a bullet feels more **authentic** than press the return key. Turning a plastic steering wheel feels more immersive than relying on a thumbstick. Consider the lockpicking mechanisms in **Skyrim**, where you need to rotate thumbsticks to control the tension wrench versus the pick. It feels more like the real activity than 'press X to pick the lock' ever could. All mechanisms in a game are abstractions, but there is a benefit that comes from a clear abstraction that maps neatly onto the real world. A quality emerges sometimes from the specific way in which a game mechanism is triggered through a game control scheme. This is a truism that carries through to the tabletop.

This is a complicating factor unique to games because nobody cares if they choose a menu option to print or click a button with a printer icon. The experience of printing a document isn't meaningfully impacted by the interaction through which it is actioned. Sometimes an accessibility solution in a game comes at the cost of verisimilitude. We'll see this when we talk about the translucent, coloured dice that are used in **Sagrada** (2017) or the way in which board games often use paper money at the cost of usability. **Kitchen Rush** (2021) employs egg-timers to control pacing – very appropriate for a game about cooking, but it comes at an accessibility cost. To change a component can be to change the experience.

This is something that always needs to be taken into account when we talk about the route to achieving greater accessibility in games – digital **and** tabletop. The path needs to be navigated very carefully, and its exact shape will vary from game to game.

So, we're sorted right! We know what makes game accessibility difficult – we can now move on to how to actually fix our board games?

Not so fast, I'm afraid. We've only just dealt with the main complication in **game** accessibility. It's even more difficult for **board game** accessibility. Our job isn't just on hard mode. It's **nightmare** mode.

The Continual Reinvention of User Experience

I genuinely believe that accessibility in board games is the single most interesting usability problem domain that exists. It's a completely different beast from video game accessibility. Just as inaccessibility is bound up in fun, **complexity of inaccessibility** is an unavoidable side effect of what a board game **is**.

Within video game accessibility, we have some constants that make life easier. We know how to make accessible video games, by and large. I won't say it's a solved problem because we see every year that there is still work to do. But it is a **solvable** problem because we know the size and boundaries of the problem domain. A video game comes with a control scheme (keyboard/mouse, controller, motion control wand, whatever) and an output system (monitor, speakers, virtual reality [VR] headset – again, whatever). For a given system, 99% of the games that are played will use these interface features in the same way. The exact specifics of consequence will change from game to game, but you move a joystick, you click a button, and you look at a screen. 'The exact specifics' contain complexities, for sure. But at least you can make some assumptions and that allows for things like the Xbox Adaptive Controller, remappable control schemes, and all the genuinely great guidance to be found in the Game Accessibility Guidelines[2]. There is **consistency.**

We don't have that luxury with board games. Every single board game reinvents its interface anew. There might be shared features or informal conventions, but the innovation of a board game is often tied up in the novelty of its interface. Games may share a common component list (dice, tiles, cards, and tokens) and still have no commonality in how those components are used.

Tiny Epic Galaxies (Figure 1.1) uses a set of custom dice that are used as a currency for actions that may be taken in a round.

Archaeology – The New Expedition (Figure 1.2) has relatively standard cards – some played to the table and some held in hand.

FIGURE 1.1   Some of the pieces in Tiny Epic Galaxies. (Photograph by the author.)

FIGURE 1.2   A hand of cards in Archaeology: The New Expedition. (Photograph by the author.)

FIGURE 1.3   A pile of tokens for Race for the Galaxy. (Photograph by the author.)

Race for the Galaxy (Figure 1.3) has a fixed set of scoring tokens – you add these to the score attained by playing cards at the end and sum up to find your final point tally.

Catan (Figure 1.4) has a modular board made of tiles, where their relative fecundity is determined at setup with randomly assigned numbers.

Dice, cards, score tokens, and tiles. All used in one way to create the game interface. But …

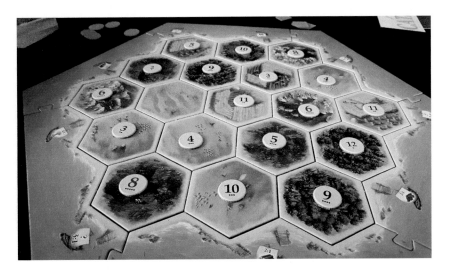

FIGURE 1.4 Catan, the board laid out for future exploitation. (Photograph by the author.)

FIGURE 1.5 Lords of Vegas. (Photograph by the author.)

Lords of Vegas (Figure 1.5) uses dice as area control as much as for generating random numbers. The ownership, value, and meaning of these dice (and the tiles in which they are embedded) will all change constantly through the course of the game.

Tigris and Euphrates (Figure 1.6) has chips for scoring just like Race for the Galaxy. But you don't add the points to your tally at the end – you get the points from the category of score in which you have the *smallest* number of chips. With **Race for the Galaxy**, you can just look at your chips and know what they mean. **Tigris and Euphrates** has

FIGURE 1.6   Some of the tokens in Tigris and Euphrates. (Photograph by the author.)

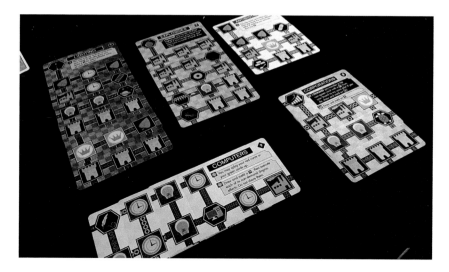

FIGURE 1.7   Cards in Innovation. (Photograph by the author.)

ownership of chips as a kind of elastic game mechanism of progress. The combination you hold will influence the way you play the game. You don't need to get 'more'; you need to get 'more of the one of which you have fewest'.

Innovation (Figure 1.7) makes use of cards, but the direction in which they are splayed (as in, how they are fanned out) has huge gameplay impact because it changes which symbols on which cards are visible and thus how many of those symbols you have access to in order to fund game actions. This splaying system is fun, and interesting, but certainly 'non-standard' as far as the use of cards in games goes.

FIGURE 1.8   Tiles in Hive. (Photograph by the author.)

Hive (Figure 1.8) shares features with Catan in that it has a modular board made of tiles. However, this board will shift and move, slithering across the table in response to the decisions taken by each player. Its size, shape, and configuration are all going to evolve over play like insects crawling over each other in a … well, a hive. **Catan's** board is fixed. Hive's board is forever shifting.

Dice, cards, score tokens, and tiles. Each game uses them differently, and it is in this variety of experience and utility that we find the joy – and difficulty – in tabletop gaming. Games exist that use egg-timers (such as **Kitchen Rush**) and that make use of scratch-and-sniff cards (**the Perfumer**). There are games that use marbles (**Gizmos** and **Potion Explosion**), games with meeples that you place on boards (**Village**), and games with meeples you balance on top of other meeples (**Meeple Circus**). There is no end to the way in which games will vary the way you use their components. Within board game accessibility, we can't even rely on the anchor of how a game interface works.

The Cult of the New

One thing you will undoubtedly notice as we go through this book is that I seem to be taking pot-shots at a lot of old games, games with designers that couldn't possibly have known better, and games from the early oughts or the 90s. Each game we talk about is cited with its first publication date. That may give an impression that the scholarship of this book, such as it is, may be overly focused on antique insights. The truth is that old games haunt the present like ghosts. Fun, exciting, and interesting ghosts … but ghosts nonetheless.

All of the games discussed during this book were commercially viable within at least the last five years. Many are still available, in the editions in which I reviewed them, right now. When they are not, I have confined my comments only to those elements that remained unchanged between editions. Our investigation has to be broad – the 'cult of the new' may be overpowering within the hobby, but it is in the more established games that we tend to see staying power.

One of the many factors that differentiates board gaming from video gaming is the extent to which board games hold their value. This is true when it comes to the second-hand market and when it comes to cultural relevance. **Catan** (1995) was still the third best-selling hobbyist game in 2022[3]. **Ticket to Ride** (2004) was the fifth best-selling game. For context, the video game **Command and Conquer** was released in 1995, the same year as **Catan**. When was the last time you saw **that** trending on Twitch?

Pandemic (2008), **Carcassonne** (2000), **Codenames** (2015), **Splendor** (2014), **Dominion** (2008), and many others continue to sell in large quantities many years after their release. It's pretty obvious why tabletop games can demonstrate this degree of persistence – they don't suffer from platform incompatibilities or require out-of-date technology. If you try to play **Wing Commander** (1997) on modern hardware, you'll find that it runs hundreds of times faster than it did at the time of release. The speed of the game loop was tied to the speed of the central processing unit (CPU). Board games are cardboard computers, and all their hardware architecture comes preinstalled in the box.

Even if the games discussed in this book weren't commercially relevant, and by and large they are, they are not selected on the basis of being 'the games we need to fix'. They are chosen instead because they stand in for a class of recurring accessibility problem. They encode common anti-patterns of inclusion, of a sort. The issues they encapsulate resurface, again and again. Luckily, the solutions remain stable. The games are selected because of their relevance, not because of their recency. The games selected are not necessarily picked for being the most egregious or even most notable. They are the ones that can stand in for many: Archetypes, of a sort. For any example given, there are a dozen others available.

Roll for Initiative

So, let's start bringing all this together. Here's a restatement of our problem:

1. Inaccessibility is where fun comes from.
2. There is no such thing as a consistent board game interface.

There is though no reason to be gloomy! You've got this book. I've got you, fam, as I believe the kids say and, I assume, always will.

By focusing our attention on unintentional inaccessibility, we'll find that almost every game can be meaningfully **more** accessible than it was before. It's certainly true that fun comes from inaccessibility. It does not follow though that inaccessibility is in itself fun.

I'm not a believer in the principle that every game should be accessible to every person. That's because I don't believe every game **can** be accessible to every person. But I do believe most games can be **more accessible** with appropriate attention paid to their design and production. Every time a barrier is removed from a game, it adds a whole new demographic to the potential player base. The audience might get 10% bigger through just adding an icon to a card. It's sometimes **that easy.**

Perfect is the enemy of the good, and aiming for an impossible goal (all games, for all people) means that we will never get anywhere. We'll aim to make things better, as best we can. That's all we can really do.

From our perspective, great design is that which leaves only the intentional inaccessibility intact. But also, there's a level above that and it's the one that transcends our earlier discussion regarding accessibility and difficulty. The difficulty of Dark Souls is a clearly *intentional* inaccessibility, but I think to accept it as great design does a disservice to the wider context of the discussion. Great, *empathic*, design requires us to dig deeper into that intention. It recognises that intentional inaccessibility in a design is a complex function that changes based on external factors. Our assessment of intentionality and its value must always come with psychological error bars. Part of great design is looking at inaccessibility and saying 'Yes, but ... does this *intention* map on to what I really *want* to accomplish?'. Sure, you can't have the authentic **Dark Souls** experience within configurable difficulty levels ... but how much do you care about the authentic **Dark Souls** experience? How much do you just want people to be able to play your game?

None of this is easy.

Addressing inaccessibility in game design is a complex process that requires designers, developers, producers, and players to step out of their comfort zones and experience discomfort. Sometimes it means making difficult decisions about cost and value.

One of the other difficulties we have in the area of tabletop games is that accessibility decisions often come with a per-unit cost. If you want to change the size of an interface component on a video game, it doesn't keep costing you money with every subsequent sale. If you change the size of a card in a board game to accommodate a larger font, that means more cost per card. It maybe means a larger box, which in turn means higher shipping costs. A larger box may mean stores can stock fewer of the game at any one time.

In this book, I will talk over your options, what you can do to address inaccessibility, and make some suggestions as to the implications. In the end, the extent to which you can and should make these compensations is something for you to contemplate and decide upon. Any accessibility adjustment you make will expand your potential audience. It does us no favours though to pretend there aren't implications for everything you decide to do.

You've embarked upon a difficult journey here, but I think you'll find it very worthwhile!

Before we crack on though, there's another thing we need to address ....

Accessible Games versus Games that Are Accessible

A reader picking up this book may immediately have one particular thought that I think we need to spend a bit of time deconstructing – 'aren't there already loads of accessible board games on the market'?

The answer there is 'sort of'. You'll find Braille **chess** sets and Braille **Scrabble**. You'll find giant, tactile versions of **Connect 4**, large print playing cards and visually accessible **Monopoly**, a version of **Twister** especially adapted for the blind, and a special edition of **Uno** that is designed for people who have colour-deficient vision. There are audio versions of **Sudoku**. You might even find specific versions of modern hobbyist board games that are designed for accessibility (a handful) and modification kits (such as available from 64 Oz Games) that permit Braille to be overlaid onto a whole bunch of modern titles.

There is a role for all of these approaches, but this is not the destination for which we're aiming in this book. Our goal is not to explain how to make accessible board games. My view is that accessible games are **segregated games**. I don't want people creating 'accessible games', except in those circumstances where they are realistically the only option. I want people to be thinking of how we can make **all games** more accessible.

For a lot of my life, I have been a developer on Multiuser Dungeons (MUDs). I did this **long after** they faded into cultural irrelevance. If you've never encountered one, imagine **World of Warcraft** and an Infocom text adventure had a baby. There is still a small (tiny and really) dedicated cadre of gamers who play these, and by and large they have been doing it for decades. One of the largest groups who remain are blind gamers because the design of a MUD (mostly entirely text) meshes very well with the functionality of a screen reader. MUDs were designed for everyone (at the time, they were incredibly popular); they never set out to be 'accessible games'. They are **games** that are **accessible**.

Consider in comparison the genre of *audiogames* – games played almost entirely through sound. They began as a way to create an accessible format for gaming that would work for people with visual impairments, and over time, they have become both a) awesome and b) interesting to other categories of gamers. These are **accessible games.** MUDs and audiogames started at different ends of that dichotomy. They meet though in an intersection because they are niche, obscure, and lack the cultural penetration of more mainstream genres. That's not only their strength but also a problem.

Games are like books, movies, and television shows. They are where we find many of the most popular expressions of modern culture. **Fortnite** is more an online platform than a game now – it hosts concerts and television tie-ins. **Minecraft** is as much a revolution in education as it is a playground for creativity. Sometimes inaccessibility means being prevented from engaging with important forms of culture, and that is profoundly exclusionary.

Just think back to how our city streets looked when **Grand Theft Auto 5** was about to be released – its imagery plastered everything from billboards to bus stops. That was a conversation starter. We don't just consume popular culture – we are active participants in constructing its meaning. The Marvel movies (of which I'm sure we all agree there are too many) are part adaptation of comics and part the collaborative construction of a modern mythology. There are factions that debate the nature of superheroes with an almost theological reverence, and this comes along with all the attendant scriptural schisms. When each episode of Game of Thrones aired, it was immediately followed by an extended period of discussion, debate, prognostication, and contextualising. Popular culture is perhaps best enjoyed collaboratively. Games fall into that frame.

So … what happens if you can't enjoy them at all? The effect is that someone who can't play a game is cut out of the cultural commentary around that game. Disabled hobbyist board gamers don't want to play a Braille version of Monopoly. They want to play **Gloomhaven** (2017). They don't want audio Sudoku. They want **Wingspan** (2019). They want to play the games that everyone else is playing and talk about the games everyone else is talking about. There is not the same collaborative enjoyment to be had within an accessibility cul-de-sac. In those circumstances where disabled gamers **do** want to play the accessible games, most want that as an option – not a necessity. If nothing else, it's easier to get people to come over to play **Ticket to Ride** (2004) than it is the colour-blind accessible version of **Uno** (2017).

Accessible games also carry with them an additional negative property – that of stigma. People generally don't like to be singled out, and having to convince your friends to play a game on the basis of its prominent accessibility features requires a discussion around what may be an uncomfortable topic. Much as with children avoiding glasses, or older adults refusing accessibility software for their computers, there is a natural tendency amongst people to avoid distinguishing themselves by their need for special treatment. Accessibility features designed into the broader landscape of mainstream gaming do a much better job of including disabled gamers by all measures and in all categories.

There is a problem though of framing this work as being about disability because by and large that's not what this book is about. You will be forgiven for being sceptical about that if you've skipped ahead to other chapters, so bear with me for a few moments.

Part of the philosophy of the work I have done over the past few years has been to focus on what tabletop games ask of their players, not which players can and cannot play particular games. This may sound like an arcane distinction, but it's critical to a respectful approach to accessibility for those of us who are abled or, at least in my case, **relatively** abled. This is something I have included as a disclaimer on every game teardown I have published. It is persistently the thing that makes me most uneasy about the work I have done.

I say 'relatively abled' advisedly. I have various minor ailments as a consequence of aging. I am diabetic, with high blood pressure. Those two occasionally flare up in a way that impact on my ability, or willingness, to play games. I have chronic shoulder pain which makes certain physical interactions uncomfortable, and perhaps impossible, depending on how the symptoms are manifesting on a day-to-day basis. I am profoundly short-sighted. I am aphantasic, which is to say I cannot form pictures in my mind.

All of these things make a difference in my life, and the combination of them creates the unique set of impairments that is **me.** But none of that is the same thing as living with profound, non-correctible disability.

We need to make a distinction here between a kind of 'academic' knowledge of disability – which I have as someone who works in the area – and an **embodied** experience. There are those that would say that anyone relatively abled working in this area are actually committing harm to people with disabilities. This often comes with an exhortation – 'stay in your lane'. Stick to what you know. This is not our debate to commandeer.

It's not a universal viewpoint, but it's also one that you may well come into contact with and so I want to spend a little time unpacking it. It's safe to say I disagree with this conclusion, but I also think it deserves a meaningful and respectful discussion. It's not an unreasonable position for people to take up. It's also, in my view, not a helpful one … and indeed, if followed through to its logical conclusion, it's not a **wise** position. Beyond a superficial assumption that 'accessibility' and 'disability' make up a single region of a Venn diagram, it's not even an **applicable** position.

What Is Accessibility Anyway?

Let's start right at the very core. What **is** accessibility anyway?
We've already got a working definition of **inaccessibility**: 'An inaccessibility is an obstacle that stands between someone and a goal they want to perform'.

Accessibility then is the **absence** of those obstacles. Accessibility though isn't just an end-goal. It's a process – one of identifying obstacles and dealing with them. In essence we're looking to find the mismatches between people and their intentions. Those do not necessarily stem from a mismatch between people and their capabilities. Even if there was no disability there would still be a need for accessibility. Obstacles to goals would still exist. We'll see that as we go on.

There is obviously a tight relationship between disability and inaccessibility, and throughout history, we have seen dozens – hundreds even – of situations where addressing disability has improved accessibility for everyone. At the University of Dundee, there was a general philosophy that greatly shaped my conception of this topic:

> Extraordinary people in ordinary circumstances have many of the same needs as ordinary people in extraordinary circumstances.

I know that's not very catchy, but hey – it was a university. Nonetheless, I think it's an observation of real genius. Someone trying to type a text message on a mobile phone while standing on a rickety bus will benefit from many of the same accessibility features as someone with Parkinson's disease sitting on a sofa. An oil-rig worker in a storm will similarly have many of the same needs as someone with severe visual impairment on a sunny day.

But those **extraordinary circumstances** don't even have to be all that extraordinary. Poor overhead lighting can create many of the same issues as colour blindness. Sun in your eyes at the wrong angle can be profoundly visually impairing. A neighbour inconsiderately drilling at a billion decibels will leave anyone thankful for subtitles on the movies they watch. The truth is that good accessibility makes things better for everyone.

Have you ever found yourself pushing some heavy luggage towards a train station and breathed a sigh of relief when the pavement dips down to the road? You can thank disability activists from the 70s for that – it was originally an innovation to help people with wheelchairs navigate inaccessible cities. It just so happens that these 'curb cuts' were a blessing for almost everyone – for cyclists, for postal workers with mail carts, for the elderly, and for parents with prams and strollers. This is the concept of the 'curb cut effect'. When changes are made to products, places, and services to aid disabled people, it often ends up helping everyone else. Important to our philosophy here though is that if there were no people with disabilities, **all of those other groups** would still benefit from a curb cut.

That's what we're looking for in this book – for you to build 'cardboard curb cuts' into the work you do. None of this is to diminish the importance of disability within this topic but rather to highlight accessibility as not an issue of disability alone.

What Do We Mean by Disability?

Some of you, looking back a couple of paragraphs, may have reacted quite viscerally to the choice of words. 'Disabled people', which is a form of what's known as *identity-first language*, is something many of us have been trained out of using. Teachers, academics, politicians, bureaucrats, and more have been trying to bring about a change in how language around disability is used. 'Person with disability', we are often told, is the more appropriate term. That is *people-first language* or sometimes *equity language*.

About two thirds of 'abled' people writing about disability will prefer to use people-first language, and many will correct the use of identity-first language as a dehumanising relic of an older age. It is 'person with disability' or sometimes PwD.

The problem is about two thirds of 'people with disabilities' prefer 'disabled people'.

That's a bit awkward, yeah? No matter which style you use, you will annoy a third of your audience. My approach upon realising you can't please everyone has been to use the two forms interchangeably. I can't make everyone happy, but I can try to ensure everyone is equally **annoyed**.

Equality can come from many different directions.

All of the equity language discussion – despite it being contrary to what the majority of disabled people prefer – is well meaning. It's a reaction to the different model we used to use when it came to disability in general. Within this book, we'll be adopting what's known as the *social model of disability*, which has largely come to take over from the previous *medical model of disability*.

The medical model of disability was one where disabilities were seen as something intrinsic to the individual. Social exclusion was to be countered through intervention by addressing the perceived wrongness in the body. The disability belongs to the person, and what cannot be fixed must simply be accepted.

The social model has a different perspective – that disability does not exist in a vacuum. When someone in a wheelchair encounters stairs, it is the presence of the **stairs** that are disabling. Stairs don't occur naturally in cities – someone chooses to build them over the other alternatives. In the medical model, we might simply decide that someone in a wheelchair has to accept not being able to ascend steps. In the social model, we look for ways to collaboratively solve the problems – with ramps, lifts, or perhaps the relocation of services to the ground floor.

In the medical model, we see solutions such as segregated schooling and assisted living communities, with the corresponding gradual isolation of people with disabilities from popular culture. We see 'accessible games'. In the social model, we see specialist support teachers, financial support for independent living, audiobooks, and wide-spread closed captioning. And, of course, 'games that are accessible'.

There are other considerations around language. Nobody is **afflicted** with a disability, and accessibility support tools are not a negative. Someone is a 'wheelchair user', not 'confined to a wheelchair'. You want to be very careful when you talk about 'curing' disability since as the identify-first preference suggests, there are a lot of disabled people who do not consider their condition to be something that needs curing. Some of those who ascribe to 'Deaf Culture' for example have remarked that 'fixing' deafness amounts to little more than a form of cultural genocide.

Got that? Good, but remember that every disabled person is unique and there is no such thing as the perfect, archetypical person with a disability. There is no common consensus on any of these topics amongst any community. For everyone who reacts strongly against the idea that their disability is a weakness, there is another who feels equally strongly to the contrary. Most important about all of this is that everyone is unique. You can't get any of this right all of the time with all of the people. All you can do is your best. Be respectful, willing to listen, and also make sure not to fall into the trap of thinking there is such thing as a single monoculture that will tell you the 'right' way to do things. Oh, there are people out there who will act as if there is. Those people are not correct.

Yeah, there's a lot you need to be aware of when you want to have a conversation about this topic. And if you don't feel comfortable in addressing accessibility in the frame of disability, then that's understandable. Not everyone has the time to master the intricacies of the debate. You don't have to stray from your lane, and in most cases, it's probably wise that you don't.

This is why the work I do comes with so many caveats and disclaimers. My focus is not on what people can and cannot do. I'm just not qualified to comment. But I **do** have a lot of experience in analysing what games **ask** of their audiences. That in the end is how I recommend those without embodied experience of disability approach this topic – you are perfectly qualified to assess what a game asks of its players. You can tell people what a game needs in order to be played. You just can't make any judgements of any specificity regarding what that means for any individual player.

In my research, I have seen blind board gamers who play Catan on a whiteboard. I have seen people who play fighting games at a competitive level using only their feet. I have seen deaf gamers who rock out at Rock Band and others who have completed games using nothing but sound cues. In my experience, the only true comment on whether a game is playable by someone with disabilities is 'it depends on how much they want to play it'. If people want it enough, they'll find a way to make it happen.

What **we** can do is help them along the way.

Before we get back to the idea of ordinary and extraordinary players, I want to spend a little bit of time exploring the logical conclusion of 'stay in your lane' when it comes to accessibility – mainly because it's a topic close to my heart. I have spent a lot of time feeling concerned about all of this. I'm not going to allay your shared concerns, but I do hope to put them in some context. It's important that we don't let perfect become the enemy of the good because there is no world in which the work of accessibility in games **can** be conducted perfectly.

Within the Meeple Centred Design project, I work through a kind of heuristic framework – a systematic approach that allows me to iterate over various categories of inaccessibility and the way in which they manifest in board games. It's not a secret as to how this approach works – this whole book is your blueprint for how to do it yourself. But in the end, I tend to adopt a 'publish then revise' model. I publish my observations – explicitly to start the conversation – and then I adjust the conclusions based on feedback from the audience. This has worked reasonably well – I receive fewer emails about errors than I do about how the work has helped find games for complex use cases. In the end though, this (largely) is a single, relatively abled academic making judgements that lack embodied experience.

It would unquestionably be better if I had embodied experience – expertise, even – in a specific category of disability and I focused on that. And I am delighted that – in the wake of Meeple Like Us – several people have started to do that very thing, inspired to do a better job than me in their own niches of expertise. **Sightless Fun**, run by Ertay Shashko, explores the intersection of board gaming and blindness. **Colourblind Games**, run by Brian Chandler, does the same thing for colour blindness. **Rolling With Two** is a YouTube channel run by Sarah Reed and Will Reed, and it reviews games with the benefit of Will's experience of blindness. These are wonderful resources, and I think any serious student of the topic will plunder them for all the insights they can.

The cost though is a fracturing of the analysis space. Ertay can offer expert guidance in blindness. Brian can give you the skinny on colour. But neither of them can expand their expert offering into other categories of accessibility. What we need then are maybe eight sites, run by eight people with eight different kinds of disability. And to ensure full coverage of each game, they all need to play and review the same games. That way, you get embodied expertise in all the different categories we look at within the Meeple Centred Design project.

Except that's not really true. As we've already discussed, there is no one person who is the archetypical representative of a disability. There is more 'intra-category' variation in a group of people with a disability than there is in the general population as a whole. That means you need someone who is totally blind doing their reviews, someone partially sighted, some with protanopia, and someone else with tritanopia. You need someone who uses a wheelchair and someone who has fine-grained motor control issues. You need multiple representatives across the whole spectrum of each category of disability. And then, you need them to buy games they likely can't play (review copies for board games are hard to come by) which is a significant financial outlay. And then, you need to keep them motivated when the audience figures are as low as you'd expect from a niche, inside a niche, inside yet another niche.

You could maybe alleviate some of these problems through a shared platform, but you can't get away from the fact that to accurately review a board game for accessibility you need a team of several dozen people working in harmony towards a shared goal. I've sometimes said that the eventual final evolution of the Meeple Like Us Pokemon is to a crowd-sourced site of this nature, but that comes with problems of its own.

Given the difficulty of attaining the perfect, I have been able to justify the focus on what I do within the Meeple Centred Design Project. It is not perfect in any category, for any game. But it's **good enough** with **enough breadth** to inform others in a meaningful way. The site may not 'write what it knows', but I have been working long enough and diligently enough in this area to say that by and large 'it knows what it writes'.

Stay in Your Lane

There is another reason why this book stresses **accessibility** within this framing – our analysis isn't constrained to the realms most often considered within the catchment area of disability. We also address sociological factors and economic factors, which means we talk about aspects such as business models and representation. These do not, and should not, be mentally linked to the definition of disability.

Severing the explicit connection between disability and accessibility is necessary. Otherwise we're going to be guilty of alarming implications when ethnicity, socioeconomic status, gender, and sex are considered. We break the link to avoid uncharitable interpretations of our overall thesis. Our focus is **inaccessibility**, for which disability is a massively important consideration but is not the only one. Cutting this link between disability and accessibility is necessary for the analysis to follow. It is not to diminish but to be more inclusive in the context.

With all of this said … what does it even mean to 'stay in your lane'? How do you justify your interest in accessibility if you have no corresponding disability to call upon?

I give unto you the tool I have had the greatest success with in convincing people as to why accessibility matters to them. I have used it successfully with students and corporations, with research projects and personal advocacy. I call it the Grid of Enlightened Self Interest (Table 1.1).

I know it doesn't look like much, but trust me – this is the key that unlocks the relevance of accessibility to even a sceptical audience. It's not limited to board games – it's a general-purpose lens for understanding the scope of accessibility work. It's certainly been most reliably drafted into the cause of tabletop accessibility, but I and others have had success elsewhere.

TABLE 1.1

The Grid of Enlightened Self Interest

	Colour Blindness	Visual	Cognitive	Physical	Socioeconomic	Emotional	Communication
Permanent Always relevant, will probably never go away although severity may modulate	• Protanopia • Deuteranopia • Tritanopia • Monochromacy • Aging • Brain Damage	• Blindness • Short-sightedness	Dementia • Alzheimer's	• Loss of a limb	• Social classification • Under representation	An emotional control disorder	Deaf/Hard of Hearing (HoH) Mutism
Temporary Short term, will eventually go away	• Concussion	• Eye infection • Wearing an eyepatch • Getting used to new glasses	• Being drunk • Bad night's sleep	• Broken arm • Sprained ankle	• Unemployment • Forgotten your wallet • Being in 'the wrong neighbourhood'	Received some bad news	Broken jaw A noisy bar
Situational Intermittent, will phase in and out of relevance	• Bad lighting • Wearing sunglasses	• Bright sunshine in your eyes	• Being distracted • Being in an open plan office	• Carrying something heavy • On a juddering train	• Contactless payments not working	Irritation at a loud conversation in the background	With a group of mixed-language friends

Along the left-hand column, we see three key scenarios in which someone might be impaired in some way, shape, or form. This categorisation comes from the Microsoft Inclusive Design Toolkit[4] with a few adjustments.

First of all, we have what people generally assume disability to be – a permanent state of affairs. It's always relevant, and while it may modulate in severity, it will likely never go away. For a lot of disabilities, it's a case of 'good days and bad days', or even sometimes 'good minutes and bad minutes'.

Underneath that are the temporary impairments. They are just as impactful as permanent impairments but – all things going well – will eventually go away. Here we don't see things like 'an amputated limb' but instead 'a severely broken arm'. The broken arm will probably heal. We have all, almost certainly, experienced a temporary impairment that has had accessibility implications.

Most complex and common is the category of situational impairments, which are the ones where one may shift in and out of the state of being impaired. Someone carrying heavy shopping cradled in one arm may share similarities with someone who has a broken arm. The difference is that the shopping can be put down and picked up again or shifted from one arm to another. We all experience situational impairments constantly.

Along the top of the grid are the different columns that identify the significant categories of accessibility that we will discuss in this book:

- *Colour blindness*: This is relating to one's ability to differentiate hues, tones, and colour frequencies as versus the colour differentiation of the general population.
- *Visual impairments*: This is relating to broader difficulties of perceiving or differentiating visual information. Can include everything from short-sightedness to total blindness.
- *Cognitive impairments*: This is encompassing conditions relating to fluid intelligence (essentially cognitive processing) and crystalised intelligence (related to memory and 'wisdom').
- *Physical impairments*: This is encompassing both fine-grained and gross motor control issues. Can relate to dexterity in the hands or the ability to move without assistance.
- *Socioeconomic impairments*: This is relating to issues of economics and sociological representation. Everything from having no money to having a 'foreign sounding surname' can come under this category.
- *Emotional*: This relates to issues of control, frustration, and self-perception associated with interaction.
- *Communication*: This encompasses expression (speaking and sign language) as well as reception (understanding vocabulary and deafness).

What we have here is a grid (hence the name) that allows us to pinpoint what kind of impairments map onto which kinds of scenarios.

I'll spare you a deep dive into the top row because as I say it's where we see the most common manifestation of disability. It's the other two rows that open up the discussion to the 'abled' and the relatively abled. Again, I'll spare you the details, but we can pull out a few choice examples.

When I switched over from normal glasses to varifocals, I spent several days both visually and physically impaired. That was a temporary impairment, but everything from standing up straight to walking, to focusing, and to driving – all of these things became more difficult to do. That wasn't because I had something wrong with my eyes but because my eyes were having to adjust to the new reality of my advancing years. Studies show that a bad night's sleep can be as cognitively impairing as a few units of alcohol. I'm a career insomniac, and it means that I am temporarily impaired on an almost permanent basis. Losing your wallet means you're economically impaired in a way that is indistinguishable (temporarily) from poverty. Having received some bad news means you're more likely to lash out at others. All of these are temporary impairments that impact on your ability to function in the same ways as those with permanent impairments in the same column.

In one of the houses we once lived, my partner and I had a kitchen with exceptionally poor overhead lighting. This house was in Scotland, which is in darkness most of the year and perpetually overcast when it's not. The lighting was so bad that we often couldn't tell the difference between blues and greens in some board games (**Memoir 44** being one particularly bad offender). We could fix it by moving rooms or adjusting lighting, but it still left us effectively colour blind when we were there.

I sometimes describe myself as 'the situational impairment in any conversation'. I work in Sweden, and while all of my colleagues and students are exceptionally gifted at speaking English, I am still aware this is a second (or third or fourth) language for most of them. As we sit together in groups chatting, the need to shift in and out of English for my benefit creates a communication inaccessibility. People struggle for the English translation of a word they want to say or have to reinterpret a common phrase in a comprehensible manner. I, on the other hand, work hard to speak slowly and anglicise my Scottish accent. For fun, I occasionally startle friends and students by addressing them in full-speed, full-flavour Dundonian to illustrate how much shared work we're all doing to be understood.

The key observation here is not in any individual intersection of impairment category or situation but rather the understanding that we are all impaired at one time or another. And importantly, even those of us who are abled are only temporarily so. As we age, we accumulate impairments on a regular basis. It's possible none of these are significant enough in themselves for us to self-identify as disabled, but they may still reach the criteria of requiring accessibility support. Many of us get a little bit colour blind as we get older. Our hearing becomes less able to differentiate between tones. Our fluid intelligence goes down while our crystalised intelligence goes up. We all change in complex ways as time goes by. Our needs become more profoundly **intersectional**.

And of course, we're all only one bad car accident away from needing extreme accessibility support **right now**.

I often look at my board game shelves with a sense of wistfulness. 'When I retire', I think, 'I'll finally have time to play all of these games'. Or perhaps, more cynically, 'when the bombs fall, that's my time to enjoy myself'. There are more than a few games on my shelves I have yet to take out of the shrink wrap. Life just gets in the way. There are work responsibilities and family responsibilities. Home repairs that I think 'that's a half-hour job' and subsequently spend three days at the Do-It-Yourself (DIY) shop trying to buy the adapters and connectors I had no idea I needed. So, it all gets deferred. When I retire. When **we** retire, right?

If we do want to be able to play those games that we have been accumulating in our collections, then we need them to be accessible. And if we want them to be accessible **then**, we need to start making the case for them to be accessible **now**.

A big user group for accessibility is to be found amongst disabled gamers – both the ones that are ready to play now and the ones who will be ready to play once we meet them half-way. Don't forget the long-term benefit to you. Every cardboard curb cut put in place now means another game you're going to be able to play when the sun is shining in your tired eyes as you warm yourself in your retirement villa on the coast of Lisbon.

The Tabletop Accessibility Guidelines

Over the next few chapters, we're going to follow a pretty regular structure as we explore the way that inaccessibility is threaded through tabletop game design. We'll begin with a brief introduction to how the impairments in a specific category tend to manifest, debunking some common assumptions as we go. These are intended to be primers – they are not comprehensive and do not delve into the deeper complexities of each topic. They are there to help conceptualise what we are talking about when we refer to impairment. They are the briefest, shallowest of overviews of what are incredibly complicated topics.

We'll then take a tour through some significant examples of the problems observed in each category, drawing these from the body of work that is freely available to you on the site Meeple Like Us. We'll also look at some of the best practise that we've observed as well as a few interesting examples that don't neatly conform to simplifications like 'good' or 'bad'.

We'll end each chapter with design guidelines. In those guidelines, we're going to condense down all the observations, discussions, and evidence from the work of Meeple Centred Design into something actionable that can be applied by individuals. These will be categorised broadly under subheadings, and these subheadings will be compatible across all guidelines for all categories.

It is important to note here that all of these guidelines are advisory. The exact nature of your game will dictate which are possible, which are **feasible**, and which are desirable. Chapter 9 talks about how to apply these Tabletop Accessibility Guidelines (TTAG) in the context of the real world, where we are often choosing between the lesser of evils and deciding which compromises we can make. It's also important to note here that some of these guidelines may seem contradictory when viewed against those in other categories. We'll talk about that more in the final chapter, but nothing in life is ever easy. Sometimes in improving things for one group of people, you'll make it harder for others. One examples of this is digital text-to-speech – wonderful for those with visual impairments, but its synthesised nature makes it more cognitively expensive to process than real speech. By improving things for one group, you may find yourself disadvantaging another.

All games listed as examples in the guidelines have full accessibility analyses (and reviews) available. URLs are notoriously prone to link rot, so my advice is go to the search engine of your choice and find the links there. That way if the site moves, you'll still be able to get access (Figure 1.9).

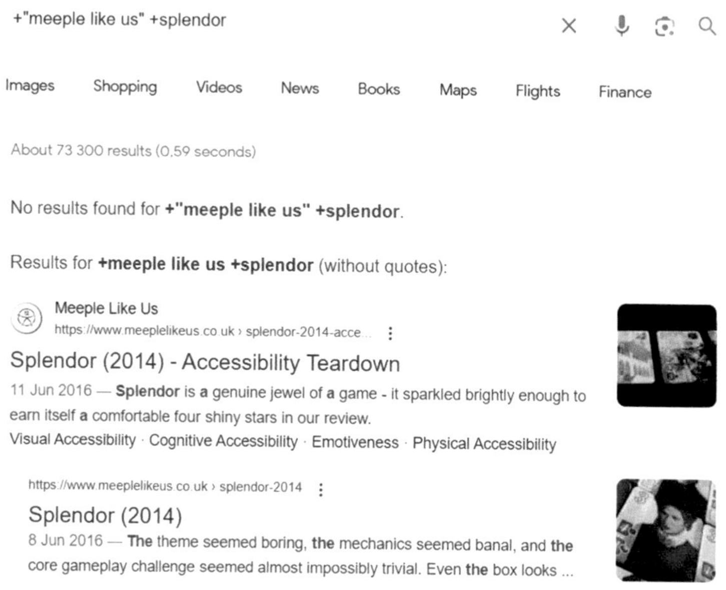

+"meeple like us" +splendor   ✕ 🎤 📷 🔍

Images   Shopping   Videos   News   Books   Maps   Flights   Finance

About 73 300 results (0.59 seconds)

No results found for **+"meeple like us" +splendor**.

Results for **+meeple like us +splendor** (without quotes):

🧩 Meeple Like Us
https://www.meeplelikeus.co.uk › splendor-2014-acce ... ⋮

Splendor (2014) - Accessibility Teardown
11 Jun 2016 — **Splendor** is **a** genuine jewel of **a** game - it sparkled brightly enough to
earn itself **a** comfortable four shiny stars in our review.
Visual Accessibility · Cognitive Accessibility · Emotiveness · Physical Accessibility

https://www.meeplelikeus.co.uk › splendor-2014 ⋮

Splendor (2014)
8 Jun 2016 — **The** theme seemed boring, **the** mechanics seemed banal, and **the**
core gameplay challenge seemed almost impossibly trivial. Even **the** box looks ...

FIGURE 1.9   URL rot is a real thing – you can find almost every referenced game with a search in your
engine of choice. (Screenshot by the author.)

Okay, that's more than enough preamble! Let's start digging into the real meat of this
book. Let's talk about how to make games accessible!

Notes

1. Kids, ask your parents.
2. https://gameaccessibilityguidelines.com
3. https://icv2.com/articles/markets/view/53652/top-hobby-channel-board-
   games-fall-2022
4. https://inclusive.microsoft.design/

BIBLIOGRAPHY

Andrews, E. E., Forber-Pratt, A. J., Mona, L. R., Lund, E. M., Pilarski, C. R., & Balter, R.
    (2019). #Saytheword: A disability culture commentary on the erasure of "disability".
    Rehabilitation Psychology, 64(2), 111.
Blackwell, A. G. (2017). The curb-cut effect. *Stanford Social Innovation Review, 15*(1),
    28–33.
Crabb, M., Heron, M., Jones, R., Armstrong, M., Reid, H., & Wilson, A. (2019). Developing
    accessible services: Understanding current knowledge and areas for future sup-
    port. *Proceedings of the 2019 CHI Conference on Human Factors in Computing*

Systems, 1–12. https://dl.acm.org/doi/abs/10.1145/3290605.3300446?casa_token=
RxVchYP2FlIAAAAA:zhRObV3K5ZC4UHTMZxIJVuJ0z6EGSR7UQu3fkBD
LLt_ski-tuFCgvRt9GOWrtllo2C3GQZGZfoX

Dunn, D. S., & Andrews, E. E. (2015). Person-first and identity-first language: Developing psychologists' cultural competence using disability language. *American Psychologist, 70*(3), 255.

Heron, M. (2013). "likely to be eaten by a grue"—the relevance of text games in the modern era. *The Computer Games Journal, 2*, 55–67.

Heron, M. J. (2015). A case study into the accessibility of text-parser based interaction. *Proceedings of the 7th ACM SIGCHI symposium on engineering interactive computing systems*, 74–83. https://dl.acm.org/doi/abs/10.1145/2774225.2774833?casa_
token=4vNAVap5pSgAAAAA:FMfITYswN4NzqZ1JYxo4KuK_4vYY_705zcjgrTJaT
CjayG4Rjir7IqQTQZJbcABre7KkraLCiVw

Heron, M. J., Ellis, K., Leaver T., Kent, M. (2022). The sociological accessibility of gaming. In *Gaming disability* (pp. 144–154). Routledge.

Heron, M. J., Belford, P. H., Reid, H., & Crabb, M. (2018a). Eighteen months of meeple like us: An exploration into the state of board game accessibility. *The Computer Games Journal, 7*, 75–95.

Heron, M. J., Belford, P. H., Reid, H., & Crabb, M. (2018b). Meeple centred design: A heuristic toolkit for evaluating the accessibility of tabletop games. *The Computer Games Journal, 7*, 97–114.

Heron, M., Hanson, V. L., & Ricketts, I. (2013). Open source and accessibility: Advantages and limitations. *Journal of Interaction Science, 1*(1), 1–10.

Heron, M., Hanson, V. L., & Ricketts, I. W. (2013a). Access: A technical framework for adaptive accessibility support. *Proceedings of the 5th ACM SIGCHI symposium on Engineering interactive computing systems*, 33–42. https://dl.acm.org/doi/abs/
10.1145/2494603.2480316?casa_token=_0R6PM19XlkAAAAA:HYqedVfbk_
uWTOglbeKz3xIwazF0Q5eINcK8_zH2upSgGIt1rNgzzh4kl3tVWAxERsCKhnef5ri

Heron, M., Hanson, V. L., & Ricketts, I. W. (2013b). Accessibility support for older adults with the access framework. *International Journal of Human-Computer Interaction, 29*(11), 702–716.

Padden, C. A., & Humphries, T. (2005). *Inside deaf culture.* Harvard University Press.

Rovithis, E. (2012). A classification of audio-based games in terms of sonic gameplay and the introduction of the audio role-playing-game: Kronos. *Proceedings of the 7th Audio Mostly Conference: A Conference on Interaction with Sound*, 160–164.

Shakespeare, T. (2006). The social model of disability. *The Disability Studies Reader, 2*, 197–204.

2

Colour Blindness

We'll begin with some relatively low-hanging fruit – colour blindness, also known as colour vision deficiency. The former is the term most commonly used, so it's the one we'll be sticking with throughout the text. Colour is obviously a major factor in board game design – colours are **everywhere**. They're in the box art; they're in the card design. They're part of the basic vocabulary of tabletop gaming. 'What colour do you want?' is one of the first conversation topics when it comes to setting up. There are people who always pick a certain colour when playing; others are happy with anything. Colour is part of the culture of gaming. Board games have become a lot better over the years at accommodating colour blindness in their design, but that's partially because the situation began from a quite low baseline. Even as recently as the year of writing this book, I have seen new releases that still lack basic accessibility for people who are colour-blind.

We begin with this category for several reasons:

1. It's highly impactful. Around 8% of men are colour-blind, although prevalence differs by ethnicity. Women are much less likely to be affected at around 0.5% of the female population. Colour blindness is estimated to be a factor for around 300 million people worldwide. That's a **lot** of people.
2. It's probably the most accessible of the accessibility categories we'll discuss. It's easy to grasp, easy to observe, and easy to see how it affects game design.
3. It is, usually, **so easy to fix**.

More often than not colour blindness is a genetic condition. Our eyes come equipped with a **retina**, which is the part of our visual system where the photoreceptive cells are located. Those cells broadly separate into two categories – the **rods**, which identify light but don't do anything about colour, and the **cones**, which are sensitive to different wavelengths of visible light. There are more than 90 million rods in the eyes, but it is the approximately 6 million cones that are responsible for colour vision. These get separated further into three types – red or 'long wave' (about 60% of them), green or 'middle wave' (about 30%), and blue or 'short wave' (the rest). When working correctly, combinations of cones are what allow us to see a range of approximately a million different shades of colour.

Colour blindness then is a catch-all term for the condition of having a weakness in one (or more) of these types of cones. Red and green colour blindness is the most common type, as might be expected by the fact they make up 90% of the cones in your eye. The genes for colour blindness are carried on the X chromosome, which explains why it is so

DOI: 10.1201/9781003415435-2

much more prevalent in men than in women. Colour perception can come in pretty much any form, but we'll focus on a few key examples in our discussion here:

- *Fully chromatic vision*: This means you see colour just fine.
- *Protanopia*: The condition of being unable to distinguish light in the red wavelength and thus an inability to see the colour red.
- *Deuteranopia*: The condition when the problem is associated with the green cones.
- *Tritanopia*: The condition in which the problem in the blue cones.

You will notice here that the condition of seeing no colours (something usually referenced as *monochromatic vision* or *achromatopsia*) isn't one of these categories. That might be surprising. When colour blindness is discussed in popular culture, the term is often a short-hand for 'sees in black and white' or, in terms of the architecture of our eyes, 'has no working cones and relies primarily on the rods'. However, despite the common assumption, this is actually a tremendously rare condition, impacting on only around one in every 33,000 people.

There is a spectrum of severity for each of these cone deficiencies. *Protanopia* (red-blind) means 'few working red cones', but there is also *protanomaly* which means a weakness in, rather than an absence of, the ability to perceive red light. The other conditions have equivalents. We have here a range of different conditions, each of which may be of varying severity.

But there's a problem!

This is what we normally think of in terms of genetic colour blindness – the kind people are born with. Colour blindness can emerge from a number of different causes and manifest in different parts of our perception system. Degenerative eye diseases can introduce colour blindness into late life. Brain trauma, or brain disease, can impact on colour perception. There are medicines and toxins that can create temporary, or permanent, state of colour blindness. Many of us will find that simply getting older will gradually change the range of colours that we can perceive.

The non-genetic causes of colour blindness manifest in different ways. Damage to the cerebral cortex may result in a complete lack of ability to distinguish colour (such as in *cerebral achromatopsia*), or it may result in colour perception being 'scrambled' (*colour agnosia*). Damage at the cortical level may result in information being lost about the wavelength of colours. It's possible for colour blindness to manifest in such a way that someone can't perceive the colour purple, for example, but has no difficulty with other hues.

All of this cuts away at a common assumption about making things 'colour-blind accessible' – that there is a combination of colours that exists that everyone (save for those with *monochromacy*) can perceive. The truth is, there is no such thing as a colour-blind accessible colour palette, although there are certainly colour palettes that are more accessible than others. Masatake Okabe and Kei Ito have put together a set of eight colours that can offer unambiguous differentiation for all the genetic categories of colour blindness[1], and one might argue 'eight colours ought to be enough for anybody'. There also exist a 12-colour palette and a 15-colour palette, and even a 24-colour palette, devised by Martin Krzywinski[2]. These don't solve the problem, but they do mitigate it under a lot of circumstances.

Straight up 'unplayable' games are rare when it comes to colour blindness. People find a way to play even if the game fights them every step of the way. Some homebrew solutions include the following:

- Replacing problematic game pieces with accessible variations.
- Tying coloured thread around pieces to make them differentiable.
- Painting pieces a different colour.

As you can imagine, all homebrew solutions come with compromises. Board games hold their value tremendously well on the secondary resale market, but that's not true if you've gone over all its bits with your paint gun. The thin channel of information represented by coloured thread lacks the visual distinctiveness of raw colour when viewed at a distance. Not all games have pieces that can easily be replaced.

So, that's colour blindness – it's an issue that affects a lot of people; affects different people in different ways; there's no colour palette that will work for everyone, and it impacts on gameplay and aesthetics across the board. Pardon the pun.

Problematic Colour Design

One thing that *Days of Wonder* does tremendously well is 'production value'. Every *Days of Wonder* game I own feels like a product of love, carefully designed and immaculately put together. Once upon a time, the philosophy behind their publishing model was to put out a single game a year but to make sure each of those games had the reasonable expectation of becoming **evergreen**. That is to say, a game that sells consistently well year on year rather than has a bunch of sales on release before fading into obscurity.

When **Yamatai** (2017) was released, it's fair to say it had certain expectations upon it. For my part, in 2017, I was expecting a game that was broadly colour-blind accessible. *Days of Wonder* is certainly aware of colour blindness – **Ticket to Ride** (2004) in its original forms was often criticised for its unadorned colour design.

Figure 2.1 shows one of the photographs I took of Yamatai, and it's fair to say I think that it is visually striking. It looks genuinely beautiful on the table, made up of all kinds of nice and interesting pieces interacting in fascinating ways.

FIGURE 2.1   The colourful board of Yamatai. (Photograph by the author.)

FIGURE 2.2   The board of Yamatai as seen through CVS. (Photograph by the author, CVS used under the MIT Licence, Massachusetts.)

But let's look at that exact same board game state as it might be experienced by some-one with *Deuteranopia*. Figure 2.2 shows the image above once it has been put through the (genuinely excellent) tool Chromatic Vision Simulator (CVS). I thoroughly recom-mend you add this to your game design toolkit.

Right away, you can see the issue – what was a vibrant, exciting board of colours and possibility has become a largely undifferentiated mess. With ideal lighting, it might be possible for someone to get up close to the board and identify which are the red and which are the orange pieces. It **might** be. But imagine having to do that every time some-one makes a move and hold all of that information in your memory. It's just not feasible. And worse, those colours are also used on the tokens that tell players what they need to spend. Figure 2.3 is a quad view that shows the same image four times, with 'fully chromatic' (C) vision in the top left, (P) *Protanopia* in the top right, (D) *Deuteranopia* in the bottom left, and (T) *Tritanopia* in the bottom right.

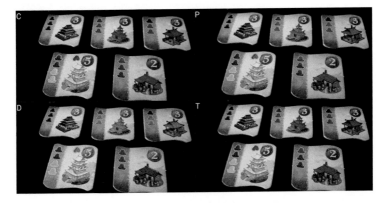

FIGURE 2.3   Tiles of the game Yamatai as seen through CVS. *Abbreviations*: C: Fully chromatic; D: Deuteranopia; P: Protanopia; T: Tritanopia. (Photograph by the author, CVS used under the MIT licence.)

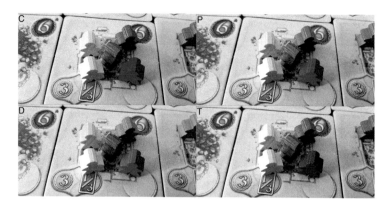

FIGURE 2.4   Five Tribes, meeples and board, as seen through CVS. *Abbreviations*: C: Fully chromatic; D: Deuteranopia; P: Protanopia; T: Tritanopia. (Photograph by the author, CVS used under the MIT licence.)

We see similar issues in Figure 2.4, which shows **Five Tribes** (2014), also from *Days of Wonder*, and also the four-quad view from CVS. Also consider the dice in **Lords of Vegas** (2010, Figure 2.5). Or the spices is **Century: Eastern Wonders** (2018, Figure 2.6). And the cards of **Iota** (2014, Figure 2.7).

The problem with all of these games is that they use colour alone as a channel of information – the only way to tell one thing from another thing is by colour. This is known as *single coding*, and it's the cause of 99% of issues in colour accessibility. It's frustrating because the solution to this problem – and again, 99% of colour blindness accessibility issues – is to *double code*. It's not enough to pick good colours (and indeed, these games don't even do that). You have to eliminate the idea that colour is a reliable way to provide information to a player. But also, you need to do it correctly.

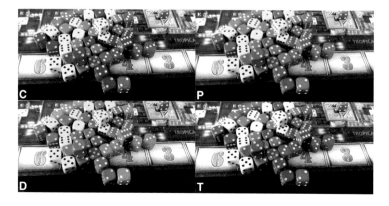

FIGURE 2.5   The dice of Lords of Vegas, used to indicate player ownership of casino tiles. *Abbreviations*: C: Fully chromatic; D: Deuteranopia; P: Protanopia; T: Tritanopia. (Photograph by the author, CVS used under the MIT licence.)

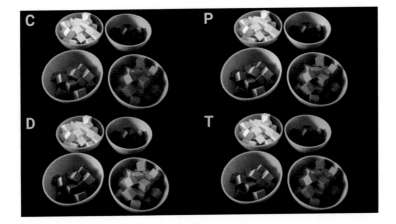

FIGURE 2.6 Spice in Century: Eastern Wonders as viewed through CVS. *Abbreviations*: C: Fully chromatic; D: Deuteranopia; P: Protanopia; T: Tritanopia. (Photograph by the author, CVS used under the MIT licence.)

Games with Good Colour Design

Coloretto (2003, Figure 2.8) – as you might guess from the name – is a game about colours. You lay out cards and collect sets. You get scored for every set of colours you create, but the quirk of the design is that you don't necessarily get scored **positively** for each set. You pick three sets that serve as your baseline score, and the value of all the other sets subtract from your total It's important, in other words, to be very mindful what sets you create, which you build, and which you neglect. It uses eight different coloured sets, and these include reds, greens, and blues. In other words, it includes all the problem colours that we identified earlier. And yet, I regard it as being 'fully accessible' for people with colour blindness.

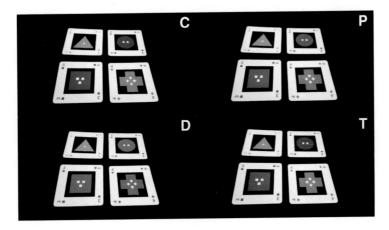

FIGURE 2.7 Iota as seen through CVS. *Abbreviations*: C: Fully chromatic; D: Deuteranopia; P: Protanopia; T: Tritanopia. (Photograph by the author, CVS used under the MIT licence.)

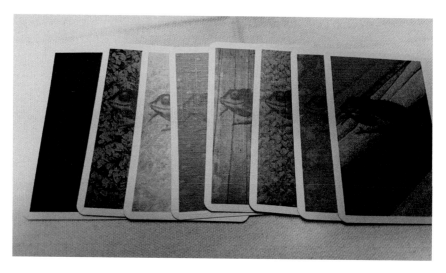

FIGURE 2.8   Coloretto as seen through CVS. Note the use of double coding to indicate different sets. (Photograph by the author, CVS used under the MIT licence.)

Note that every colour comes with a pattern in the background. Those that can't rely on the colour can instead rely on the texture associated with the card. This is *double coding* – providing the same information (to which set a card belongs) in two forms (texture and colour). You can even *triple code*. Colour, with a texture, and with an icon. Or more! There is though a certain point at which coding becomes too visually busy to be accessible, but double coding is almost never going to be a problem. **The Resistance** (2009) is an example of a game that uses *triple coding* (Figure 2.9). It uses colour to indicate team membership as well as an icon and a character portrait that indicate uniqueness of the

FIGURE 2.9   Triple coding as employed in The Resistance. *Abbreviations*: C: Fully chromatic; D: Deuteranopia; P: Protanopia; T: Tritanopia. (Photograph by the author, CVS used under the MIT licence.)

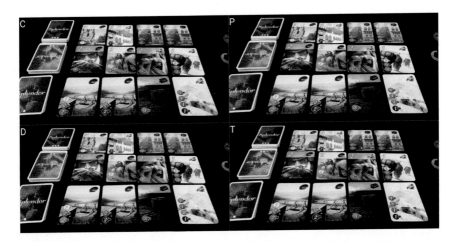

FIGURE 2.10 Splendor – Does the right thing but still perhaps not accessible. *Abbreviations*: C: Fully chromatic; D: Deuteranopia; P: Protanopia; T: Tritanopia. (Photograph by the author, CVS used under the MIT licence.)

team. The character portraits will only really become useful as players become familiar with the whole roster available, but it's an additional way to tell your role that detracts nothing and indeed adds to the experience.

We'll have cause to return to The Resistance in other chapters.

In **Splendor** (2014), you collect gemstones to buy gem production, and the more gem production you have, the cheaper all your future purchases become. The goal is to reach 15 points before everyone else. Certain cards on the table yield those points, and combinations of gem production may also lure nobles (worth a hefty three points each) to your home. Again, a game in which collecting the right combination of things is important.

Splendor accompanies each colour of gem with an icon for that gem (Figure 2.10), which you can see in the top right of each card. It also uses a smaller version of the icon on each of the cost markers at the bottom left. It *double codes* the information. However, it's included here not because it *double codes* but to show some of the risks that go along with following accessibility instructions without the knowledge of context.

Just because something is an accessibility solution doesn't mean it can be applied without thought or consideration. Guidelines alone are not sufficient for achieving accessibility – if they are improperly applied without reference to their motivation, they can end up causing more problems than they solve. That's not the case with **Splendor** – the inclusion of its icons doesn't make anything worse. The icons though for displaying cost are quite small and difficult to make out at a distance. If you have colour blindness that intersects with a visual accessibility issue (short sightedness, for example), you may find yourself having to examine the available cards quite closely before you can make an intelligent decision. And, problematically, the more you examine the table, the more likely it is that other players will deduce your intentions and may act to undermine them.

Some games too, it has to be acknowledged, don't need explicit double coding even if they use colour exclusively because they indicate all the pertinent game state through other routes. **Perudo** (1800, Figure 2.11) is a classic dice game that shares a close design

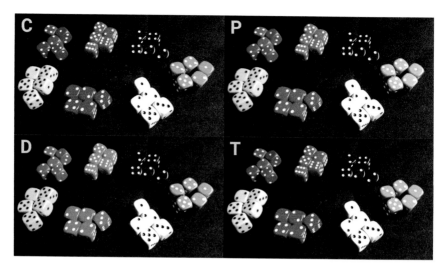

FIGURE 2.11   Perudo and its dice. *Abbreviations*: C: Fully chromatic; D: Deuteranopia; P: Protanopia;
T: Tritanopia. (Photograph by the author, CVS used under the MIT Licence.)

lineage with **Liar's Dice**, the perrenial gambling game of buccaneers if Disney's Pirates
of the Caribbean is to be believed. You can play it with handfuls of dice you happen to
have around the house (five per player), but you can also buy a box that comes with dice
that are coloured in sets. That colour information is purely decorative because each die
fulfils the same role in the game – a way to generate a random number. The dice that
belong to you never leave the proximity of your play area, unless they are discarded. This
is an **implicit** *double coding* because you get – for free, without designing anything –
the double coding of physicality.

Perudo is a game of attrition, in which hubris gradually robs each player of their dice
until only one player (the winner) has any dice left at all. However, if you play very well,
you might – very rarely – get one of those dice back. The only role that colour has in the
whole game is that returning dice from a pile into the rightful player's pool may be difficult if everyone at the table has the same kind of colour blindness. In the end, it doesn't
matter if you're using a mismatched set of dice – the game plays exactly the same.

Games with Especially Interesting Colour Design

Accessibility is too complex a topic for us to divide games into **good** or **bad**. Every game
contains multitudes. We come back here to the discussion we had in Chapter 1 – every
game reinvents the idea of an interface. It is only to be expected that games innovate
with how colour is used as much as they do with anything else.

But also, board games are simply nice objects to play with. Beauty is not necessarily a functional requirement of a game, but it's increasingly a quality of life expectation. Games from even a couple of decades ago tend to look drab and dull on the table.
They don't **pop.** And games these days need to pop if they're going to stand out from
an increasingly competitive crowd. We've focused so far in this chapter on the idea of
colour as a channel of information. We can't neglect colour as a channel of beauty.

FIGURE 2.12 The translucent dice of Sagrada. (Photograph by the author.)

The games in this section aren't picked for being exemplars or cautionary tales. Rather they are selected because of how they add richness to the discussion because of the ways in which their colour use manifests. Let's start with the only game where I have ever said 'You know what, maybe this **can't** be colour-blind accessible without losing something important in the process'. That game is **Sagrada** (2017), which is a game of using translucent coloured dice to build stained glass windows.

Figure 2.12 shows the importance of **aesthetics** in the game. Everything about it evokes the intricate glasswork of devotion. You fit coloured dice into the slots based on their face value, the placement restrictions of the window pattern you have chosen, and colour proximity. You cannot have a die of the same value, or the same colour, orthogonally adjacent to another. **Sagrada** is a game of tightening a noose around your possibility space, with the easy choices of the first round giving away to torturous compromise in the middle, and frustrating failure at the end.

It's great.

But you can see, I'm sure, the accessibility issue. If not, we can certainly show it (Figure 2.13).

It's the single coding problem once more. Each die is identical except for its colour, and colour is an important channel of information for play. Our solution, as we have already outlined, is simple – right? We double code.

Double coding dice is a little more difficult than double-coding a card or a board. There are though ways to do it. Some dice use dots to indicate their value (as **Sagrada** does). Some use roman numerals. Some dice are transparent. Some are opaque. Some are opaque with marbling or transparent with flecks. Some are plastic. Some are wood. Some are metal. Some even **light up.** There are five colours of dice in Sagrada, and you can quite easily come up with a set of five possibilities that implement double coding:

- Transparent, with dots
- Transparent, with numerals

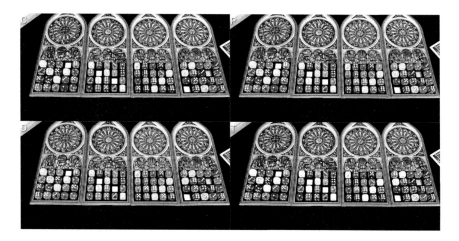

FIGURE 2.13   The dice of Sagrada as seen through a colour blindness filter. *Abbreviations*: C: Fully chromatic; D: Deuteranopia; P: Protanopia; T: Tritanopia. (Photograph by the author, CVS used under the MIT Licence.)

- Opaque, with dots
- Opaque, with numerals
- Opaque, with numerals, with marbling

The problem here is the marriage of game design, to game theme, to game aesthetics. The uniformity of the transparent dice creates a visual impression that evokes a strong sense of the goal – to create beautiful stained glass windows. That tight knot of synchronicity would not survive the change to different kinds of dice. **Sagrada** is definitely a game that **could** be made colour-blind accessible. It's the only game though where I think the cost might be too high for most players to bear.

That's not to say there aren't solutions. Sagrada doesn't use full-sized dice, but you can buy bags of mini-dice pretty easily off the Internet, and an accessible blend of these could certainly be put together. I just wouldn't want to play it, and I suspect that's true for most people. Sometimes the solution I recommend for players is to just play something else. **Roll Player** (2016) is a very similar kind of game, and it absolutely would survive having its boring inaccessible dice (Figure 2.14) swapped out for accessible alternatives.

Sagrada poses us a deeper question about accessibility, which is 'What are you prepared to lose in order to make this game colour-blind friendly?' As I say, the question doesn't come up often – most games can easily be made colour-blind accessible without the sacrifice of anything of importance. However, like the stained glass windows upon which it is designed, I think a reasonable person could say **Sagrada** is too fragile an artefact to stand much tampering.

Not all games have inaccessibility as a result of their colour choices. Sometimes their problems emerge as a result of cultural association with colour. In the west, white is a colour often associated with weddings. In other countries, white is the colour of mourning. More pertinently though to our discussion, the meaning of colour is a product of the people at the table. I may associate a bright orange with the falling leaves of autumn.

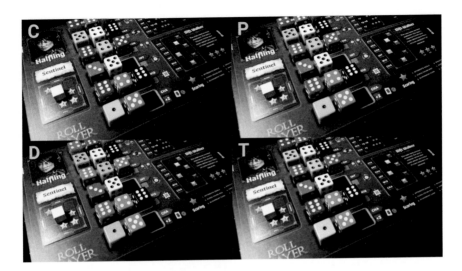

FIGURE 2.14 Roll player as seen through colour blindness filter. It may not be very accessible, but there is no cost to replacing the dice with ones that are. *Abbreviations*: C: Fully chromatic; D: Deuteranopia; P: Protanopia; T: Tritanopia. (Photograph by the author, CVS used under the MIT licence.)

My mind is hard-wired to make that connection because I have seen the passing of many seasons. Someone with colour blindness may not make the same immediate association as their experience of the changing palette of the seasonal calendar is different.

So when we have a game like **Dixit** (2008) or its darker spiritual twin **Mysterium** (2015), we find games that are completely colour-blind accessible but also complex from a colour perception perspective. Both games are about communicating through abstractions. In **Dixit**, you are dealt a hand of cards containing whimsical imagery. The active player tells a 'story' about that card in the form of a phrase, or a gesture, or a sound. Everyone else looks at their hand and plays down a card that is the closest match to the expressed story. Everyone then votes on what they believe the storyteller's card was. The storyteller only gets points if some, but not all, of the other players vote for their card. As such, they want to be vague enough to avoid being obvious, but not so vague that nobody makes the connection.

Figure 2.15 shows a sample of cards, and what we can instantly see is that the colour palette experienced by each player will create different associations. No information is lost here. Every player has the same art. They just see it differently and will be *semantically primed* in different ways. If you've never encountered the idea of *semantic priming*, it's basically that your brain operates on a kind of 'just-in-time' system. If someone says the word 'dog' to you, your brain begins to nudge all the dog-adjacent neurons out of their sleep. 'Wake up!', it yells. 'You might be needed in a bit!'

Mysterium is a very similar kind of game to **Dixit**, except that one player is a ghost trying to lead players to conclusions about their murderer. The ghost gives players clues in the form of dreams, and those dreams are made up of cards that contain associations (of the ghost's choosing) that link up murderer, murder location, and murder weapon. Let's say a ghost is trying to map the central card to the in-hand options (Figure 2.16).

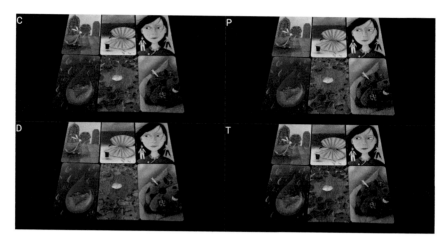

FIGURE 2.15   Some of the whimsical art of Dixit as seen through a colour blindness filter. *Abbreviations*: C: Fully chromatic; D: Deuteranopia; P: Protanopia; T: Tritanopia. (Photograph by the author, CVS used under the MIT licence.)

In the absence of anything more solid, they try to communicate a colour clue – linking the colour of the bedspread to the colour of the dream. Unfortunately, the ghost has Protanopia and those connections may not be shared by others at the table (Figure 2.17).

The extent to which someone with colour blindness will rely on colour as a clue language is obviously dependant on players. People can work to avoid these kind of associations. But that's why these are games with interesting features for people with colour blindness rather than games that have problems. They just show the complexity associated with dealing with accessibility in a board gaming context.

FIGURE 2.16   Mysterium, as seen through a colour blindness filter. Centre card represents a clue given by the ghost to the players. *Abbreviations*: C: Fully chromatic; D: Deuteranopia; P: Protanopia; T: Tritanopia. (Photograph by the author, CVS used under the MIT licence.)

FIGURE 2.17   Mysterium, showing the fragility of clues around colour. *Abbreviations*: C: Fully chromatic; D: Deuteranopia; P: Protanopia; T: Tritanopia. (Photograph by the author, CVS used under the MIT licence.)

Double coding is never likely to be a bad thing. It always exposes more information to more players. It's just that double coding **alone** is not in and of itself a solution to your accessibility problems. It always needs to be considered in the context of how it'll be used in the game. For example, I have occasionally seen people recommend **Hanabi** (2010) as a colour-blind accessible game. To be fair, it does exactly what I say a game should do – it double codes its colour information as we can see in Figure 2.18.

Hanabi is a game of collaboratively building a firework display. Its design is that you hold your hand of cards **face out**. You never know what cards you have, but you do know

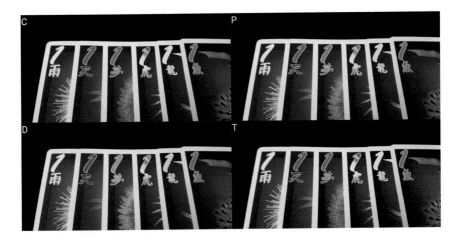

FIGURE 2.18   The cards of Hanabi, and their problematic double coding. *Abbreviations*: C: Fully chromatic; D: Deuteranopia; P: Protanopia; T: Tritanopia. (Photograph by the author, CVS used under the MIT licence.)

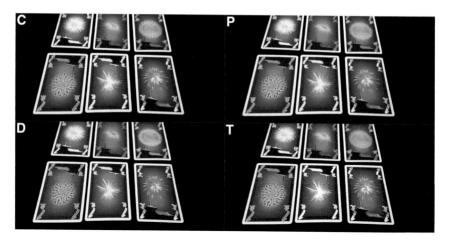

FIGURE 2.19 The cards of Hanabi once more, and their equally problematic triple coding. *Abbreviations*: C: Fully chromatic; D: Deuteranopia; P: Protanopia; T: Tritanopia. (Photograph by the author, CVS used under the MIT Licence.)

what everyone else has. The group collectively has to play out sequences of cards in the right colours. Knowing the face value **and** number of the card is important, as is being able to communicate this to other players. In recognition, **Hanabi** actually triple codes its different kinds of fireworks (Figure 2.19).

Here we brush up against another issue that comes with *double coding*, explicitly within the frame of being able to communicate with other people. Double (and triple) coding can sometimes thrive, or not, on the basis on how easily you can **describe** the coding to other people. The use of Japanese kanji (while certainly thematic) is a troublesome choice here for those that don't know the proper words for the characters in use. As is the description of the fireworks:

> This card in your hand is a 4, with a spherical firework pattern and a character that looks a bit like a fox with a tail but not like the fox with the tail that leans to the left, or the fox with the tail that has too many legs.

Familiarity – as with the *triple coding* in The **Resistance** – will help alleviate this. A group of people who play **Hanabi** regularly will build up a vocabulary of description. The problem is that if you do have a colour-blind player participating for the first time, they will find it difficult to play. The triple coding isn't really communicable in the way it needs to be to gel with the design. Hanabi then is an example of good intentions, combined with a correct implementation of a guideline, that solves little because it doesn't cohere with the way the information is used in the game.

Finally let's consider the **Unlock** (2017–2023) series. The conception and design of these games represent a compelling problem for accessibility. For those who haven't encountered these fun 'escape rooms in a box', the pitch is simple. There are dozens of scenarios, each of which are purchased separately. You get a deck of cards. Each card has a numeric value on it. Combining the value of these cards lets you explore the intersection of their interactions via arithmetic. A crowbar (15) used on a door (11) is (15 + 11 = 26). If there's a card 26, then congrats – you've unveiled a bit more of the puzzle.

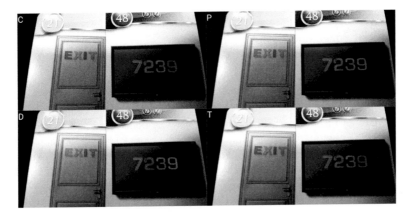

FIGURE 2.20 A puzzle from the Unlock tutorial. Colour perception is important to its timely solution *Abbreviations*: C: Fully chromatic; D: Deuteranopia; P: Protanopia; T: Tritanopia. (Photograph by the author, CVS used under the MIT licence.)

The **Exit** games (2016–2023) work similarly. They all share a common core of a solution wheel and a set of cards and other 'feelies' that represent the escape room. They also come with a booklet that will contain many of the puzzles. You explore the environment through cards where clues and other puzzles may be displayed. When you think you know the solution, you dial it into the solution wheel and may find yourself rewarded with more cards, more puzzles, and parts of the solution to other puzzles. Each scenario takes maybe a couple of hours in a group, and nobody knows in advance what the puzzles are going to be. Each is an inaccessibility of accessibility – in order to tell people what accessibility considerations are part of the puzzle, they would invariably need to spoil their own design.

That's true of both sets of games – I include them in the colour blindness section not because that's where they are most likely to demonstrate this issue. It's just that colour is a common aspect of puzzle design. Consider this example (Figure 2.20) from the Unlock tutorial adventure (which I don't feel bad about spoiling):

It's a trivial puzzle – the code is the numbers, in the order it is outlined on the door. Except it's only trivial if you have fully chromatic vision. Everyone else – good luck with working out the logic of an impossible puzzle. Sometimes puzzles are hard because the design is unforgiving. Sometimes they're hard because you haven't found all of the information you need and you have to go hunting for what's missing. Here, it's impossible because there is no more information to come, it's just that the information you need is unavailable **to you.**

Guidelines for Colour-Blind Accessibility

- *Games to look to for inspiration*:
  - Codenames/Codenames Pictures, Wingspan, Sushi Go, Splendor, Second Chance, Modern Art, Jaipur, Isle of Trains, Ingenious, Imperial Settlers, Coloretto, and Arboretum.
- *Games to look to as cautionary tales*:
  - Iota, Yamatai, Lords of Vegas, and Takenoko.

Icon Design

Make Icons Large and Easy to Tell Apart

When using icons to support colour blindness, make them as large as possible so as to ease game flow. The less people need to closely examine the board to find key information, the more fun they'll have.

One of the ways our eyes can pick up information is through comparison with its context. Gestalt theory gives us some useful ways of understanding how we interpret information. To summarise though, the simplest way to make it easy for people to identify things at a distance is to ensure that their outlines (or silhouettes) are distinctive. A rectangle versus a square is not very distinctive at a distance. A circle versus a triangle on the other hand is difficult to mix up.

- Make use of all available and appropriate component real-estate for icons.
- Emphasise distinctiveness of different icons.
- Compare each icon in your game against others to identify silhouette overlap.

General Aesthetics

Double Code All Your Information

This is the big, important guideline in this category. Avoid the use, as far as is possible, of colour as the sole channel of game information.

- Make use of texture, shapes, materials, symbols, or other visual differentiation to supplement colour information.
- Employ transparency and opaqueness as a method of differentiating physical components.
- Examine your game through a colour blindness tool to identify missed opportunities for double coding.

Make Icons Easy to Describe

Many games require players to communicate gameplay information to others. This is especially true when you consider the intersection of disability categories – a colour-blind player who cannot reach over a board to move a piece, as an example. Make sure that it's easy for people to describe pieces, cards, board elements, and such with reference to your double- (or triple-)coded design.

- Ensure each icon has a clearly describable shape.
- When introducing icons in rule-books and reference cards, give them a name that players can use.

Use a Colour-Blind Friendly Palette

Colour-blind friendly palettes do not work in all circumstances (hence why we recommend double coding so heavily), but they certainly help. At the very least, avoid using red, green, and blue in combination as these three choices map onto the cones of our eyes and will be a problem in all circumstances of colour blindness.

- Use one of the colour-blind friendly palettes as outlined above as the baseline for your colour profile.
- Where red, green, and blue must be employed, try to use them for non-critical components and aesthetics.

Rules

Describe by Role, Not Colour

Avoid formally linking colour to game role, for example having the blue meeple associated with a blue card which outlines role and powers. While this aids in identification for fully chromatic players, it makes everything harder if tokens must be swapped around or replaced.

Colours may not mean the same thing to different people. Avoid where possible relying on colour names as a consistent element of disambiguation in rules or examples. Instead support this with the use of other descriptors such as player names or player roles.

- Avoid the use of language such as 'the red player moves their piece' in manuals and instructional material. Instead consider role-specific wording such as 'the medic player moves their piece'.
- When encoding links between roles and player pieces on the board, make that link based on iconography rather than colour.

Game Layout and Experience

Minimise the Busyness of the Board

Consider how easy it is to tell game elements apart when they are mostly densely arranged. Consider too compounding issue of density of game pieces and distinctiveness of pieces. Even very easily differentiated pieces can become inaccessible if observed within a mess of others. The density of a game is one of the primary ways in which inaccessibility can manifest.

- Make use of modular boards where possible to help manage the density of the game layout.
- If appropriate, consider verticality (stacking pieces for example) as a way to convey game information in an otherwise underused axis.

Meeples and Miniatures

Give Miniatures Some Unique Identifier

Make sure each meeple and miniature has, as far as is possible, some way to be differentiated other than through colours. Either have completely unique form factors associated with each player piece or some additional physical double coding through tokens, stickers, or other physical annotations.

- If possible, make use of add-ons such as stickers and accessories to provide a way to differentiate pieces that are identical save for colour.
- Consider the use of player-specific miniatures (for example, the car, the ship, and the wee scotty dug) to eliminate colour-based differentiation.

Dice and Randomisation

Make Use of Different Channels of Differentiation

If using colour to indicate differences between dice, consider alternating between transparencies, textures, and die faces to offer additional channels of differentiation. A standard die for example may be opaque or transparent. It may employ Arabic numerals or dots. It may be embossed or recessed. Combining these allows for double coding in circumstances where it would otherwise be difficult.

- Consider all your game components in combination, and make use of all opportunities to differentiate.
- Consider varying aesthetics to convey information in which colour is critical and double coding is otherwise difficult.

General Component Design

Offer Supplemental Identifiers as Opt-In

If colour cannot be easily altered to be accessible, consider providing stickers or other (optional) supporting adhesives for those that require them.

- Allow players to semi-permanently annotate game components with stickers or provide spaces in which annotations can be written.
- Consider the use of slots in the base of a miniature that allow for identifying tokens to be slotted into place.

Notes

1. Available at https://jfly.uni-koeln.de/color/
2. This is available at http://mkweb.bcgsc.ca/colorblind/palettes.mhtml#projecthome.

BIBLIOGRAPHY

Aslam, M. M. (2006). Are you selling the right colour? A cross-cultural review of colour as a marketing cue. *Journal of Marketing Communications, 12*(1), 15–30.
Cowey, A., & Heywood, C. A. (1997). Cerebral achromatopsia: Colour blindness despite wavelength processing. *Trends in Cognitive Sciences, 1*(4), 133–139.
Dell'Acqua, R., & Grainger, J. (1999). Unconscious semantic priming from pictures. *Cognition, 73*(1), B1–B15.

Ichihara, Y. G., Okabe, M., Iga, K., Tanaka, Y., Musha, K., & Ito, K. (2008). Color universal design: The selection of four easily distinguishable colors for all color vision types. *Color Imaging XIII: Processing, Hardcopy, and Applications, 6807*, 206–213.

Karhulahti, V.-M. (2012). Feelies: The lost art of immersing the narrative. *Proceedings of DiGRA Nordic 2012 Conference: Local and Global–Games in Culture and Society*, 1–9. http://www.digra.org/digital-library/publications/feelies-the-lost-art-of-immersing-the-narrative/

Kinsbourne, M., & Warrington, E. K. (1964). Observations on colour agnosia. *Journal of Neurology, Neurosurgery, and Psychiatry, 27*(4), 296.

McNamara, T. P. (2005). *Semantic priming: Perspectives from memory and word recognition*. Psychology Press.

Milne, S., Dickinson, A., Carmichael, A., Sloan, D., Eisma, R., & Gregor, P. (2005). Are guidelines enough? An introduction to designing web sites accessible to older people. *IBM Systems Journal, 44*(3), 557–571.

Pinckers, A. (1980). Color vision and age. *Ophthalmologica, 181*(1), 23–30.

Simunovic, M. (2010). Colour vision deficiency. *Eye, 24*(5), 747–755.

Wong, B. (2011). Color blindness. *Nature Methods, 8*(6), 441.

3

Visual Accessibility

Visual impairment covers a wide spectrum, ranging from 'slightly short-sighted' to 'totally blind'. It is though perhaps misleading to think of it in this way, as really, it's a spectrum with a largely binary state change at one extreme. Think of visual impairment as impacting on precision and range of sight and specifically the degree of reflected light that can be processed by the eyes and the brain. The thing is that the difference between seeing 'some light' and 'no light' is so significant than it moves people into an entirely new and different way of interacting with the world.

First of all, let's deal with a common assumption. When people say 'blind', or 'legally blind', there is often a belief that blindness is the same thing as darkness – as in, when someone is blind what they see is nothing. We talked about a similar assumption with regards to colour blindness – that the cultural definition is that those who are colour-blind see only in monochromacy even though that is very rare. In truth, it is approximately only one in five of the people who are 'legally blind' who have the condition of being **totally blind.** That is to say, of the estimated 284 million blind people in the world, fewer than 55 million of them can see nothing. Of those that are legally blind, around 80% of those affected are in the 50+ age category.

The legal definition of blind centres around visual acuity. We sometimes talk about 20/20 vision as being the baseline for normal sight – which is to say, at 20 feet you can clearly make out the second last line on a traditional eye-chart. European opticians may instead talk of a 6/6 baseline, which is that you can see at six meters what the average person can see at the same distance. Figure 3.1 shows the standard North American Snellen chart for reference.

One counts as legally blind in many jurisdictions when visual acuity is 20/200 or worse or, in less clinical terms, when someone sees at 20 feet what someone with 20/20 vision can see at 200 feet. Alternate definitions of legal blindness centre on someone's field of vision – if someone can see a region in front of them smaller than 20 degrees as opposed to the 90 degrees of the baseline population. The majority of people classified as blind can still differentiate between light and dark, and some may have more precise visual acuity at angles or on the periphery of their vision. Individuals with *macular degeneration* for example will usually experience the condition as a large dark patch in their central vision, but the edges will often be packed with colour and light information. *Retinopathy* (such as is often associated with diabetes) manifests as dark patches across the entire visual field. *Glaucoma* is almost the inversion of *macular degeneration*, with visual detail packed into the centre field of vision with almost nothing at the periphery. Other forms of blindness act like a curtain, dulling everything into muted shadow and

DOI: 10.1201/9781003415435-3

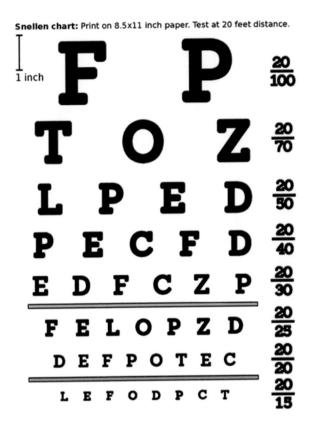

FIGURE 3.1 The standard Snellen chart used in tests of visual acuity. (From Universal Public Domain Dedication licence. Available from https://commons.wikimedia.org/wiki/Category:Snellen_charts under the CC0 1.0.)

somewhat perceivable colour. To provide a kind of framework for these different manifestations of sight, we usually talk about two main categories:

1. Total blindness, which is the 'total darkness' of cultural expectation.
2. Low vision, where someone is able to differentiate lights, colours, and shapes but with significantly reduced accuracy or precision.

Blindness may come about in later life (from disease, injury, or aging) or be *congenital* – which is to say, impactful from birth. Those that are born blind adapt to society differently from those that have to shift from a reliance on visual information to acceptance of its absence. In all cases, the lack of visual information is often accompanied by other symptoms such as discomfort or dryness in the eyes, pain or discharge, and occasional physical manifestation in terms of discolouration of the cornea. Figure 3.2 shows some examples of visual impairment.

The causes of blindness, like its manifestation in life, are varied. The most common cause of blindness in children is *cerebral visual impairment* (CVI) – a brain-based

FIGURE 3.2   These images show several kinds of visual impairment. (a) We have tunnel vision. (b) This shows macular degeneration. (c) This shows cataracts and (d) shows glaucoma. (As work produced through the US Federal government, all images are in the public domain.)

disorder that impacts on the processing of visual information. It often comes with an associated visual impairment in the eyes. However, because it is largely a processing-based disorder, it can manifest in different ways for different children. Children with CVI have sometimes described the world as a kaleidoscope or as a mass of shifting colours.

- *Macular degeneration*, which comes in both wet and dry variations, derives from a disease that results in damage to the part of the eye responsible for sharpness in straight-ahead vision. The dry version of this condition involves a thinning of the tissue in the *macular* (the part of your eye that handles central vision) as a result of its inner layers breaking down. In its early stages, it may result in visual distortions, a difficulty with low light levels, or problems in identifying faces. It can manifest in one eye or in both eyes. It is often linked to age, but it also has a genetic component. Smoking, obesity, and cardiovascular disease all contribute to the risk of developing it. There are treatments, but no known cure and it tends to be progressive – getting worse over time. The dry variant is by far (around 80–90%) the most common form of *macular degeneration*.

  The wet variant is linked to problems in the blood vessels, resulting in them leaking fluid or blood into the macula. This is the rarer variant, and it is marked by the rapidity of its progression – whereas *dry macular degeneration* is slow, progressing over several years, *wet degeneration* is severe and rapid. Retinal scarring and photoreceptor damage are the primary ways in which it impacts on vision. Despite its rarity (10–20%), it still accounts for around 90% of the most significant loss of vision associated with the broader condition of macular degeneration.

- *Retinopathy* has its own range of symptoms. It's caused by a weakening of blood vessels in the retina, which will then – as with *wet macular degeneration* –

leak blood and fluid. This time, as the name suggests, it leaks directly onto the retina. In some cases, the condition may end up triggering the growth of scar tissue, which can pull the retina away from the back of the eye. This is often accompanied with flashes of light and vision loss. Vision may worsen slowly over time or be suddenly absent. Such loss may be temporary or permanent. *Retinopathy* is associated with 'floaters', which are shapes that manifest across the whole field of vision. It can progress to total blindness.

- *Cataracts*, which manifest as cloudy areas in the lens of the eye, are a very common form of visual impairment particularly in the elderly. They result in blurry vision, faded colours, issues with light sensitivity, and double vision. They are often, but not always, correctable through surgery.

- *Glaucoma* is the catch-all name for a group of related eye diseases that impact on the optic nerve. Most cases of glaucoma are categorised as 'open-angle', which is related to pressure that impacts on the optic nerve in the back of the eye. This pressure, as time goes by, damages the nerve, which in turn damages the person's vision. High blood pressure is a predictor of *glaucoma*, as is diabetes. However, *glaucoma* can also occur in people where there is no unexpected pressure on the optic nerve (*normal tension glaucoma*) or from congenital conditions that stop fluid draining properly in the eyes. Often *glaucoma* is a condition in itself (*primary glaucoma*), but it may also be linked to another medical condition (*secondary glaucoma*).

Of course, we cannot forget the good old near-sightedness (*myopia,* Figure 3.3) and far-sightedness (*hyperopia,* Figure 3.4), both of which are related to the shape of the eye

FIGURE 3.3 This image shows an example of how myopia manifests. (As work produced through the US Federal government, all images are in the public domain.)

FIGURE 3.4   (a) An example of hyperopia or far-sightedness. (b) Normal vision. (Image by David Jueng, made available under a CC BY-SA 4.0 licence. https://en.wikipedia.org/wiki/Far-sightedness#/media/File:Hyperopia_comparison.jpg.)

and are usually correctible by contact lenses or glasses, or *strabismus*, where the eyes don't align with each other – this often comes with a corresponding lack of reliable depth perception.

All of this is to say – as we will repeat like a mantra in this book for all categories of accessibility – there are a lot of causes of visual impairment, and it manifests in a lot of different ways. It's one of the most significant barriers to play associated with board games. But we **can** make things better!

Problematic Visual Design

For understanding how visual impairment impacts on play, it's important to first consider how people may compensate in day-to-day life. Sight is generally the last thing people are willing to relinquish – they will fight tooth and nail to retain visual information as their primary way of experiencing the world. People will bring books right up to their eyes, for example, before they decide to switch to learning braille (or turning to audiobooks, these days). They will use screen magnifiers before they switch to text-to-speech. As such, many of the compensatory strategies people use are focused on enhancement – increasing the size of something through magnification or viewing angle. Within Meeple Centred Design, we refer to this as **close inspection.**

The most obvious way in which games offer problematic visual design is simply in the size of important game elements in **Scotland Yard** (first published in 1983, Figure 3.5).

The sheer size and complexity of this board are its own problems. It represents a transport network made up of buses, taxis, and subway lines. Moving around the board requires the spending of a ticket, and different tickets are applicable at different locations. To understand what makes a sensible move, someone must understand not just the options they have immediately but the options they have a turn, or two turns, or three turns, in the future.

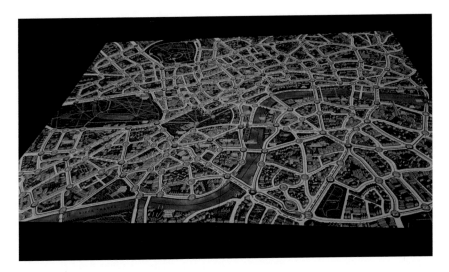

FIGURE 3.5 The board of Scotland Yard. Note how complex it is and how difficult it is to make out specifics at a distance. (Photograph by the author.)

Now let's look at that board up close (Figure 3.6). Stops indicate their valid ticket types by their colour coding and show available routes by the lines between adjacent stops. It's not possible to take a bus from stop 122 to stop 94 as there is no connecting line. You can't take a subway car from 93 to 74. A visually impaired player must hold a phenomenal amount of information in mind to make meaningful decisions, and that's a direct consequence of the density of the board. The closer you get to the elements, the less surrounding context you have. Close inspection is possible, but it doesn't help all that much. What also doesn't help is the way in which the

FIGURE 3.6 A close up of the Scotland Yard board. (Photograph by the author.)

numbering functions – to the left of stop 95 is stop 94. To the right of stop 95 is stop 77. Even to find a particular stop then is an act of visual interrogation.

But I choose **Scotland Yard** as an example here for another reason, and it's one especially important in this category. **Sometimes you don't want people to know what you're looking at.**

Scotland Yard is what is known as a *hidden movement* game. One player takes the role of a mysterious scoundrel (Mr X), and the others play police officers trying to deduce where Mr X might be. This is possible because the hunted player must inform everyone else of what they did on their turn. 'I just moved by taxi', they might say. 'I just caught a bus'. By linking together these revelations – along with what they imply about how far a player might travel – the net can close around the target as police officers examine the network of the city. Again, it is difficult to do if you're relying upon close inspection.

The larger problem though is that an easy way for Mr X to reveal themselves is to direct police attention to the region of the board where they are located. A visually impaired player is then forced to pantomime, looking closely at a range of areas even when they only need to know about one. Such deceit must be convincing to throw others off the scent, but no matter how convincing it's going to be difficult to avoid giving some additional hints as to where the police should be hunting. That's due to the complexity of the board, of its movement rules, and of the possibility space of stealth.

This then is a tremendously good example of the intersectional nature of accessibility in board games. It's not just about what information is available; it's about the implications associated with wanting to know the information.

The board of game isn't the only place where we find problems though. A common feature of many board games is the inclusion of custom dice which make use of specially designed symbols to convey game-specific information. **Blood Bowl** (2016, Figure 3.7) and indeed most *Games Workshop* titles are an example of this.

We can also see them in the **Star Wars X-Wing Miniatures Game** (2015, Figure 3.8).

FIGURE 3.7   The custom dice used in the Games Workshop game Blood Bowl. (Photograph by the author.)

FIGURE 3.8   The dice used in the X-Wing Miniatures Game. (Photograph by the author.)

Dice rolling is not, in itself, necessarily a problem for visually impaired players because they have strategies for dealing with it. They might use custom, accessible dice as shown in Figure 3.9.

Perhaps they use a dice roller app on their phone, or they can even say, 'Siri, roll five six-sided dice'. The problem with custom dice, or even standard dice used in a custom way, is that those strategies no longer reliably work. Instead, one must construct a lookup table. Table 3.1 shows an example lookup table for the **X-Wing Miniatures Game** across its two different types of custom dice (green and red, which are defence and attack).

FIGURE 3.9   This shows two accessible dice – a d20 and a d6. Regular-scale dice are shown for reference. (Photograph by the author.)

TABLE 3.1

A Constructed Lookup Table for the X-Wing
Miniatures Game

Result	Attack	Defence
1	BLANK	BLANK
2	BLANK	BLANK
3	HIT	BLANK
4	HIT	EVADE
5	HIT	EVADE
6	CRITICAL	EVADE
7	FOCUS	FOCUS
8	FOCUS	FOCUS

'A one means this, a two means this, a three means this'. This massively increases the cognitive complexity of making game decisions because it adds a layer of translation. The more the dice rolled, the greater the additional mental toll. Some games – such as **Yahtzee** (1956) and the many modern board games that use its dice-saving mechanism – require combining, separating, and interpreting dice in sets. In fact, let's do a quick example. With the **X-Wing Miniatures game**, we can trade off hits against evades – they cancel each other out. Table 3.2 shows the result of a pair of dice rolls – attack versus defend.

How many hits got through?

'I will grant you this is not exactly an impossible calculation. It's also a simpler scenario than in the actual game, as you can probably guess by the presence of focus and critical results in Table 3.2. The actual game often involves comparing these dice in sets against special cards, ship abilities, and pilot skills. It might need you to do this 20 or more times in a given round of the game. You can see the additional costs that come from custom dice **even if you had five accessible dice available to roll.** Most people don't have a cupboard full of oversized d6s, and many fewer have even one accessible d8 much less five of them.

Here we see one of the trade-offs that we discussed in an earlier chapter. Custom dice make a game more cognitively accessible, for the exact same reasons that accessible dice can make a game more cognitively complex. However, this additional cognitive accessibility comes at the cost of visual accessibility.

Nothing in life is ever easy, right?

But again, this is just one area in which visual inspection becomes a problem due to design decisions. There's one that impacts on almost every game, and that's the use of **tokens,** such as we might see in **Tigris and Euphrates** (1997, Figure 3.10).

TABLE 3.2

An Example of a Roll that Must Be Calculated with Reference to the Lookup Table in Table 3.1

	Die 1	Die 2	Die 3	Die 4	Die 5
Attacker	4	1	5	6	4
Defender	2	3	5	1	6

FIGURE 3.10   Tiles and tokens as they are presented in the game Tigris and Euphrates. (Photograph by the author.)

One easy way in which tokens can be made accessible is by allowing them to be differentiated by touch – which is to say I should be able to tell each different token apart using nothing more than my fingers. Think of the coins in your pocket, and how they usually follow an accessible design. Lower value denominations are smaller, and they will usually progress in size and shape from that.

Reaching into a pocket means someone can work out – with high accuracy – the total value of their coins. And they can do that because the form factor of each is distinctive enough and carries enough representational information (bigger means more valuable) that you don't even need to look at them. Now look back at Figure 3.10 and the Tigris and Euphrates point tokens and tiles. You can tell tiles from points. You can't tell different kinds of points apart or different kinds of tiles apart. Now look at the coins from **Merchants and Marauders** (2010, Figure 3.11).

Even the money doesn't follow the real-world design of coins. **Merchants and Marauders** is far from a lone offender in this category – it happens more often than it doesn't. But it's an especially interesting example because it would have been, thematically, so much cooler to be accessible. This is a game of pirates and traders, and we all know what a 'piece of eight' is. As a memetic link to the theme, it's almost perfect. But the piece of eight, as the name implies, was actually a coin that had been fractioned from another coin. They'd be clipped to create smaller denominations. Coins at the time had value linked to their precious metal composition, so to cut a gold coin in half was literally to make it worth half as much. A Spanish dollar was worth eight reales, and so you'd cut it into eight pieces to make a coin worth a single real.

You can already see where this is going – it would be a lot more evocative of the theme to genuinely play with a piece of eight than a coin that is indistinguishable by touch. Even old-timey pirates were making accessible design choices.

Then, we have a particular gameplay design choice that has massive implications for accessibility full stop. One thing you may have gleaned from these discussions is that accessibility compensations take time, and they take care. Examining every inch of a

FIGURE 3.11   Cardboard coinage in Merchants and Marauders. (Photograph by the author.)

board is a slow process. Contemplating the relationship between two cards when you can only perceive part of one at a time – that's a ponderous task. And it only really works when players have the time to do it – and that, in itself, may require a table of players who have more than the average amount of patience.

There is a family of game where nobody gets the time for accessibility compensation – *real-time games* – or games where reaction time is important. For many of these, the accessibility can only ever truly come from the design of the game. The other compensatory options just won't survive the frantic pace of play or sometimes the imposition of certain game rules. **Magic Maze** (2017, Figure 3.12) is a prime example.

FIGURE 3.12   A close up on part of the Magic Maze board. (Photograph by the author.)

FIGURE 3.13 The board of Magic Maze, shown at a distance. Note how much information must be managed by each player. (Photograph by the author.)

Within **Magic Maze**, everyone is collaboratively trying to get the pawns to a particular location by acting upon the single direction in which they are allowed to move things. This is done to a time limit, and there are all kinds of restrictions on the board as to who can go where and what happens when a pawn steps upon individual squares. That would be difficult enough to do under ideal circumstances, but Magic Maze also introduces a silence clause. Most of the game, all you get to do is communicate by passive-aggressively banging a piece in front of someone else.

It happens across a board that is visually complex and one that sprawls as new elements are added (Figure 3.13). The pawns are distributed across the board, within a context where the wrong move can be disastrous. Close inspection just isn't a possibility here because there's that time limit. And you can't even ask for help because of the silence rule.

I rated **Magic Maze** as 'literally unplayable for people with visual impairments', and that's a judgement I rarely attach to a game for the reasons we discussed in Chapter 1 – namely, it's **almost** always incorrect.

Every accessibility issue that exists is made more pressing by the presence of a time constraint – whether it's in the design of the game or informally imposed by an impatient table. We're all familiar with the problem of what is sometimes called *analysis paralysis*. When faced with too many options, or possibilities with too many permutations, many people have a tendency to freeze in a process of intense contemplation as they weigh up what are often incomparable choices. A player prone to indecision can add a layer of frustration to an enjoyable gaming experience unless a game is designed to allow a certain parallelism of actions. Otherwise, the game moves at the pace of the slowest player. Accessibility compensations can function like this, and players with impairments can feel pressured at the table even if there isn't a timer slicing away at the precious seconds of the round.

And then, there are games like **Escape: The Curse of the Temple** (2012, Figure 3.14), which take two inaccessibilities and blend them together. This is a game of collaboratively exploring an expanding temple, rolling dice to move and unlock the

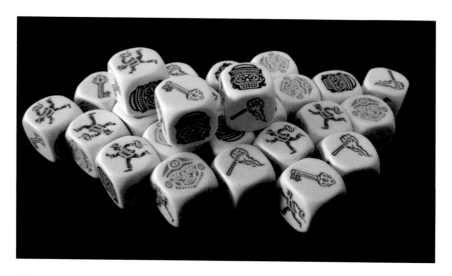

FIGURE 3.14   The dice from Escape: The Curse of the Temple. (Photograph by the author.)

secrets found within. Every player rolls a pool of five dice, and these may allow movement, solving challenges, and opening doors.

When a player rolls a black mask, that die is locked and can't be rolled again. A golden mask can unlock two locked dice, and it can unlock the dice of anyone in the same room. The game is played to a tight time limit, and every so often players must return to the central chamber within 30 s to avoid catastrophe – the permanent loss of one of their dice. But if most of your dice are locked, you probably won't be able to do that. So you yell across the table, saying 'I'm locked! I need someone to come help me!' and then someone has to roll the dice they need to get to you, roll enough golden masks, and then go back to what they were doing. And of course, it's only fate that is stopping them from blocking themselves in the process.

It sounds hectic, but what makes it **especially so** is that you don't take turns in **Escape**. No – you all roll the dice as often as you can, as fast as you can. And you better be quick because there's virtually no time to do anything.

My partner (referenced throughout Meeple Like Us as 'Mrs Meeple') is the underappreciated co-author of much of the work in this book because she's the one with whom I play most games. Conversations with her inform almost every observation throughout this text. She's also a keen fitness fanatic, and she's in such great shape that her resting heart-beat lies a few whiskers above 'probably dead'. Because she is obsessed with the topic, she wears a fitness tracker at all time. After we played **Escape: The Curse of the Temple**, her heart rate had spiked up by 40 beats per minute. That is to say – we have conducted quantitative experiments that demonstrate clearly that this is a game so stressful it can literally kill. It is though fun enough to be worth the risk.

Imagine how that works together – custom dice, rolled in combinations, against a tight time limit, and in real-time. One of these elements wouldn't necessarily render the game unplayable. It is the combination here that makes it an issue for visually impaired players. Inaccessibilities can compound in unexpected ways.

Then we have the issue of games that don't use tokens for their currency and instead rely on paper money. Paper notes tend to be printed from lesser paper stock than actual currency, with numerous effects. Notes are hard to differentiate, hard to form into the requisite combinations, and hard to count.

'Ah', you might say, 'You are wrong there because blind people use paper money all the time', to which I reply 'I live in Sweden, nobody here has touched a paper note in years. But yes, you are right – and it still doesn't help anyone playing a board game'.

One of the common techniques blind people will use to deal with paper money is what's called the *folding method*. The smallest denomination of money goes unfolded. The next higher is folded lengthwise. The next is folded by width. The next still is folded by length and then by width. If there are still unaccounted for denominations, they get held in a separate compartment of a wallet or a pocket. In essence, notes get folded based on how often they're likely to be used.

That works in real life because by and large few of us are regularly making it rain with our phat stacks. As I believe the kids say. We use money occasionally, mindfully, and generally only a few times in a given period. As such, the 'ramp-up' cost of actually handling the folding is something that can be borne by the day's activities. It doesn't work in a board game because money is exchanged far more quickly, in far more complex quantities, and between far more people.

All of this is before we get to the really common offenders with regards to visual inaccessibility – *size*, *distinctiveness*, and *contrast*. I leave these for last because they are, by far, the most significant and common problem in graphical design for board games.

In **Blood Bowl** (2016), we can see this in the design of its board. The game is one of grid-based fantasy football. **Literally** fantasy football, as you have orcs tackling elves while trolls are eating the goblins. The contrast between the grid-lines and the artwork sometimes makes it difficult to place pieces where they should go. Each of these sectioned white lines (Figure 3.15) actually represents a 3 × 3 region of squares, but you'd be forgiven for not seeing the little crosses that indicate them.

FIGURE 3.15 The board of Blood Bowl. You can probably make out the white lines that separate regions of the board. You may find it more difficult to see the little crosses that indicate individual spaces that will be occupied by pieces. (Photograph by the author.)

FIGURE 3.16   Cargo items that will be carried by the ships in Merchants and Marauders. (Photograph by the author.)

This contrast ratios (the difference between one colour and another) are not a major problem for people with 20/20 vision. You can make it out, on the green side of the board, easily enough if you're close enough. They do increasingly become a problem as colour differentiation becomes less reliable or as visual acuity diminishes.

Merchants and Marauders demonstrates another problem – the size element. You can see on the board when tokens are placed on each port, and these correspond to a demand for goods that you can deliver for a bonus (Figure 3.16).

Now, take a look at Figure 3.17 and tell me which good is currently in demand in St John.

FIGURE 3.17   The distance view of the Merchants and Marauders map. Note how difficult some goods are to distinguish at a distance. (Photograph by the author.)

FIGURE 3.18   Tiles in Exodus: Proxima Centauri. Nothing here is inaccessible in itself, but in combination, it becomes a challenge to parse game state. (Photograph by the author.)

The goods markers are all different, but they're not **different enough** to be able to identify at a distance. Close inspection here will reveal 'Michael wants to sell in St John, so I am going to beat him there'. The tokens are not **differentiable** because they're too small.

That's not even necessarily just an issue of the tokens by themselves. Sometimes visual differentiation is made difficult by sheer complexity of state. **Exodus: Proxima Centauri** (2013, Figure 3.18) absolutely floods each of its (reasonably sized) hexes in information, bits of which will obscure other bits.

There's a lot of information contained on every single hex:

- Victory point value.
- Type of resource.
- Numerical direction indicators.
- Initial number of resources.
- Current number of resources (the dice).
- Ships in the area.

One hex by itself is a baffling blend of information. The board is made up of many hexes, each of which also add **contextual** information such as implied by their adjacency to others. Regardless of how accessible any individual hex may have been, the **combination** of them would still end up being inaccessible.

Finally, then we get to the issue of size with regards to text. **Lords of Waterdeep** (2012, Figure 3.19) has cards with text that is so small that someone would need a magnifying glass for their magnifying glass to make it out.

In its defence, the smallest text is also the least important for play. It's what's called **flavour text**, which is to say descriptive text that is there to set context and unveil relevant lore. Even at its best though many of these cards are text heavy in a way that is a visual accessibility challenge.

FIGURE 3.19   Some of the cards in Lords of Waterdeep. (Photograph by the author.)

If a trade-off must be made, it's better for flavour text to be inaccessible so that game-relevant info can be visible. The trade-off though should ideally be avoided because of the message it sends. 'You can have a subset of the game' is perhaps not the inclusivity standard for which we should be striving.

Games with Good Visual Design

So, what games offer especially **good** visual design that may offer a path towards accessibility?

Some obvious examples feel a little cheap to bring up because complexity of the game design itself has an impact on how feasible solutions might be. **Cards Against Humanity** (2009) has an almost perfect visual design because it is literally just some words on some cards. The cards are black and white, as is the text, offering almost perfect contrast.

You may think I chose **Cards Against Humanity** just so I could show a photo (Figure 3.20) of the best round I ever played out. You may very well think that. I couldn't possibly comment.

But the aesthetic of Cards Against Humanity is used in a lot of different games of similar style. **Funemployed** (2014, Figure 3.21), for example, is the same aesthetic and largely the same game experience. It's just that you have to argue why you should be given a ridiculous job on the basis of a comical CV. It's the game I usually recommend to people who like Cards Against Humanity and are looking for something a little more skill based and a little less … emotionally confrontational. These kind of social games have little mechanical complexity, and thus little game state they need to convey on the cards. They are (almost) optimally accessible because they have an easy job to do. Even so, there is room for improvement. There's usually **a lot** of unused space on these cards that could be used to increase the font size even farther.

FIGURE 3.20 Answer and questions cards for Cards Against Humanity. This may be the single round of any game I am most proud of playing out. (Photograph by the author.)

Most games though have more game state to represent, more complexity of state to communicate, and more interaction between gameplay elements. They also have to take into account deeper aesthetic considerations. The visual accessibility associated with these designs offers perhaps more generalisable guidance. **Billionaire Banshee** (2014, Figure 3.22) could be thought of as the next step up – it's still a game primarily about conversation, but it has more information to convey on each card. The game is about navigating a kind of fantastical version of Tinder where you are presented with exotic individuals with interesting blends of 'quirks' and 'perks'. Your friends try to guess if

FIGURE 3.21 The cards of Funemployed. (Photograph by the author.)

FIGURE 3.22   The cards of Billionaire Banshee. (Photograph by the author.)

this is a person you'd actually date. Structurally it is very similar in its design to the games we've already discussed, but more complex in its aesthetic.

The trick here is that the game works well even if the current player cannot see because verbalising the traits on each card can be done by anyone. A visually impaired player can have their options read aloud by someone else, and in many cases, that actually increases the fun of the game. The alternative is playing out two cards and then everyone has to get up and read the contents privately. The narrated version ensures that everyone gets to contemplate their erotic opportunities with nothing more than their ears – a kind of aural sex, in other words.

This solves a problem with the cards themselves – the text is dense and complicated, and the ALL CAPS form makes it difficult to read. It is the style of play, rather than the card design, that creates the accessibility opportunities.

Tokaido (2012) ensures visual differentiation through both game and art design. This is a game that, depending on your frame of mind, is about taking a nice serene holiday or being stuck queueing during a commute. The current player is the one that is farthest back on the track, and they can move wherever they like forwards on the board to an unoccupied space until they are no longer the current player. At each stop, they can reap whatever benefits are available. The game then is a balance between getting lots of things and getting the things you need before someone blocks them.

Figure 3.23 shows the full board, which is long and meandering. Figure 3.24 shows all you really need to pay attention to in any given turn. You technically can go right from the starting slot to the end slot for the stage, but realistically you are making a single decision each turn, which is 'What is the least distance I can travel while still getting something I want'. As such, all you really need to know is where **you** are and where there are available slots. It's still not perfect – the meeples can't be differentiated by touch and there's a lot of white space on the board that could have been used to make the stops easier to see. However, with a single sighted player at the board the game becomes fully playable through discussion.

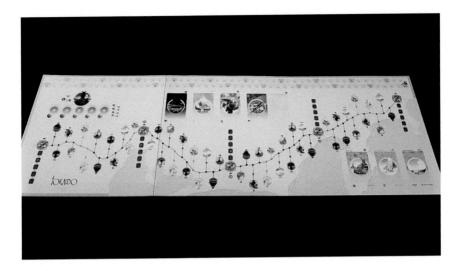

FIGURE 3.23 The board of Tokaido – note how much of it is given over to white space. (Photograph by the author.)

To see a game that neatly solves Tokaido's issue with the meeples, we can look farther back in time. **Monopoly** (1933, Figure 3.25) has been optimally accessible for player tokens since the very early days, where each player would be represented by a piece taken from a charm bracelet. People form strong associations with the different player pieces in Monopoly. 'I'm always the race car', or 'I want to be the wee Scottie dug'. The charms are, well, charming. They are also the best example of how player pieces should be handled in a board game because each and every one of them is fully differentiable by touch. A blind player doesn't need to rely on others to help them find their piece. All they need are fingers.

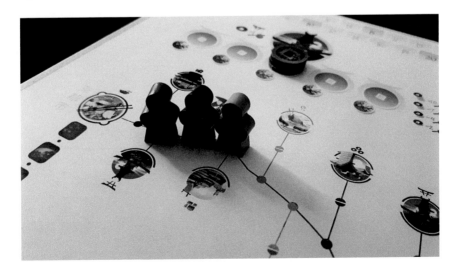

FIGURE 3.24 A close up on the Tokaido board. (Photograph by the author.)

FIGURE 3.25   The player pieces from Monopoly. The past has many design lessons we should take seriously. (Photograph by the author.)

Monopoly is a very accessible game, all in all – you don't get to be the juggernaut of the hobby for almost a century without understanding the value of including as many potential players as possible. It's not perfect – few games are – but it has a surprisingly large number of accessibility features that have evolved over the years. It's well worth taking some time to study it even if it's not quite what we might think of as a 'modern board game'. As in any discipline though, it's worth studying the classics. We'll have cause to revisit this idea – chess, poker, and others still have wisdom from which we can benefit.

Returning to the modern era, **Cottage Garden** (2016, Figure 3.26) has a board design that makes it almost fully accessible to visually impaired players. You have a number

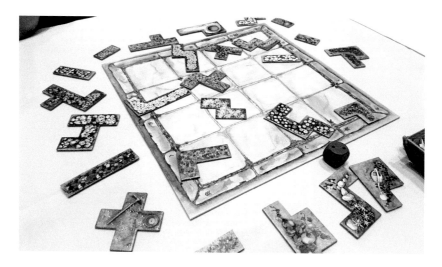

FIGURE 3.26   Cottage Garden. (Photograph by the author.)

FIGURE 3.27   A piece from the game Patchwork. Note that it has no indication of what is up and what is down, and thus some numbers can be confused. (Photograph by the author.)

of garden plots, each of which are 5 × 5. Tetris-style polyominos are used to fill up a plot so that its rich crop of victory points can be harvested. Each of these pieces has a distinctive shape that can be explored with fingertips. It all comes together to create a very physical representation of game state – the fixed parameters of the board, of the available pieces, and the tactility of simply placing things atop another thing. It allows for a player to interrogate their game state by simply running fingers along the different parts of the board. It represents something of an evolution over **Patchwork** (2014, Figure 3.27) by the same designer.

In **Cottage Garden**, none of the pieces contain actionable information that needs to be visually perceived. In **Patchwork**, each piece has a time cost, a button cost, and a 'button income'. As they used to say in the mafia, you need buttons to make buttons. The face information is visually encoded in a way that is going to be difficult for a visually impaired player to interact with, especially when it comes to orientation. Figure 3.27 is actually eight buttons and six time, rather than nine time and eight buttons. That kind of uncertainty is why it is now traditional to include a line at the bottom of the six and the nine, to indicate which way 'up' is.

There's a reason though that **Patchwork** is in the 'good design' section of this book, and it's because it comes with a kaleidoscopic nightmare of a time tracker. Figure 3.28 shows it in all its garish beauty.

That is a mighty fine piece of inaccessibility – it lacks distinctiveness in the size of spaces, in the texturing of each space, and in the contrast between. Why is it in the section on good visual design for accessibility? It's because of one simple fact – the board can be flipped over to a much starker, much cleaner aesthetic (Figure 3.29).

I cannot express to you how much I love this – those who want the full coloured experience can have it, and those who want a more minimalistic option can simply flip the thing over. This is a solution adopted in other sections of this book too. It's fair to say that if there's a compromise that must be made between aesthetic design and accessibility, a regular and reliable solution is 'give the option to your players'. That doesn't

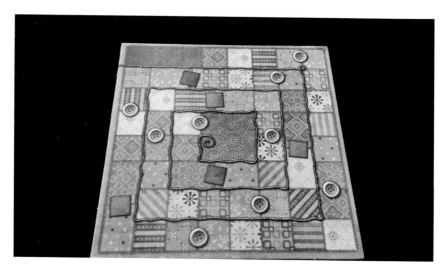

FIGURE 3.28   The garish board of Patchwork. (Photograph by the author.)

necessarily mean bundling multiple copies of every component into a box. Print and play conversion kits that are freely available and signposted in the game manual can offer a route to accessibility that economic factors may otherwise make infeasible. The growing availability of 3D printers in the home and at accessible commercial spaces too is ripe for exploitation.

Takenoko (2011, Figure 3.30) sets its 'players' as a gardener and a panda, both of which are differentiable by touch in the style of the varied pieces of **Monopoly**. Mainly though the game's accessibility is a consequence of the visual design of the hexes (which

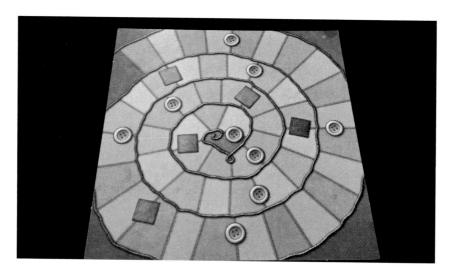

FIGURE 3.29   The other side of the Patchwork board – accessibility as a choice of the player. (Photograph by the author.)

FIGURE 3.30 Takenoko – a pretty game with numerous accessibility features. (Photograph by the author.)

are large, brightly coloured, and with clearly contrasted icons) along with the way in which changing state is indicated. There are 'bamboo shoot' pieces that click together to give a completely tactile way to explore the map. It requires care to do this without upsetting the game state but less than you might think. Even if that's not an option, the fact that the bamboo becomes notably taller as it grows means that as long as there is some ability for a player to differentiate light levels, it's much easier to assess the game than it would be with cards or cubes. It makes good use of verticality in a way few other games do. Similarly with irrigation – this is handled via blue blocks that are clearly differentiated from the sides of the hexes they occupy. It makes for an accessible approach that, in turn, creates for a striking amount of presence when the game is set up on a table. When people pass a game of **Takenoko** in play, they say 'Oh, that's pretty! What is it?'

It's accessibility as an advertising feature. It's hard to imagine a bigger win-win situation.

Games with Especially Interesting Visual Design

Let's take a look at some games that have **interesting** visual design – not necessarily good, not necessarily bad. Just worth discussion because of how they explore the intersection of accessibility and design and the compromises one must sometimes make.

Barenpark (2017, Figure 3.31) has many of the features that we've identified from **Cottage Garden** – a game of tactility and constrained areas that make for accessible play. And where it makes the Patchwork mistake of encoding visual information on the tiles, it does so in a way that is predictable and doesn't leak gameplay intention with inquiry.

Players take sections of a bear park in construction (Figure 3.32), and as they place pieces onto the park to complete a section, they'll cover up icons that confer special benefits upon them.

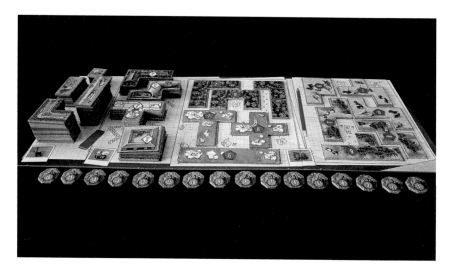

FIGURE 3.31   The supply board for Barenpark. (Photograph by the author.)

The interesting aspect here is that this is a game where information is fully available when decisions are made and then fully invisible when it is no longer relevant. When a portion of the park is covered with a tile, it's a permanent game decision. The icons are never re-used. This is an interestingly nuanced way to handle the trade-off between accessibility and inaccessibility – the trade-off is in time and relevance rather than 'I will make this cognitively more difficult to play so as to make it visually simpler'. It's not a perfect solution – once a piece is covered up, you still need to remember what special effects it had and that can create a memory burden on players. For my own sake, I

FIGURE 3.32   Park boards, upon which players will place pieces from the supply. (Photograph by the author.)

sometimes need to lift up a placed tile to make sure I remembered things correctly. But even that creates a temporal 'bubble' of inaccessibility that only exists at the inflection point where visible information becomes hidden.

Well, **I** think it's interesting.

NMBR 9 (2017) is a game of placing tiles shaped like numbers on top of a personal play area made up of other tiles shaped like numbers. You try to build up layers, leaving no gaps between one level and another, with your score depending on the face value of tiles multiplied by the level you got them to. You want a construction where small numbers are foundations on the lower levels so that you can place the big-ticket numbers atop them. What makes it a difficult challenge rather than a simple stacking exercise is that each tile must be adjacent to another on the level (unless it's the first), and each must overlap at least two other tiles on the floor below. What you end up with is a kind of home improvement project where you are working with cold, unfeeling arithmetic rather than cement.

Figure 3.33 shows off a lot of interesting accessibility features. The design of the pieces, like in **Barenpark** and in **Cottage Garden**, is enjoyably tactile and the game state can be explored by touch. We can even explore the edges between pieces (important for placement) because they create perceivable seams. And the shape of each piece maps on to the number it represents, and that in turn is the point value. You know when to spend a valuable nine and when to rely instead on load-bearing ones and twos.

There is a deeply awkward word to describe this feature of the design – **skeuomorphism.** This is when the design of a thing mirrors a real-world counterpart. This is the principle that explains why your media player's control console looks like it comes from the front panel of a VCR[1]. It's why the calculator app on your phone still looks like a physical desk calculator. It's why modern cars have engineered sound associated with closing the doors. They're a kind of cultural clue as to expectation, and they help people construct mental models of interaction.

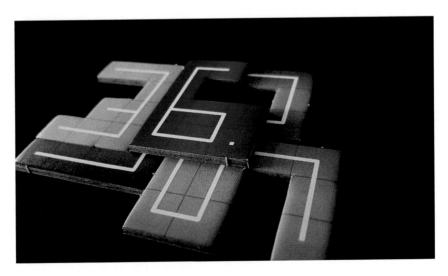

FIGURE 3.33   A game of NMBR 9 in progress. (Photograph by the author.)

FIGURE 3.34   The box of NMBR 9. It's as much part of the User eXperience (UX) as anything else. (Photograph by the author.)

So, the skeuomorphic design of the pieces here is actually an accessibility feature, and the whole board is made up of tactile, differentiable elements each of which convey their point information through physical design. That's super interesting! That by itself is enough for me to send you to try out NMBR 9 to see how it works and plays.

NMBR 9 though has a second accessibility feature that I adore, and one that I wish more games built their design around (Figure 3.34).

I'm sure we've all experienced playing with the three kinds of players when it comes to laying components on the table.

1. The person who pours everything into a pile and then searches through that pile when they need a specific token. The one that cashes in the time-saving benefits during setup for a kind of perpetual, low-grade frustration sure to erupt in a tantrum along the lines of 'WHY ARE THERE NEVER ANY BLUE TOKENS WHEN I NEED THEM??'

2. The person who immaculately arranges tokens into neat piles by size, shape, and function. And the one who then spends the rest of the game tidying each pile every time someone makes a withdrawal, and who will also need to repeat their activities when neatly arranged columns get knocked over.

3. The wise sage, beloved by all, who portions out pieces into containers. I do that, in case you weren't sure.

But this is more than just a particular philosophy of game play – this is an accessibility issue. Searching through undifferentiated piles of tokens is a visual accessibility problem. Trying to extract a piece from a neatly arranged pile or a container is a physical accessibility problem. The latter is also often a cognitive accessibility problem because the arrangements of piles and containers may not follow any obvious ordering scheme. Or if it does, the ordering may not be compatible with everyone's mindset.

FIGURE 3.35 Bowls in Century: Spice Road. They are not easy to work with. (Photograph by the author.)

Figure 3.35 shows the plastic bowls that come with **Century: Spice Road** (2017). Approximately 98% of my playtime in Spice Road is spent trying to get my spices as I attempt to slide a smooth cube out of the shifting quicksand of the other cubes, up a smooth side of a smooth bowl.

It is wonderful to see **NMBR 9** solve the accessibility issue of playing at the table by turning its inlay into a kind of component tray. It's cleverer too than it might seem even if the actual accomplishment seems obvious – it's so obvious that almost every game overlooks it. It's like when you ask someone 'what's the nearest star to the Earth' and they completely forget the existence of the Sun.

Look at how it works – the inlay creates a natural column for each piece, allowing it to be lifted easily out of place. It's in order, which means you always know where the next piece is to be found. It still allows for the tactility of the piece to be determined by touch but also adds a predictability of placement. The neat piles can't be knocked over because they're anchored into the inlay. Yes, all of this is painfully obvious, but it is also painfully obvious that hardly any other game takes advantage of the box in this way. **NMBR 9's** genius is in realising that its box **is part of its user interface** (Figure 3.34).

Seriously, I love this so much. Not every game can turn its game pieces into its game board. Almost every game though comes in a box and it can do more than just hold the pieces in place.

One final topic worth considering is the use of braille in board games, as this is often a solution suggested by those brainstorming ideas for how to make visual inaccessibilities less problematic. 64 Ounce Games make braille conversation kits for a wide variety of board games, and while this is an excellent solution in a number of situations, it is a) expensive and b) not appropriate for those with nerve damage in their fingers since they can't read braille. Coupled with that, braille literacy has been dropping steadily for decades. In 1960, around half of legally blind school children in the United States were able to read braille. Braille literacy is currently lower than 10%. Similar patterns of decline can be seen internationally – the rise of audiobooks, text-to-speech, and image to speech algorithms has made the case for learning braille increasingly difficult to make.

In all of this, we're actually discussing the accessibility issues as if their compensations exist in isolation. One of the leading causes of *retinopathy* is diabetes, and one of the compounding symptoms of diabetes is *peripheral neuropathy* or, in less clinical terms, damage to the nerves in the hands and feet. This can cause weakness, pain, and numbness in the extremities. So, when we talk about tactility as a way to solve the problems of visual accessibility, we have to remember that many people who are visually impaired may also be neuropathically impaired as well.

This is one of the profoundly complex **intersectional** implications of accessibility. People often aren't impaired in a single way. Conditions can and will compound, and solutions that work in one category (visual impairment) may not be effective when taken in conjunction with issues in another category (physical impairment).

Guidelines for Visual Accessibility

- *Games to look to for inspiration*:
    - Coup, Skull, Funemployed, Trial by Trolley, Love Letter, Takenoko, and Photosynthesis.
- *Games to look to as cautionary tales*:
    - Galaxy Trucker, Magic Maze, Scotland Yard, Iota, Yamatai, Dobble, Five Tribes, and Inis.

Text

Aim for High Readability of Text

One of the most important things is to ensure clear, crisp, and well-sized writing that minimises ambiguity and maximises contrast. A contrast ratio of around 4.5:1 is generally considered appropriate for accessibility purposes, and this is a solid target for which to aim. If that's not feasible in all cases, contrast between important game elements should be primarily stressed.

- Use larger fonts of the biggest font size that can be incorporated; 14-pt is considered an acceptable minimum.
- Maximise the contrast between text and background.
- Make use of standard font categories to improve the utility of Optical Character Recognition (OCR) tools.
- Keep font size consistent within semantic groupings. If flavour text is small in one place, it should be small in another. Revise text to fit if needed.
- Use bold to highlight key game information in text passages.
- Indicate orientation of numbers by underlines or dots.

Limit the Amount People Need to Read to Understand the Game

Not every piece of information is equally important in a game. Some information is used regularly, some only infrequently, some is supplementary, and some of it is thematic or ornamental. Limiting the amount of information someone **has** to read in a game can make it much more accessible:

- Keep flavour text separate from gameplay-relevant information through positioning or with a letterbox (a boxout specifically designed to add contrast).
- If separation is employed, be consistent with positioning of that separation. If flavour text is at the bottom of the cards, it should also be at the bottom of the board.
- If large passages of text are present on cards or in rules, consider the use of QR codes that link to voiced sound files that permit players to receive the information aurally.

Provide Easy Access to Accessibility Support Tools

Supporting materials for specialist accessibility purposes are wonderful, but they're not always appropriate or cost effective to include in the box. Some solutions (braille, as an example) are only going to be useful for a subset of people. As such, it is possible to minimise the logistical and financial cost of accessibility by making support tools available digitally. However, this approach often involves players having to cross-reference between the game and external resources, so it's important to make sure that can be done easily.

- Provide access to braille sleeves and braille version of rules. If that is not possible, provide a formal link to a service that can provide braille sleeves as an additional extra.
- If using custom dice, consider making available downloadable stickers or lookup tables for those using accessible alternatives.
- Consider providing 3D printable alternatives for inaccessible components.
- Provide manuals in a screen-reader-compatible digital format for download.
- Provide an online digital reference (such as a photo lookup table with alt-text) for game components so that they can be examined through digital accessibility tools.
- Ensure each part of the game can be uniquely described to permit cross-reference between online tools and physical play. Be consistent with your own conventions.

Icons

Aim for Easy Differentiation of Icons

Icons should be possible to tell apart at a distance, which means that they should be – as far as is possible – meaningfully unique. This helps everyone, but particularly when someone is visually impaired. Bear in mind too that the orientation at which someone may view a board is not necessarily the ideal case of 'straight ahead, right way up'.

- Make icons as large and visually distinctive as possible.
- Ensure silhouettes are distinctive.
- Aim for consistent sizes of icons.
- Aim for consistent placement of icons.
- Avoid using outlines or halos around game icons to indicate a different state or behaviour. Use separate iconography instead.

- Duplicate icons at alternate orientations to ease gameplay for people at opposite sides of a table.
- Consider the use of icons that read the same in multiple directions.

General Aesthetics

Separate Game Information from Theme Information

As with text, it is a good idea to keep thematic content as separate as possible from gameplay content. A square of a board that mixes these up will be harder for someone with visual impairments to separate into what they **need** to know and what they **want** to know.

- Keep aesthetical flair separate from gameplay-relevant information.
- Where possible, be consistent with the layout of separation.
- Consider the use of letterboxing or clearly delineated regions of the board to ensure 'game areas' versus 'board aesthetics' are identifiable at a distance.

Ensure Aesthetic Considerations Do Not Override Information Clarity

Part of what makes information easily processed is clarity – specifically, consistency of how information is presented. Small icons interleaved with text are a powerful way of reinforcing gameplay mechanisms. They tend to be so small though that even those with distinctive silhouettes may not be obviously interpretable if using an assistive aid. Similarly, clear and simple fonts without a lot of flourishes are more easily read than decorative fonts. Such ornate typography can help reinforce a setting, but it does come at the cost of readability. There is a similar issue to be found when it comes to texturing the background of text – to make it look like old parchment and such. These flourishes add to the aesthetic while detracting from the accessibility. A good solution is to add a letterbox text.

- Avoid mixing text and icons together unless unavoidable.
- Employ a clearly readable font for gameplay important information.
- Limit ornamentation of fonts and icons.
- Add a letterbox to the background of game text and icons.

Give Yourself Room to Incorporate Accessibility

White space is good for clarity, but it can be a waste from an accessibility perspective. If possible, consider making all available use of what space you have on each component. Unused borders around cards and components are sometimes a necessary artefact of production, but if you have the choice, make use of every spare millimetre you can access while retaining clarity.

- Use full-bleed art to provide more room for larger text and iconography.
- Fit text to component size, rather than to conform to some larger aesthetic design.
- If feasible, employ larger boards with larger spaces rather than smaller boards that are too densely packed.

Ensure Clear Presentation of Information

Clearly presenting all game information is important – this is not just for text but for everything that appears in the game.

- Aim for a good contrast ratio for distinctive game play elements – 4.5:1 or better, ideally.
- Aim for consistent placement of gameplay information – locate it in the same location and orientation whenever possible across different components.
- Replicate information at alternate orientation if possible.
- Cluster semantically related information together – stats across the top rather than distributed around a card, for example.
- When there is an explicit link between two bits of game information, be consistent in how they are presented. If stats are in a bold, serif font on a card, they should be bold and serif in the manual.
- Avoid incorporating key game state information into the graphical design of the background. Make it clear what is game and what is artwork.
- If feasible, provide low-clutter alternatives for game components and boards. If necessary, these can be provided as downloadable overlays or as purchasable extras.

Rules

Give Players Formal Approval for Accessibility Support

Later on, we will talk about the stigma that often goes along with seeking out accessibility help. Players asking for special dispensation are occasionally treated negatively at the table, or may be unwilling to ask for it. Within the game rules, it is important to make the seeking of accessibility a supported part of the system. It carries more weight if it's permitted in the manual, and not handled via table conventions or house rules.

- Within the rules, encourage players to narrate their activities.
- Where game information does not **need** to be kept secret, encourage or formally support people to play openly so the table can assist with visual accessibility problems.
- Consider the inclusion of rules that can mitigate players leaking intention to the table. For example, allowing players to bagsy a card or place a token that temporarily prevents others taking action on a part of the board.

Provide Alternatives to Sight-Based Game Mechanics and Components

Some games make use of additional components or gameplay conventions that explicitly reference eye contact or line-of-sight. Wargames often use physical line-of-sight between miniatures to determine if one unit can shoot another. Deception games with a 'day' and 'night' phase may require confederates to secretly 'make eye contact' so as to indicate collaboration. Such techniques are problematic for a visually impaired player.

- Avoid game mechanics that require the use of eye-contact. Provide a range of possible ways for people to secretly indicate game roles. Placing hands in the centre of the table, for example, can reveal team mates as well as indicate their relative position.

- Minimise game mechanisms that emphasise a physical, real-world line-of-sight and provide tools that help manage it when required. Emphasise alternatives such as laser pointers that can be more easily audited.
- Provide an accessible digital copy of the rulebook to allow for the use of digital accessibility tools such as text-to-speech. Ensure that digital rulebooks conform to PDF accessibility guidelines and are not made up of images alone. Prominently indicate digital resource availability in the manual.
- Test all your digital material with a text-to-speech tool to ensure that they are usable for non-sighted players.

Game Layout and Experience

Simplify Interaction with the Game Board

Players often have to reach over a board to move pieces, examine game state, or understand a competitor player's intentions. If this is combined with the need for a compensation regime such as close inspection, it can be uncomfortable and cumbersome.

- Make use of an accessible system for storing game tokens so as to allow them to be identified quickly.
- Try to focus interaction within an arm's length of each player. Assume interactions at longer distances will be actioned by others and design for that.
- Consider the trade-off between board size and distance of important game information. Cluster shared information in the centre, rather than the periphery, of the table.
- Limit sprawl of game state as much as is possible. Where a game board will grow in response to player actions, build restrictions as to how lop-sided it can be.
- Make it easy for players to verbalise the state of the game as it pertains to them or another player.

Game Boards

Make the Board Easy to Interpret

The less ornamented a board, the easier it is read. The easier it is to read, the easier it is to understand. Larger icons, unornamented fonts, minimalist design – all of those improve the visual accessibility of a board game. But so too does making sure information is available only when it is needed. Predictability of information matters too. Consider the standard scoring progression of 1, 2, 4, 7, 10, and 15 for example – that may require a novice players to regularly consult a reminder where 1, 2, 4, 8, and 16 wouldn't.

- Avoid hiding gameplay information under other gameplay components unless in doing so you remove obsolete information from the game.
- Ensure guidelines on boards are as highly contrasted as possible to make spaces and hexes visually distinctive.
- Consider making use of double-sided boards and components – one side that is fully aesthetically ornamented and another that is stripped down to core information.

- Make sure everything on the board is well contrasted against the background, making use of letterboxing if necessary.
- Indicate different regions of the board through high contrast against its surrounding regions.
- If using non-standard progressions of numbers or symbols on a board, document the pattern of progression so it can be reconstructed mentally.

Employ Tactility and Verticality in the Board

A flat, undifferentiated board is an accessibility opportunity – a canvas for investigating double coding through texture, indentations, seams, and embossing. Thin cuts, slots, sockets, and more all encode information deeply into the physical part of the game in a way that makes it more accessible to a visually impaired player. Similarly, employing components that stack or click together can offer a richer tactile environment that aids in accessibility.

- If possible, offer tactile guidelines on boards between spaces or transition points in game state. Let people track location and progression with their fingers.
- Offer slots, sockets, and depressions in game boards to permit components being anchored in place.
- If there are opportunities to make use of verticality in game systems, employ them.

Tokens and Currency

Make Tokens and Currency Tactile and Visually Distinctive

Consider all your game tokens in the same way as we've talked about coinage – it should be accessible in terms of its form factor and sizing. Be inspired by real-world coinage – having everything the same size and shape is an accessibility barrier, and the solution template is already in your pocket.

- Provide tokens that alternate size and shape for different denominations.
- If it is necessary for players to hide which tokens they have, consider providing a player screen rather than having tokens that share the same size, shape, and obverse.
- Make use of large tokens to aid players in identification at a distance.
- Avoid transparent tokens, including coloured transparent tokens, that might be lost against the board. If transparent tokens must be used, make them especially visually distinctive.
- For game tokens where orientation is important, include notches or indentations that indicate top and bottom.
- Limit, or eradicate, double-sided tokens (where they can be flipped to reveal different game information) since these make it difficult to find key game components at setup and in play.
- Avoid the use of paper money.

- Aim to have standard denominations of in-game currency or victory points that map on to real currency. Consistency here permits players to make use of alternate accessible currency where possible. Units in 1, 2, 5, 10, 20, and 50 are traditionally suitable for this.

Meeples and Miniatures

Ensure Bespoke Miniatures and Figures can be Substituted for Accessible Alternatives

If it's not possible to make your game use different form factors for meeples and miniature figures, ensure that they can be replaced with external, accessible variants. Essentially this means limiting (or eradicating) game-specific information that is represented directly onto figures. It also means avoiding a tight mapping from game components to game board. If there are non-standard slots on a board into which player pieces are placed, for example, other options may not fit.

- Limit the amount of irreproducible information on components and miniatures.
- Permit players to substitute in accessible variants where possible.
- Conform as far as possible to standard dimensions regarding dice, pieces, and miniature scale so as to make your game compatible with widely available alternatives.

Make Your Figures Feel Different to the Touch

A great accessibility benefit comes from allowing players to map the physical parameters of a figure or meeple to identify ownership and role information. At a minimum, a game should allow a player to identify to whom a piece belongs by touch. Role information and other game-specific nuances can often be communicated by posture or equipment of a piece. If you do have different figures, distribute them between players – each player having four different figures is less accessible than each player having four figures that are the same, but each player having a different set of four.

- Where meeples and other components are used to indicate game information, ensure they have a meaningfully different form factor that permits for identification by touch.
- If this is not possible, provide some embossing, stickers, attachable parts, or other indicator on the components that can be used to identify them.
- If employing variation of figures in the game, try to ensure that it is expressed between players rather than within an individual player's components.
- Consider socketed bases for miniatures so as to allow differentiating accessories to be slotted in place.

Dice and Randomisation

Support the Use of Alternative Dice

As discussed above, custom dice may be fun and thematically effective. However, custom dice create wall-to-wall accessibility problems for people with visual accessibility impairments and the compensatory solutions that exist are often inappropriate except in simple scenarios.

- Try to avoid the need for non-standard die faces because accessible dice are not a good replacement for these.
- Try to ensure that dice used in your game are of the standard form factor, as alternate forms are harder to swap out.
- If using non-standard dice, try to make use of embossing, indenting, or some other tactile indicator that can be used to tell different faces apart.
- If this is not possible, consider the provision of a voiced digital dice roller tool.

General Component Design

Physically Annotate Your Components

As with the game board, much otherwise visually inaccessible information can be provided through physical annotation of components. Embossing, indentation, stickers, and shaping can be employed to reveal details that can be used to identify, by touch, different elements of the game. They can also highlight and prioritise, allowing key information to be brought to the fore.

- Consider embossing key game information elements on boards and components.
- If embossing text on game components, ensure it is visually distinctive at all angles.
- Raise or emboss important parts of the game board or cards.
- Raise or emboss important letters and symbols on game components.
- Accompany as much visual information as possible with a tactile and/or auditory component.

Aim for High Durability of Components

There is a durability cost to physical investigation of game components and close inspection of boards. Many games, produced with an eye to per-unit implications, may sacrifice paper and card stock thickness for financial efficiencies. However, bear in mind that accessibility often involves more rigorous and imprecise handling of components, and low-quality components will impact on the experience for impaired players. Over time, cards can become ragged and boards may become frayed.

- Make use of hard-wearing materials that can stand a lot of physical manipulation.
- Aim for the thickest possible card stock.
- Aim for the thickest possible paper stock.
- Consider post-assembly production processes that improve the longevity of game components.
- Ensure cards conform to the sizes that are supported by standard card sleeves.

Note

1. I'm not sure how to explain any of these to any younger folks reading. A VCR was a device used for playing video tapes, which were precursor technology to DVDs. Oh, wait – imagine you could take a Netflix movie and convert it into a shiny disc, and then you could fire lasers at that shiny disc to make the movie play on your television. That was a DVD.

    Oh, yeah. Televisions were what people had before mobile phones. Think of them like a massive version of your phone screen, with zero apps.

    Anyway, video tapes were sort of like DVDs except they used magnetic tape and fired light through them or something.

    Look, ask your older siblings about DVDs, and then get them to ask your parents about video tapes.

BIBLIOGRAPHY

Bourne, R., Steinmetz, J. D., Flaxman, S., Briant, P. S., Taylor, H. R., Resnikoff, S., Casson, R. J., Abdoli, A., Abu-Gharbieh, E., Afshin, A., Ahmadieh, H., Akalu, Y., Alamneh, A. A., Alemayehu, W., Alfaar, A. S., Alipour, V., Anbesu, E. W., Androudi, S., Arabloo, J., … Vos, T. (2021). Trends in prevalence of blindness and distance and near vision impairment over 30 years: An analysis for the global burden of disease study. *The Lancet Global Health, 9*(2), e130–e143.

Chang, M. Y., & Borchert, M. S. (2020). Advances in the evaluation and management of cortical/cerebral visual impairment in children. *Survey of Ophthalmology, 65*(6), 708–724.

Fazzi, E., Micheletti, S., Calza, S., Merabet, L., Rossi, A., Galli, J., Early Visual Intervention Study Group, Accorsi, P., Alessandrini, A., Bertoletti, A., Campostrini, E., D'Adda, N., Franzoni, A., Fumagalli, E., Scalvini, E. G., Martelli, P., Marras, M., Molinaro, A., Motta, M., … Semeraro, F. (2021). Early visual training and environmental adaptation for infants with visual impairment. *Developmental Medicine & Child Neurology, 63*(10), 1180–1193.

Lim, L. S., Mitchell, P., Seddon, J. M., Holz, F. G., & Wong, T. Y. (2012). Age-related macular degeneration. *The Lancet, 379*(9827), 1728–1738.

Menzel, S. (2004). *Cobs, pieces of eight and treasure coins: The early Spanish-American mints and their coinages, 1536–1773.* American Numismatic Society: New York.

Roodhoft, J. M. J. (2002). Leading causes of blindness worldwide. *Bulletin of the Belgian Society of Ophthalmology, 283*, 19–25.

4

Cognitive Accessibility

As with each of the categories of accessibility we are discussing in this book, cognitive accessibility is a broad catch-all term relating to a wide spectrum of conditions. At the core of cognitive functionality is the brain – the meaty processor that handles how we reason, remember, and perceive the world around us. An impairment in cognitive faculties can impact across all categories of accessibility – we already saw a hint of that in the previous chapters. Similarly, physical and emotional impairments can have their root cause in the brain but we'll discuss those in the appropriate chapters. Here we're going to talk about those factors of accessibility that relate to brain function, specifically when people have trouble learning, retaining information, concentrating, or processing information.

A full treatment of the various theories associated with how the brain works is well outside the scope of this chapter, but we are going to build our discussion around a model of cognition introduced in 1963 by Raymond Cattell. Cattell's theory takes the concept of 'general intelligence' – the overall quality of cognitive performance – and views it through two separate but interrelated lenses. Important here though is the observation recorded by George Box back in 1976 that all models are approximations. Or, as the popular rephrasing goes, 'All models are wrong, but some models are useful'. For our purposes, what we need is a way to assess problematic game design as it pertains to the mind. The fidelity of the model to reality is a secondary factor.

Cattell's model of intelligence is, in my view, both illuminating **and** useful. Primarily, its utility to us comes in separating out cognition into two key elements – *fluid intelligence* and *crystalised intelligence*. *Fluid intelligence* is concerned with reasoning, learning, abstraction, and the ability to solve problems. *Crystalised intelligence* is about recall, vocabulary, and drawing inferences from accumulated knowledge. *Fluid intelligence* handles mental activities that are about thinking with speed and making conclusions fluidly (hence the name). *Crystalised intelligence* is about making use of developed skills and drawing upon storehouses of past experience.

Closely related to each of these measures are other complementary aspects of cognitive processing – *working memory, short-term memory*, and *long-term memory*. *Working memory* is the small cache of information that is held actively in mind while the brain is processing cognitive tasks. Working memory is in turn linked to *short-term memory* – memory that is held in attention for a few seconds to aid in the processing of what is currently being cogitated upon. *Long-term memory* is the huge set of data that one accumulates across our entire lives. *Working memory* is the primary engine of *fluid intelligence*, and *long-term memory* underpins *crystalised intelligence*.

Again, none of this is **true.** Our benchmark is **useful.**

The relationship between information processing and information retention is too complex to fit neatly into this kind of separation, and that's why within this chapter we talk about cognitive impairments as if they are unitary conditions. There is a sophisticated relationship between *fluid* and *crystalised intelligence*, and each real-life cognitive

DOI: 10.1201/9781003415435-4

task will draw upon both types of 'smarts' in different proportions. If one has high *fluid intelligence*, then you may process data into information more quickly, which can then be processed more readily into the knowledge that fuels *crystalised intelligence*. *Fluid intelligence* can be enhanced in turn by *crystalised intelligence* when general problem-solving skills are employed to aid in the processing of new information.

One can even compensate for the other – much scientific evidence shows that *fluid intelligence* decreases as we age and cognitive decline begins. At approximately the same time as *fluid intelligence* declines, *crystalised intelligence* increases. The general effect is that older people draw more heavily on skills and knowledge than they do processing and reasoning, but functional general intelligence remains at roughly the same level.

If this still doesn't make a lot of sense, imagine yourself as a Dungeons and Dragons character. Fluid intelligence is your **intelligence** stat. Crystalised intelligence is your **wisdom.**

How does all of this impact on cognitive impairment? Let's take the two things in isolation.

Impairments in *crystalised intelligence* relate to 'knowing things'. They may result in reduced vocabularies, problems with comprehension, and a smaller domain of general knowledge. These traits have several knock-on effects – it becomes harder to understand things simply because the context of understanding itself is restricted. Learning is a process of encoding information in a form that can be later accessed in context. This in itself relies upon relating new information to previous models, concepts, and experiences. Impairments may also impact on the ability of an individual to execute upon instructions or follow sequential processes. Mathematical and verbal reasoning are often compromised, including with regards to the processing associated with basic arithmetic (addition, subtraction, multiplication, and division) and seriation versus classification[1].

Impairments in *fluid intelligence* can relate to following instructions, making use of information for a task under active consideration, and multitasking across two or more processes. They can impact on the ability to focus attention on a task as well as the speed at which data can be processed into information. Someone with reduced *fluid intelligence* may struggle to make connections between data points with which they are presented. Pattern recognition and creativity may be impaired.

As usual, there are intersectional considerations. Planning requires both *fluid* and *crystalised intelligence*, as does executing upon strategy. In games, we often talk about two different kinds of planning – **tactical** and **strategic.** Strategy is the broad plan that sets the trajectory from a current position to an intended destination. Tactics comprise the specific actions that will take someone along the strategic path. Both approaches blend *fluid* and *crystalised intelligence*, with tactics being proportionally more impacted by *fluid intelligence* and strategy by *crystalised intelligence*.

Cognitive accessibility is served when people are able to play a game at all. However, an additional factor is whether people will be able to **play well.**

Much cognitive impairment comes from aging, and the process begins early. Our cognitive faculties rise until the age of around 24, level out for a little while, and then begin to decline at around the age of 27. This decline manifests slowly at first, but it accelerates as time passes. Performance on certain cognitive tasks declines by around 0.8% a year from age 25, with that decrease compounding significantly over time.

Medical frameworks for categorising cognitive disability usually assess impairment across three key areas – conceptual, social, and practical life skills. Positive diagnoses will usually categorise these into one of four severities – mild, moderate, severe, and profound. Around 85% of those diagnosed with cognitive disability fall into the mild category, but as always, there is a massive amount of variation within each of these group-ings. Many people too will have *fluid* or *crystalised intelligence* impairments without ever considering themselves to have a disability. or at least, not something they would consider an 'intellectual disability'. Common 'everyday' conditions include aphasia, autism, atten-tion deficit hyperactivity disorder (ADHD), dyslexia, and dyscalculia. More severe condi-tions include traumatic brain injury, strokes, Alzheimer's disease, and dementia.

There is a general progression of how we grade the severity of cognitive impairment.

No cognitive impairment (NCI) can be described as when people do not see them-selves as having any perceivable decline in their real-life experience of *fluid* and *crys-talised intelligence*. On average, it's at age 30 that people begin to shift into the next category, where individuals will notice some real-world decline in their cognitive capac-ities. They'll notice they are forgetting things, or don't learn things as quickly as they used to. This is the stage which most people will occupy for the rest of their lives, as it encompasses normal cognitive decline due to aging. This is sometimes known as *subjec-tive cognitive impairment* (SCI).

Mild cognitive impairments (MCI) encapsulate the point at which normal aging no longer explains a decline in cognitive abilities around language, reasoning, memory, and data processing. Those with MCI can still engage in independent living although learn-ing new skills although engaging in complex activities may pose problems. The largest concern is that in certain forms of cognitive disease, such as Alzheimer's, people will progress from MCI into dementia over an average of seven years. Dementia is a severe condition with substantial and wide-ranging quality of life implications. Well-practised skills – including those associated with basic bodily functions – decline. Speech becomes affected, as does the ability to control the nerves and muscles of the face. Independent living becomes more difficult and in some cases impossible without significant external support and redesign of life routines.

The unfortunate truth of cognitive impairment as it relates to board game accessibility is that there is usually a minimum floor on our expectations of the mental capability of a player. There is a certain mechanical complexity required for a game to be a game – even the simplest and most straightforward have rules. For a game to be **fun** rather than sim-ply meet the mechanical definition, it usually has to offer opportunities for skilful play, which in turn requires the ability to set forth strategies for improvement and act upon those strategies. As such, profound intellectual disabilities do not cohere happily with an accessibility agenda in this area. Our compensations must focus on the 'relatively abled' categories of cognitive impairment. I am usually an advocate of the philosophy that accessible games are segregated games, as discussed in Chapter 1. Our goal is to make games accessible, not to make 'accessible games'. Unfortunately, the nature of cognitive impairment in its most severe form is that the design and aesthetic considerations require a bespoke approach and thus fall outside the remit of this book.

But with that in mind, let's talk about games!

Problematic Cognitive Designs

One of the primary ways in which a board game works is through the setting out of clear, unambiguous rules. Those rules can be used to manipulate personal and shared game state in order to accomplish an understood, perceivable goal. You might even think that's a feature shared by every possible game – how could it be otherwise? How would a game even work when there are no rules, nothing that counts as 'your' game state, and no perceivable goals?

For that, we turn to the **Fluxx** family of games. Specifically in this case, **Star Fluxx** (2011). This is a game that throws all those conventions out of the window. This is how I describe the game to those that want a feel for the experience:

> Imagine rolling a die every time it's your turn. You then pick up a different die, and roll that. Sometimes you pick up ten dice. Sometimes you pick five dice and get rid of three of them. Sometimes you roll a number and keep that die in front of you. Then, at some point, you roll your handful of dice and someone yells 'I win!'. That's Star Fluxx, except it uses cards and not dice, and it tries to hide its fundamental, uncontrollable randomness through aggressively whimsical branding.

In **Star Fluxx**, and all its many brothers and sisters, you begin with a 'basic rule' which is usually something along the lines of 'shuffle the deck, deal 3 cards to each player. Choose a first player. Take turns – on your turn, you draw one card and then you play one card'. Those cards come in various flavours. They may be a **goal**, indicating a win condition. 'You win if you are the player with card X and Y in front of you'. They may be a 'keeper', which are cards you play out to try and meet goals (Figure 4.1).

They may be 'creepers', which act as a kind of penalty for the player to which they are attached. They may be a special action, which lets you adjust the game state in a particular way as a one-off state-change independent of the stated rules.

Or they may be new rules entirely (Figure 4.2). It's the latter aspect that makes **Star Fluxx** such a problematic game from the perspective of cognitive accessibility. The rules may change hand limits, swap ownership of cards, or alter what happens as part of the game. In one turn, you may be drawing one and playing one. The next time your turn comes around, you might be drawing four and playing three, and then executing a bunch of special instructions outlined on your keeper cards. All to try

FIGURE 4.1   Some of the cards in Star Fluxx. (Photograph by the author.)

FIGURE 4.2   Examples of new rules in Star Fluxx. (Photograph by the author.)

and accomplish a goal that may not still be on the table by the time your turn comes around again. It's a game that is profoundly reactive – you can't really plan, all you can do is try to move yourself towards the goal as best you can on your turn.

It's a game though that gives the **illusion** of being able to engage strategically and tactically. Every goal is a temporary mirage. Most often it seems like you win **Fluxx** by accident. The rules are tightly **state dependant** (which requires *fluid intelligence* to process and *crystalised intelligence* to interpret a path to victory) with large amounts of variation (both in terms of rule cards and in terms of keeper abilities and creeper complications). In every new round, you need to analyse everything anew. By the time you've processed the current game state, that understanding is already obsolete. There's no regularity to the flow of the game, which can be confusing even without cognitive impairments to complicate the experience.

To be fair, this is what **Fluxx** is intended to be – an anarchic, high-energy experience much like being in a car careening across a motorway while four people fight for control of the pedals and the steering wheel. That's the fun of it, for its fans. The design though is aggressively inaccessible.

We've already spoken a little bit about **Iota** (2012, Figure 4.3) with regards to colour blindness, but its design is also worth discussing in this chapter.

Iota is one of these deceptively simple games that sounds like they're going to be straightforward but end up placing a vice around your mind. Placement rules here emerge from the creation of the start of line, which happens when any two cards are orthogonally adjacent. A full line is made up of four cards, each of which is differentiated by colour, shape, and face value. All cards in a line must **either** match on the similarity of each trait (categorisation, as we mentioned above) or on the difference (seriation). If you place a green cross next to a green square, all subsequent cards need to be green. If you place a green two and a blue three, then the next two cards must also be different in face value and in colour. The horizontal line in Figure 4.3 shows this in practice – every card is different in every axis of comparison. The vertical line works differently – they all

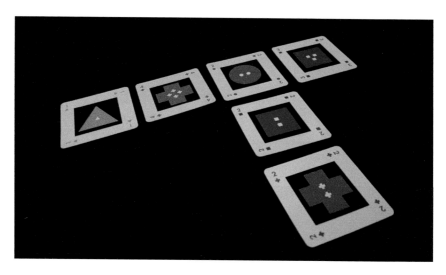

FIGURE 4.3   Lines constructed in Iota. (Photograph by the author.)

differ in shape but share a number. A card placed into the grid of the table must satisfy all placement rules of all lines it is joining.

The effect in play is that this leads to a grinding cognitive cost comparing cards in hand against all of the possible places they can, and cannot, go. *Fluid intelligence* gets a **proper workout** in this game.

The next level of strategic thinking is to consider what each move means for an opponent – as in, what placement rules does your card put into consideration for the next player. The next level above that is what all of this planning will mean when it gets back to your turn. You earn points in **Iota** by completing lines, and the more lines you complete with a card, the more ridiculously high your score gets. It's like playing **Scrabble** with tile bonuses you position yourself, making use of an alien vocabulary expressed in little more than the hieroglyphics of a colourful playschool geometry. It's possible to look at the space where a card can go and find yourself momentarily cognitively adrift as you try to puzzle out what validity of placement even means.

This highlights an issue that is often counter-intuitive in the area of cognitive accessibility – simplicity of rules doesn't necessarily mean accessibility of game. Some of the most cognitively inaccessible games are those that require the shortest rules explanation. **Dobble** (2009), also known as **Spot-It**, is one of my favourite examples of this and we'll talk about it a little later in this chapter. It's certainly true that the more complicated a game is, the less cognitively accessible it will tend to be. The reverse is, however, not true – simpler rules do not imply cognitively accessible games. You only need to look at **Go** (2356 BCE) to see the truth of that statement.

The thing about **Iota** and **Star Fluxx** is that they are processing puzzles – there is no need for a player to memorise anything to play effectively, and strategic thinking is often counterproductive. In **Fluxx**, it's frustrating to try to enact a strategy because it has to change almost every time your turn comes around. In Iota, a rule for placement that was valid one turn probably won't be valid the next. Little of the skillset associated with *crystalised intelligence* gets emphasised, other than that which is brought into scope by the act of observing and interpreting a game state. In other words, it is not the mechanisms that pose the problem. The rules aren't the issue. Complicated is not the same thing as complex.

In other games, we can see a much more obvious example of an escalating mechanical complexity that creates inaccessibility, and we can see it repeated again and again in certain kinds of card game: **Magic: The Gathering** (1993), **Dominion** (2008), **Android: Netrunner** (2012), **Game of Thrones: The Card Game** (2015), and **Arkham Horror: The Card Game** (2016). Games like this are all about achieving a particular effect through custom deck composition, and that effect is **synergy**. In these games, a player constructs a deck of cards unique to them, drawing from a broad selection of options. These options may be made available in game (such as in **Dominion**, the first game in the genre known as **Deck builders**). They may also come through the purchase of randomised booster packs (**Magic** and other Collectible Card Games or CCGs) or expansion packs (all the others, which form a category of games known as Living Card Games or LCGs). You achieve success in competitive or collaborative tasks by leveraging a deck of cards where each works in synergy with the others. If there's a simple rule such as 'If you have a card with this symbol played out in front of you, draw another card' then your deck should make use of many cards that have that symbol. If you don't, then the cards don't synergise and you don't get the benefit of these special effects.

The key thing about synergy though is that it requires a player to be able to assess each of their options for this often mystical property. **Star Realms** (2014) is perhaps the most instantly approachable game in this family as its synergies, at least in the base game, are simple to execute upon.

Figure 4.4 shows an example card which has a faction (indicated in the top left), a cost to buy (top right), and then the effects outlined at the bottom. The frigate counts for four damage, and when you play it, you pick an opponent who has to discard a card from their hand. If there is another ship with the same faction already played out in front of you, you get an additional four damage you can inflict. And if you scrap the card (get

FIGURE 4.4 A card from Star Realms. (Photograph by the author.)

FIGURE 4.5   The Star Realms marketplace from which new cards can be bought. (Photograph by the author.)

rid of it permanently), you can draw a card. In **Star Realms**, you get a certain amount of currency (from playing cards that give you spendable money) which you can use to buy ships from a central offering. The synergies you need to consider are the ones in the marketplace (Figure 4.5), and a workable rule of thumb is 'go deep on one, or maybe two, different factions'.

These games also function on the basis of deck density, which is to say that a deck should be **lean.** It should contain no dead weight. **Star Realms** involves taking your deck of cards and dealing five out in front of you. That's your turn, and the only synergies you get are the ones from the current turn. If a card isn't making synergy happen, it's taking the space of a card that could. Part of play is a conscious act of **curation**, making sure that the deck composition is such that even shuffling doesn't get in the way of spectacular results. That in turn relies on remembering what you have in your deck – both in terms of the deck as a whole and what's left to come out before you need to shuffle your discards. All of your decisions in the present (*fluid intelligence*) rely on an understanding of what's in your deck (*crystalised intelligence*) and what you need to do to maximise the deck's potential (*fluid* and *crystalised intelligence*). To make your deck work the kind of magic you require, you need a really good handle on what fairy dust needs sprinkled in.

Dominion and **Star Realms** confine the problem of identifying synergistic combinations to the table – all you need to know is in the box because that's where you find all the cards. Other games make deckbuilding from diverse sources a core part of play. Decks are defined as being 'legal' based on the extent to which they conform to composition rules, but they are otherwise a free-for-all between starter sets, expansions, booster packs, and the secondary market.

Synergy isn't a feature that exists only in card games. It's a feature of any game where taking an action has differential effect based on other actions taken previously. That in turn is a regular feature of almost every game beyond a certain complexity level. Sometimes it's a feature baked into the design, sometimes it's just a side effect of the

FIGURE 4.6 An engine under construction in Gizmos.

kind of game mechanisms hobbyist gamers tend to favour. Synergy might be heavily stressed, such as in **Gizmos** (2018) or just a natural consequence of changing the capabilities each players may have over time, such as in **Lords of Waterdeep** (2012).

In **Gizmos**, the player board in Figure 4.6 has been expanded beyond its starting ability to have a whole range of additional effects. The game is built around the collecting and spending of marbles to build blueprints, which in turn give you points and award special contextual powers. It is a game that is **rigorously algorithmic**, requiring players to build a cardboard machine that bends with their needs and preferences. Players need to work out how to slot optimal pieces of machinery into pre-defined subroutines so as to have them work cleanly together to achieve results greater than the sum of the parts. It's like programming, but without its syntactic complexities. It's a difficult process that works across both categories of intelligence – it needs a solid grasp of numeracy as well as comprehension of a symbolic functionalism that can bind together abstractions with functional payloads. It needs players to be able to analyse what different input (marbles) will mean in terms of programming blocks (gizmos). It needs both *long-* and *short-term memory* to be working optimally. The end result is a game that – while simple in its basic rules – is almost completely cognitively inaccessible.

Lords of Waterdeep is also a game about building an engine of special abilities that can work synergistically together. The basic premise of the game is that you gather up cubes that represent adventurers, and you spend those to complete quests which give you points and other rewards. Some of these quests are **plot quests**, and part of their reward is that they give you a special ability. The base game has only a few of these – **Scoundrels of Skullport**, the expansion, adds in many more, with more interesting effects. For an example of a power, perhaps any time you collect a warfare quest from the supply you get some free warriors. Or perhaps whenever you play an intrigue card (the game's espionage system), you get to draw another random intrigue card and play that too. Some quests give you more points each time you complete other quests in that category. As you play, you'll build up a unique set of interlocking abilities that help you get more out of each action than other players. Combined with your Lord card (which gives you a secret end-of-game scoring condition that is relevant only to you), it's a puzzle of constructing an engine of privilege from random parts. You need to do it quickly enough to benefit from it, but not so quickly your engine lacks power. It's a game as much about the timing of actions as it is about the sum effect of them. It might be worth going all in to get the lieutenant early, as that quest gives you private access to an additional meeple (agent) that nobody else will get. It's not worth getting it at all in the last round of the game.

This is a lighter form of synergy because the effects scale linearly. In other games, synergy may have exponential effects and this will tend to put a greater burden on leveraging it effectively. If you get a free intrigue card every time you play one down, you might want to focus on plot quests and actions that give you a regular rotation of intrigue, but you can't do that at the expense of the other systems. It changes the flavour of the game, not the architecture. But still, it's a form of synergy – identifying and leveraging it remain cognitively challenging.

Hanabi (2010, Figure 4.7), which we first encountered in Chapter 2, represents a complex memory challenge. Each player holds their hand of cards facing outwards. Everyone knows what everyone else has. Each player knows only those characteristics of their own cards that are communicated through gameplay. One of the traits of a problematic game in this category is that it contains hidden game state, but most games hide the state of **other** players with your own state being comparatively easily accessed. Hanabi inverts that paradigm.

One of the most common inaccessibilities presented by games is forcing a player to remember important things without being able to refresh their memory should details fade. These kind of games favour the cognitively abled. A **Star Realms** player with a good memory has advantages over one with a poor memory. Remembering which factions an opponent is looking to acquire, and which cards they have previously placed in their deck, can influence decision making. There is a strategic decision to be made regarding whether one should build a deck around a faction in which multiple players are interested, as an example. This is a kind of 'informal benefit' of having a good memory,

FIGURE 4.7   Hanabi cards in a transparent card holder. (Photograph by the author.)

FIGURE 4.8　The various tiles that make up an island in Survive: Escape from Atlantis. (Photograph by the author.)

and it's one that is hard to control for in game design. Explicitly building game systems around memory though is always going to be a challenge if cognitive accessibility is to be retained.

We see this in **Survive: Escape from Atlantis** (2012, Figure 4.8). Each of a player's meeple characters have a point value encoded on the bottom of the piece. The task during play is to rescue pieces by getting them on to boats and getting those boats to safety. Players earn points based on **value** of rescued meeples rather than the quantity. The meeples will move around during play, swap places, and be eaten up by events and wildlife.

Once a piece is placed, the rules state you can't look again at the value – remembering which are your high-value meeples is part of skilful play. It's what makes the game tense and exciting, but it's also something that hands a huge in-play advantage to those that have the best memories.

Many games are built around 'predictable surprises', and this often comes from drawing from a deck of cards designed to add complexity to play. Over time, the contents of that deck will become known, and the possibility space associated with uncertainty will contract. Familiarity then transmutes, through an alchemical process, into domain-specific skill. In **Lords of Waterdeep**, a game which I have played many hundreds of times, I know which plot quests work well together because I have seen them all rotate into play many times over many sessions. I may not have full knowledge of the deck's composition (cards may be squirreled away into player hands) and I will have no knowledge of the deck's ordering. But I do know – statistically speaking – whether my favourite quests and intrigue cards are yet to turn up in play and whether I should prepare myself for when they are dealt out. This familiarity relies on long-term memory and confers an obvious gameplay advantage but not one that is insurmountable. Someone can play effectively, without penalty, even if they don't know the approximate percentage chance that the 'impersonate tax collectors' quest is still to be played out to the board.

FIGURE 4.9   Some of the early cards that come out of the deck of Twilight Struggle. (Photograph by the author.)

Twilight Struggle (2005) on the other hand heavily penalises players who are not familiar with its deck composition. The game is one of nuclear brinksmanship, where political events through the course of the Cold War are manipulated and remixed to play out a tense wargame between the United States and the Soviet Union. The game is made up of several decks which represent distinct historical eras. They include things like the formation of the Warsaw Pact or a ban on nuclear testing. Figure 4.9 shows some of the cards from the early era of play. The changing context of the Cold War is contained within these deck. Your job as a player is to manage these events well. It ties gameplay to a real historical context.

Some of these cards though are viciously punitive if you don't know to expect them – they can completely undermine invested effort. While the 'US/Japan Mutual Defence Pact' card is in the deck, there is no point in the Soviet Union trying to invest influence in Japan. That card straight up gives control of the Japan region of the board to the US. If a Soviet player had been investing effort in Japan with an eye to using it as a launch-pad for other operations, then sucks to be them. Similarly, the US probably shouldn't invest in Eastern Europe until the Warsaw Pact card is played out, or they will find that investment radically fails to pay off. Cards like this lurk like landmines in the deck, and knowing that they are present and what they do is key to playing **Twilight Struggle** well. Those with good memories and deep familiarity with the game decks have an explicit advantage over those that don't.

Games with Good Cognitive Design

It is a difficult challenge to make a cognitive accessible game. Everything from the rules to the specific profile of cognitive faculties employed has an impact. Board games are built on the idea that the players are human processors executing the instruction set of a cardboard algorithm. That is always going to be cognitively taxing.

Hitting the mark for genuine cognitive accessibility is challenging, but that's not the same thing as saying **improvements** in cognitive accessibility are impractical. There are many games that have design features that – intentionally or otherwise – remove some of the inaccessibilities in this category. With accessibility, we are rarely in the position of things being all or nothing – instead, every additional accessibility adjustment opens a game up to a larger proportion of people with relevant impairments. Reducing the memory burden a little might be all it takes to push a game from 'not accessible' to 'just accessible enough'. Offering the option to play without an especially cognitive demanding rule might turn an inaccessible game into a version that can be enjoyed by larger groups. Accessibility is a quality that accumulates through small degrees.

We talked about **Star Fluxx** in the previous section and how it is almost entirely cognitively inaccessible. **Red7** (2014, Figure 4.10) is an interesting counter-example because it offers a similar kind of experience within a much more restricted possibility space.

Instead of it being a game of 'almost anything can happen, and will', **Red7** has a smaller set of rotating victory conditions which wrap around a single core rule. That rule is this: at the end of your turn, you need to be winning the game. Players can lay down cards to a palette (your personal game state) or to the canvas (the game rule). If you can't be in first place by playing a card or changing the victory condition, then you pass and you are out of the round.

It's still not a cognitively accessible game, but it is **much more** accessible than **Fluxx**. It accomplishes this by offering a tight set of constraints on how much the experience can vary – nobody gets to switch palettes or win through accident. Instead it's a kind of Judo experience where everyone is using the momentum of the other players against them. Sometimes the solution to a game being cognitively inaccessible is to add some constraints to its systems. The more they flex and bend, the more people need to think about because the possibility space becomes much larger. **Red7** shows that you can still deliver some complex experiences within such constraints.

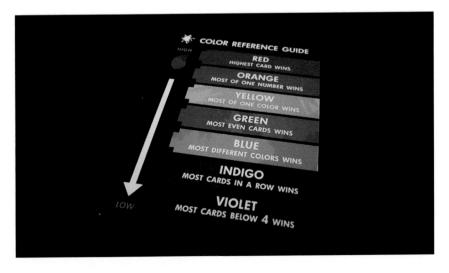

FIGURE 4.10 Win conditions in Red7. (Photograph by the author.)

That doesn't mean a game needs to be simplified from an original vision, which is an assumption many people have when they begin to consider accessibility options in their games. Those constraints can be optional or delivered as variations in the game rules. You can also handle it through a kind of loose *scaffolding* of game systems.

Scaffolding is a pedagogical term relating to a particular method of teaching in which knowledge is built incrementally over time, with each new piece of knowledge raising the learner to a higher level of understanding. Scaffolds are then progressively removed. To teach a student how to play **chess**, perhaps a teacher begins by setting up a board with pawns only. Once that student has mastered the rules of pawns, they add in the rooks. Once the rooks have been mastered, the king enters play. By the end of this process, a student has learned to play chess incrementally without someone trying to explain it all at once.

If you see a parallel there to board game manuals and 'how to play' videos … yeah.

An ideal way to implement scaffolding in board games is through the use of optional game rules and game versions. **Flash Point** (2011, Figure 4.11) – a fun game of firefighters trying to deal with an escalating calamity of fire – has a rulebook that offers two modes of play. Family mode has a deterministic setup, a more forgiving model of spreading fire, and a rescue system that works on just getting people out of the building.

It doesn't use ambulances, or hazardous material, or specialist roles. What it does though is introduce people to the core flow of play without overwhelming them with details. Once that has been mastered, the experienced mode adds in special abilities for players, ambulances, fire engines, and more. It ramps up the difficulty by introducing dangerous 'hot spots' that can rapidly advance the speed of conflagration. And it does all of this in a kind of 'plug in' style that lets you select rules based on what you want. Don't want to worry about whether an ambulance is ready to help a victim of the fire? Don't use it. Flash Point invites players to find their own sweet spot between cognitive accessibility and gameplay challenge.

This is always an option in a board game – they are the ultimate moddable gaming environments. To modify a video game, one needs to learn its internal systems and

FIGURE 4.11   Flash Point. (Photograph by the author.)

the coding architecture that can manipulate them. If you want to mod a board game, sometimes it's as simple as removing a card from the deck. Explicit scaffolding within a rulebook though serves two key goals:

1. It builds a sense of confidence that you're not going to ruin the game balance because the game designers have endorsed the approach.
2. It gives explicit **permission** to modify the game in a way that a strict rules lawyer cannot complain about.

Santorini (2016, Figure 4.12) accomplishes a similar goal by offering a wide range of different powers that can be selected at the start of play. The game is one of creating buildings while also trying to get one of your pieces to the top of a building that is three blocks tall. To stop an opponent reaching that goal, players place down buildings to block paths and 'cap off' buildings so that nobody can reach the top. This is the base two player experience, and the game rules suggest using this system for the first few games so that everyone gets comfortable. Again, this is scaffolding in action, literally, in this case, because it's hard to imagine how anyone could build the city without actual scaffolds.

Once everyone is happy with the flow of play and the rules, the God cards are introduced and these give each player special powers they can use during play. These are more interesting, from an accessibility perspective, than they may first seem.

The God cards are separated into simple gods with simple powers and advanced gods with more complexity. This gives three levels of cognitive challenge – the base game, the base game with simple gods, and the base game with advanced gods.

It becomes especially interesting though when we consider a common circumstance in playing games in mixed ability groups – as in, some with impairments and some without. In order for it to be fun for everyone, it has to be approximately equally challenging. Otherwise someone is going to find it unacceptably difficult or frustratingly simple.

FIGURE 4.12 The board of Santorini. (Photograph by the author.)

Santorini allows for players to compete in nuanced ways. One player with simple gods and another player without gods as an example – it's a balancing act that allows every group to find the perfect point at which everyone has fun. Not all gods are equally powerful, so perhaps the strongest players can use the weakest gods. Or perhaps you deal the player most likely to struggle two (or more) god cards to your one. It will require experimentation to find what works best for any given table of players, but the game is flexible enough to accommodate it.

Some games take even this idea to extremes. **Blank** (2017) is as much a game designer's playground as it is a game. You begin with a deck of cards, each with a colour and number. On your turn, you lay down cards (Figure 4.13) based on whether they match the colour, or number, of the current card in play. You also deal out some random rules at the start of the game. Unlike **Fluxx**, these rules don't change until the next game. Some cards have other effects or pictures. Most though have large amounts of blank space. The cards look unfinished, and the game **feels** similarly incomplete. Just play out your cards; first to get rid of them all wins.

The first game you play is an act of drudgery – it's not fun, and it's not interesting. It's barely a game. But something **exciting** happens when you win a game of **Blank**. **You get to design part of it**. You get to add a rule, or annotate a card, or write a poem, or … **anything.**

If a game with scaffolding offers opportunities for more cognitive accessibility, just imagine how specifically accessible you can make a game if everyone gets to make up the rules themselves. **Blank** is an extraordinarily neat approach in that it puts the design in your hands. Sure, you might screw it up. The game you make might be awful. It probably will be. But the game of **Blank** was never in the cards – it was in the modifications. If it's accessible, or if it's not, it's entirely up to you. Not every game can be a 'choose your own design' in a box though, so while this approach is powerfully effective, it may not be equally generalisable.

Other games solve the problem of complexity by changing what it means to plan and strategise. We often think of hobbyist games as primarily intellectual activities,

FIGURE 4.13   Some of the cards you might encounter in Blank. (Photograph by the author.)

but that's to discount a number of awesome games that let us engage intuitively with a game state: games that let us engage in advanced mathematics where trajectories are calculated without us even thinking about the arithmetic, or games where our bodies do the maths for us.

I'm talking about dexterity games, of course. Things like **Snooker**, **Pool**, and other table sports are outside our scope, but there are plenty of smaller games that exist happily on the table and offer a relatively low cognitive burden while also permitting plenty of fun. Physical games offer an interesting cognitive profile – the act of assessing power and direction to make an object intersect with another is computationally expensive, and yet our bodies do it largely subconsciously. Physical games encode rich, deep sophistication of game state into a largely intuitive package. We know where we want to flick something just because our bodies are constantly doing the work for us.

It's not that the games are simpler, but rather the calculation is to be found somewhere in the intersection between memory, cognition, and embodiment. *Muscle memory* – distinct from the kind of memory we have discussed so far – operates in different parts of the brain to where we tend to see the general intelligence functionality. As with *short-* and *long-term memory*, models of *muscle memory* suggest that we have a short-term period of memory encoding and a long-term process of consolidating regular motor activity into largely automatic processes.

It's not correct to say that muscle memory is not impacted by what we traditionally consider to be the architecture of cognition – the mind is too complex for that. And in turn, that is not to say that cognitive impairments do not impact on rote physical learning. Degeneration across the brain can impact on the areas that encode physical activity, and we see that in scenarios of Alzheimer's and other conditions. But since these physical memories relating to embodied calculation are encoded differently, it's often the case that they can be accessible in circumstances where other memory pathways may fail.

Mostly though, what dexterity games give is a **trade-off** of mechanical complexity against intuitive complexity. Dexterity games are often comparatively rules-light, allowing for the properties of the natural world to do much of the heavy-lifting when it comes to creating interesting game states. And in that, game components can be used to modify our expectations of how physics work. Consider flicking a penguin, as in **ICECOOL** (2015, Figure 4.14), versus flicking a cube, as in **Cube Quest** (2013). We can consider two-dimensions versus three-dimensions, wood versus plastic, different weights and textures, and flicking a piece versus balancing a piece. All of it can add nuance without complexity. **Flick 'em Up** (2015) involves sending discs at speed to knock over meeples in the style of an old timey Western shootout. **Meeple Circus** (2017) involves balancing meeples on top of each other and on top of circus animals and discs. Two dexterity games, using many of the same rough components, with completely different gameplay experiences.

This in turn unlocks another useful observation – it's possible to turn complex cognitive tasks into simpler processes aimed at the same experience. Consider how a number line turns subtraction and addition into a less cognitively demanding process – instead of working out the arithmetic, you move an indicator forward and backwards. The end result is the same, but the cognitive complexity is shifted. **One Deck Dungeon** (2016) is a game of rolling coloured dice that are then used to accomplish tasks in an exploration of a fantasy underworld. Figure 4.15 shows a typical dungeon encounter.

A shield on a box indicates that these criteria must be met before any others. A heart indicates a point of damage if left uncovered. An hourglass represents lost time. It would

FIGURE 4.14   The interlocking boxes that make up ICECOOL. (Photograph by the author.)

have been perfectly possible – easier in fact – to mark each quest in terms of a checklist with penalties, shown in Table 4.1.

The act of working out how well you can accomplish a task here becomes a complex, time-consuming operation of checking and cross-checking what you roll versus the table. That's cognitively demanding, employing a range of faculties stressing *long-term, short-term,* and *working memory.*

That's not how it works in the game though. Instead, dice are placed onto the grid when they satisfy the requirements, which means completing a quest is an act of assessing a die and placing it in the most effective box. It's effortless because the cognitive

FIGURE 4.15   An encounter card from One Deck Dungeon. (Photograph by the author.)

TABLE 4.1

A Checklist of Instructions that could also Encode the Information from Figure 4.14

Colour	Minimum Value	Effect or Penalty
Blue	2	Must be covered first
Blue	4	Must be covered first
Green	3	1 time
Green	5	1 time, 1 health
Purple	5	1 time, 1 health
Green	6	2 time

profile is shifted from calculation to assignment. Compare that to the city-builder **Suburbia** (2012, Figure 4.16), which is a game of using hex tiles and adjacency effects to build a working (or not) district made up of industrial, residential, governmental, and commercial resources.

The slaughterhouse gives some income for every restaurant in the game – as in, any restaurant in any district, not just your own. The fancy restaurant gives a big income boost when it's placed but loses value for every restaurant built **after** that one. The office building gives income for each adjacent commercial hex, and the parking lot does the same. The office building gives the parking lot a bonus, and the parking lot gives the office a bonus. The waterfront realty gives the parking lot a bonus by virtue of being adjacent, but it also doubles the money given for the lake. And that effect triggers when placed, so it will cause the lake to pay out again. In short, every time you play a hex down in **Suburbia**, be prepared to grind over the implications for you **and everyone else.** The game doesn't do anything to minimise the cognitive impact. And let's not even get started on the complex, multi-stage engines you build in **Terraforming Mars** (2016, Figure 4.17).

FIGURE 4.16 The connected hexes that make up a district in Suburbia. Note that it is full of adjacency effects and other effects that work across a whole district or across every district. (Photograph by the author.)

FIGURE 4.17   An engine under construction in Terraforming Mars. (Photograph by the author.)

Finally in this section, we return to the idea of the stigma of house rules. The culture around some games (**chess**, for example) is very strict when it comes to 'take backs'. When you touch a piece, you commit to moving that piece. You can change your mind to where you move it as long as you retain contact with it. Once your hand leaves the piece, the move is committed. Informal play may be less strict, allowing players to say 'Oh no! Can I take that back?' and the opponent accepting or rejecting the request as they desire. Etiquette at the gaming table may lean towards the severe or permissive, but there do exist players who believe that there should be a formality in play. For example, no takebacks and no claiming forgotten advantages when your turn is over. There's no right or wrong way to play a game, but strictness is often inaccessible.

Star Trek: Frontiers (2016) acknowledges its own cognitive complexity by explicitly encoding a take-back rule in the manual. Essentially as long as the game state hasn't changed, a player can take back some, all, or none of the things they have done in their turn. Having it explicitly outlined in the rules staves off any objection from those that believe in the letter, rather than the spirit, of the design. These kind of permissions, encoded as word of law within a manual, can do wonders for the general accessibility of any game.

Games with Interesting Cognitive Design

For our first example in this section, it's not that we have an interesting game but rather an interesting **pair** of games – **Codenames** (2015) and **Codenames Pictures** (2016). These are essentially exactly the same game except one uses text and the other uses

FIGURE 4.18 The playing area from Codenames Pictures. Codenames itself is largely the same, except with words instead of pictures. (Photograph by the author.)

images. In each, players form into teams. During setup, the deck is shuffled and dealt out into a fixed-sized grid on the table. One member of each team is the spymaster, who has to give a clue that connects a certain subset of cards together as defined by a separate card which shows to which team each cell in the grid belongs.

If a spymaster wanted to connect the cards 'van', 'ship', and 'limousine', they might say 'Vehicle, 3'. Their team mates then try to identify what cards were indicated by the clue while avoiding the cards of their opponent or the insta-loss assassin. Figure 4.18 shows the grid you might see in Codenames Pictures.

What makes these games interesting is not so much their design or their individual accessibility profiles, but rather they let you choose your inaccessibilities. You can choose a game that stresses visual processing and interpretation or one that focuses on linguistic dexterity and vocabulary. **Codenames: Disney** (2017), **Codenames: Harry Potter** (2018), and **Codenames: The Simpsons** (2019) all in turn subtly change the accessibility profile. The shift from abstract imagery such as in **Codenames: Pictures** to specific the employment of Disney or Harry Potter references alters the way in which interpretation works and places differing emphasis on popular cultural knowledge. Different variants of the game, in other words, offer some of the flexibility that we discussed with regards to the scaffolding in games such as **Santorini**. Finding ideogrammatic links between abstract images is a different skill to remembering narrative links between Disney movies.

The picture-based versions of **Codenames** also have elements of **Dixit** (2008, Figure 4.19) stitched into their DNA. We have already discussed **Dixit** a bit, so we won't rehash it except to remind you that it's a game entirely about personal meaning and trying to communicate whimsy via clues that are descriptive … but not **too** descriptive.

What makes this interesting is that it replaces cold, unfeeling logic with warm, subjective empathy. We haven't spent any time in this chapter talking about emotional elements – we'll get to those in a later chapter – but I think it's fair to say that gamers tend to over-value rules, logic, goals, and points while undervaluing the virtues of connection

FIGURE 4.19   A selection of cards from Dixit. (Photograph by the author.)

and understanding. We can see that quite easily in how 'walking simulators' are often dismissed as not really being video games because all you do is walk around and experience a place and a time. I've argued, largely unsuccessfully, that we should consider these kind of games 'empathic puzzlers' because they are about understanding a situation rather than solving a problem. **Dixit** is the kind of game that shows intelligence comes in a wide variety of forms.

Finally in this section, I want to talk about two different but related games. They are both powerful examples that show how easily mental processes can be short-circuited. **Dobble**, also known as **Spot-It** (2009), is basically snap on steroids. It has numerous rulesets, but they all work in a similar way – they require a player to match symbols on different cards. Fastest to match wins the card. Play until all your cards are gone or, in some variations, until you capture everyone else's cards.

Dobble is an extraordinary game because of that deceptive simplicity we've already discussed. Each card shares one, and only one, symbol with any other card. Figure 4.20 shows a sample deal of cards you might see in a four-player game. See how the bottom card has a moon on it, and so does the centre card? The right card shares a spider with the middle card. The left an igloo. The top card a snowflake. If you're matching against the symbols in another player's card (which is true in some modes), you'll see the bottom has a snowman match with the card on the right. And all you have to do, as any player, is name the appropriate matching symbol and touch the card before anyone else does.

It's almost laughably trivial, and yet this is a game that has stressed me so much I genuinely forgot the word for ice-cube and yelled out 'meltcube' instead. 'ICE HOUSE', I might yell when I mean igloo. 'BOAT HOOK' instead of anchor. It's fascinating to see a game which, through its very simplicity, shows some of the ways in which we take visual processing and vocabulary for granted. **Dobble** is sometimes suggested as an accessible game for people with cognitive impairments, but I disagree. The rules are certainly accessible – the sheer raw mental processing required to play is less so, and the real-time element makes it difficult to find an equilibrium in skills.

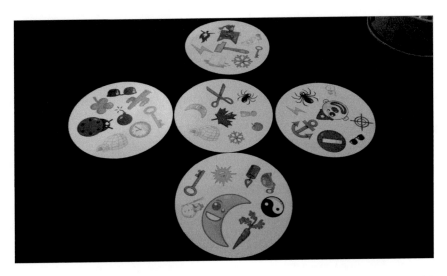

FIGURE 4.20 A game of Dobble, showing the arithmetic witchcraft that powers it. (Photograph by the author.)

In a similar vein is **That's Not a Hat** (2023), which will clearly communicate to you the fragility of our memories. Figure 4.21 shows some of the cards from the game. On the obverse of each is an arrow that shows whether a card should be passed clockwise or counter-clockwise. Everyone gets dealt a card at the start and shows it to everyone else before turning it face down. The starting player then draws another card and again shows everyone before also turning it face down. The starting player then passes their previous card in the direction indicated on the back. They say to the recipient what the card is, and the recipient either accepts the card or rejects it on the basis that the gifter is incorrect about what's on the other side. A successful rejection earns the gifter a strike

FIGURE 4.21 Some of the gifts to be passed around in That's Not a Hat. (Photograph by the author.)

against them, and an unsuccessful rejection means the recipient is penalised instead. If they accept the gift, they in turn need to pass their oldest card in the indicated direction. The game continues until someone has three strikes against them, at which point everyone else wins.

I have honestly never played a game that has made me so concerned about the diminishing sharpness of my own mental faculties. It seems impossibly easy – all you need to remember is what you were passed and what you were last passed. The problem is that you are trying to also track what other people are passing around. This ends up overwriting the *short-term memory* you're relying upon. That's why you will spend a solid minute looking at the card in front of you with absolutely no idea what it is and then pass it on to another player with a raised inflection that proves you have no confidence in what you're saying. 'This is … some … popcorn?'

From the rules, this seems like it's playable by anyone. The experience I have of playing it with different groups though seems to arrive at a general consensus. That being 'This is the most fun I've had with a game I never want to play again'. It's stressful to experience your mind blanking on something that seems this trivial. Sometimes the most valuable thing you get out of playing games is a sense of perspective.

Guidelines for Fluid Intelligence Accessibility

- *Games to look to for inspiration*:
  - Dixit, Terror in Meeple City, Tsuro, Rhino Hero Super Battle, Lanterns; Santorini, and Carcassonne.
- *Games to look to as cautionary tales*:
  - Star Fluxx, X-Wing Miniatures Game, Eclipse – A New Dawn for the Galaxy, Iota, Star Trek: Frontiers, and San Juan.

Text

Make It Obvious as to How Players Should Resolve Ambiguity

One of the common faults in manuals is when the rules are not written in a way that permits a single, unambiguous interpretation. Language is loose, and readability is often at the cost of precision. The inclusion of a reference sheet that provides examples of how to resolve uncertainty can solve this. Similarly, a downloadable FAQ or errata sheet that is easily accessed is an important accessibility feature.

- Provide easily accessed errata that helps resolve any ambiguity in game rules.
- Provide example resolution of ambiguities in an appendix of the rulebook.
- Link the manual to errata through the use of a QR code.

Aim for Text that Is Written in a Straightforward Way

Flowery, ornate text can be fun to write – I'm as guilty of it as anyone. However, if a manual is to be instructional, it should focus on function rather than form. Clever layouts and fancy vocabulary get in the way of clarity – a manual should flow simply and cleanly. Remember too that novice players may lack the literacy in game-specific terms that hobbyists take for granted. Provide meaningful introductions to terms that are unlikely to be understood by the general public. If that's too much of a sacrifice, consider the provision of a plain, simple version of the main rulebook as a downloadable PDF.

- Employ simple, descriptive language in your game text.
- Format game rules and game text as simply as possible.
- Aim for consistency in terminology across the entire game – if a game component is called a tile in one part of the rules, it shouldn't be called a token in another.
- Avoid using synonyms to indicate an activity, even if those synonyms differ in thematic heft. If the mechanism is to 'engage' an enemy, don't refer to it elsewhere as 'attack' or 'kill'.
- Decide on a naming convention for *rounds, turns, actions,* and so on and use it consistently.
- Break the description of complex mechanisms down into small steps with clear linearity.
- Reinforce the text in the manual with explanatory images.
- Limit the use of jargon and include a glossary for the jargon that is unavoidable.

Ensure Ease of Readability

The aesthetics of a piece of writing are often as important as the content in ensuring readability. White space is valuable, and the choice of font can be what makes something flow and what makes it skip over the eyes. Dealing with dyslexia falls into the general category of cognitive accessibility, and it should be borne in mind when providing the rules.

- Ensure text is large and well contrasted.
- Avoid completely black text on a completely white background.
- Avoid line width of over 70 characters to aid in comprehensibility for those with dyslexia.
- Write shorter, snappy sentences. If a sentence goes on for three lines, break it down.
- Avoid multi-line justified or centred text unless it is used to clarify a break between one section and another.
- Use an easy-read font, designed specifically for improved readability. Common candidates include Arial, Helvetica, Verdana, and Open Sans.

Include Both Reference and Instructional Rulebooks

There are two philosophical camps on how 'educational' materials are best written. One camp focuses on material as tutorial – step-by-step instructions on how to accomplish a task or follow a process. This kind of material is great for the first time you try to do something but inefficient when you want to find a specific rule. Reference material on the other hand is written in a way that allows someone to easily locate a specific element of the game but is generally a poor way to learn how to play. If your game is complex enough, consider offering two versions of the instructional material.

- Provide a tutorial manual with worked examples and clear flow of play.
- Provide an indexed reference that allows people to look up specific rules, concepts, and terminology.

Icons: Make the Meaning of Icons Easy to Understand

Icons used through the game should ideally make it clear what they represent. The semiotics of your design should ideally reinforce the link with what is represented. Make use of skeuomorphism as much as is possible and make sure iconography is consistent across the manual and game components. For example, you might represent 'hot' through a bursting thermometer or through a fire. You shouldn't try to represent it with less obvious iconography such as lines of radiated heat or a chili pepper. The latter are more easily misinterpreted.

- Make use of commonly known symbols when appropriate – rely on existing mental models.
- Minimise the use of complex symbolism that doesn't map on to real-life design.
- Employ skeuomorphism liberally to aid players to construct a mental model of play.
- Limit the level of abstraction needed to link an icon to its meaning.

General Aesthetics

Show People What's Most Important on Game Components

Some parts of your game are more important than others. The cost of a card, for example, versus the flavour text associated with it. The effect of making use of an action as opposed to its art. The design of the game should highlight the most important elements while de-emphasising the others.

- Separate out flavour text from gameplay text with spacing, letterboxing, and font choices.
- Use a prominent, distinct ornamentation (bold or italics) to indicate important terms and concepts. Use these consistently.
- Letterbox especially important text against the background of a board or other components.

Give a Consistency of Directional Reference

It's often necessary in a game to offer directions or indicate the location of an active game element, such as 'this is on the left side of the board'. This is sometimes done through the use of map references or landmarks that show where on a board something may be found. Keep in mind that the orientation of a board may not be the same for all players.

- Consider changing relative directions to absolute directions, linked to aesthetic elements on the edge of a board.

- When providing visual aids to location, explicitly anchor them to a fixed orientation and make that clear when comparing the visual aid to the board.
- For games where it is thematically appropriate, consider the use of a compass that shows where north, or up, should be expected.

Rules

Assume a Low Level of Baseline Literacy

Language independence in a board game is usually achieved by relying on imagery and iconography alone, with no need to read or interpret text on cards or the board. Limiting the amount, and complexity, of reading involved in playing a game can do wonders in making a game more accessible. When unavoidable, aim for the simplest possible phrasing.

- Avoid any reliance on players being able to read or understand in-game text.
- Do not require spelling or alphabetising in games that are not about spelling.
- Provide descriptive text in as plain language as possible.
- Limit, or eliminate, the use of jargon. When not possible include a glossary.
- Provide links (via QR code for example) to additional non-text resources where possible.

Assume a Low Level of Baseline Numeracy

As with literacy, it is safest to assume limited numeracy from players affected by cognitive impairments. Complex arithmetic should be avoided completely – even players with conditions as comparatively mild as dyscalculia will react poorly to a requirement for doing maths in their head. Arithmetic operations should be limited, and if compound calculations are required, these should be done in separate steps. Modifiers and multipliers are all likely issues here. When numeracy can't be avoided, it should be supported as far as is possible with game components – a number line for example allows for addition and subtraction without the need for calculation. Placing tokens on a board to fill missing spaces means that players know when they're done when all the spaces are filled and not because they performed a logical comparison on abstract resources.

- Limit the requirement for numeracy or convert calculation into some more physical form of representation.
- Design scoring systems that don't require explicit calculation or scoring pads.
- Limit the need to put in order or classify within gameplay systems.
- If making heavy use of probability, help players to appreciate the odds with symbolic coding where appropriate.

Give Players a Choice Regarding Desired Game Complexity

Some gamers really enjoy deep, complex games they can spend a life-time mastering. Some crave the 'crunch' of heavy titles with intricate rules. Others prefer light, breezy experiences. Some games are made up of what are essentially interconnected minigames where complexity emerges from intersection. The games that are optimally accessible though are the ones that have a simple, straightforward core upon which additional rules can be layered to deepen or broaden the experience. However, it is important to avoid the stigma of calling the simplest rules the 'basic' or 'beginner' versions – this can discourage people from using them. 'Standard' versus 'Expert' is a much more inclusive way of phrasing it.

- Provide layers of complexity in game systems. Highlight cards that are especially complex or problematic, and permit them to be removed from the deck before play.
- Scaffold your rules so as to allow people to add in additional complexity or remove elements for a simpler version of the game.
- Provide variants of your rules that allow for a simple game versus the full game. Give these different rule-sets non-stigmatising descriptors.
- Allow players to select the level of synergy expected of play – for example, by providing recommended sets of starting components or cards.
- Consider the introduction of alternate, low competition variants. For example, bands of accomplishment based on score achieved versus raw comparison of points.
- Offer an opportunity for alternate win conditions that permit for less cognitively expensive play.
- In games with asymmetrical player powers or roles, provide simpler roles that require less strategy from a player but still enable them to meaningfully compete or collaborate.

Aim for Consistent Game Flow

The more regulated a game experience is, the more understandable it is. Games that change the turn order, or turn composition, tend to be less cognitively accessible than others especially if it happens abruptly. Examples of this are games where what happens in a turn depends on the sum of player decisions in earlier phases or where clockwise play order may become counter-clockwise play through player choice or random events. This can undermine cognitive coping techniques. Consider in your design if such things are necessary.

- Try to ensure a reliability of game turns, the order of players, and the actions that make up a turn.
- Be wary of temporally decoupling actions from outcomes because players may forget or not be fully aware of the later implications.
- Try to avoid conditionals or exceptions in game rules. 'If this then that' or 'Do this unless that' are cognitively complex to accurately process.
- Provide a first-player token and have its progress around the table formally handled in the structure of a round or turn.
- Ensure that the termination condition of a game is known in advance, and it triggers at a predictable time.

Simplify Decision Making by Constraining the Possibility Space

We've all experienced play with a friend who suffers from analysis paralysis. The common cause of this is when the possibility space of 'good' choices is too large for someone to quickly process. The optimal size of this possibility space scales inversely with cognitive impairment. Too many complex choices, in too many different circumstances, can result in an inaccessible game for anyone.

- Keep the number of meaningful choices that need to be considered at any one time to a minimum.
- Try to ensure that complicated or complex mechanics are opt-in.
- Allow players to be competitive by considering the current turn, without needing to plan for what might happen several turns ahead.
- If a game does require planning multiple turns ahead, minimise how much that planning might be at risk of disruption on a turn-to-turn basis.
- Consider a hard limit on the number of temporary status effects a player might have to consider at any one time.
- Aim for the reliability and predictability of scoring opportunities. Telegraph these as far as is possible through annotation on round trackers or player aids.

Provide Alternatives for Real-Time Gameplay Elements

Every one of our accessibility categories suffers when a game is real-time – whether that's through its design or through rewarding players for acting quickly in competition with others. The pressures on any compensatory regime increase as the time to perform them decreases.

- Avoid or provide alternatives to timers.
- Consider providing turn-based variants for real-time games.

Tokens and Currency

Indicate Special Cases with Bespoke Tokens

It's often the case in a game that a miniature or meeple gains temporary attributes or should be treated as a special case for the purposes of play. When this happens, it's common to place a special token that gets moved alongside the figure to which it is attached. This can result in play becoming bogged down in additional cognitive calculation as people notice, or not, the special case token.

- Where some pieces have special powers or must be treated as a special case, consider an alternate token rather than annotating the same token with an additional marker.
- If pieces must be annotated with additional tokens, consider building slots into the base of the figure to permit ease of manipulation.

Dice and Randomisation

Limit the Need for Calculations

Calculating the sum or consequences of a set of rolled dice is an act of numeracy, which is covered in its own section above. However, with dice there is the additional complexity that comes from rolling multiple types of dice at the same time, especially if those dice have non-standard icons or numerical distribution. Rolling, for example **3d6 + 5d8 + 2d12**. Such combinations are much more difficult to predict in terms of likely output and make summing up more difficult. Tactical choices that depend on particular outcomes are likewise more difficult to assess in terms of probability.

- Attempt, as far as is possible, to avoid having players rolling multiple kinds of dice at a time.
- Provide some indication of the likely distribution of dice rolls in the game, allowing players awareness of the odds of success.
- Where players have a choice in building a pool of dice to roll, offer the option of a pre-defined deterministic total instead. For example, 'you can roll 2d6 or accept the result 6 without rolling'.

General Component Design

Make Scoring Opportunities Obvious

Scoring in games is usually very important in groups where anyone involved is playing to win, as opposed to playing to simply have fun. Sometimes scoring opportunities are hidden away on cards or emerge through certain non-obvious options on the board. Sometimes games have private scoring conditions or secret conditions that affect everyone. These all add an interesting texture to play but add cognitive complexity.

Similarly, some games change the general convention of scoring – rather than 'most points win', it is sometimes 'lowest points wins' or 'highest score, which is the sum of your smallest collection of tokens'. These games break the obvious link between 'size of my pile of tokens' and 'how well I am playing'.

- Provide a clear physical or visual approximation of score through tokens or a score track.
- Avoid secret scoring goals, especially those that impact on all players. If these cannot be avoided, make them optional.
- Try to avoid the need for score to be calculated through extended comparison and calculation at the end of a game.
- Where score **must** be calculated in several phases, provide score pads to help work this out.
- Where scoring is done on pads, have each row be about scoring a specific element of the game. Don't require cross-referencing different tokens or mechanisms.

Map Tokens to Their Meaning

As with icons, it's useful to ensure tokens are designed with comprehensibility in mind. Using unique graphics to indicate what a token represents can be aesthetically pleasing, but it loses the existing semiotic links we all regularly use within society. Using an iconic convention that is already known lowers the need for someone to learn, and work with, a new symbol in a new context.

- If possible, design tokens so that they are skeuomorphic – representing the underlying system that they abstract. Red cubes can represent apples, but so can red apple tokens.
- If using unique art to represent real-world concepts, consider modelling that art on existing symbolic conventions.
- When employing brand new iconography, support its interpretation with a lookup table.

Miscellaneous

Support Alternate Ways of Learning the Rules

Not everyone copes well with written instruction. And not everyone can work from a video tutorial. Consider supporting alternate methods of learning the game, along with supplementary material that helps people play the game. Sometimes the problem isn't learning the rules but identifying how the rules are intended to cohere.

- Provide a clear video tutorial – with subtitles – with an illustrated transcript available.
- Consider 'in-game' tutorials that teach the game through scaffolding mechanisms over several game sessions.
- Provide supporting guides that introduce players to basic strategies and techniques.

Guidelines for Crystalised Intelligence Accessibility

- *Games to look to for inspiration*:
  - Dropmix, Kingdomino, Telestrations, Forbidden Island, and Blank.
- *Games to look to as cautionary tales*:
  - Hanabi, Twilight Struggle, Iota, Onitama, The Resistance, Spyfall, Tash-Kalar, and Chinatown.

Text

Reduce the Amount of Written Information People Need to Remember

The more people need to remember, the more difficult a game is to play for everyone. One useful technique of translation is to turn the need for **remembering** into a need for **recall.** This is the difference between 'What is the capital of Great Britain?' and 'Select the capital of Great Britain from the following list'.

- Provide a crib sheet of specialised jargon.
- Include important context on cards/tokens, not just in the rulebook.
- Provide clear language references to special card powers in the rulebook or a supplemental manual. This helps mitigate the issue associated with hidden hand management.

Icons

Reduce the Amount of Iconography People Need to Remember

Translating recall into recognition is one of the most effective forms of accessible design you have available. Whenever there is an icon in the game, make it easy for people to connect it to the role it plays in the game. And in this, relying on existing skeuomorphic and semiotic conventions can do much of the heavy lifting. For example, if you require a unique icon aesthetic to represent a poison, iterate upon the triple triangles of biohazard symbology as a starting point.

- Provide a lookup table of icons and their meaning. Cross-reference this with tokens where appropriate.
- Make the design of icons descriptive as opposed to simply decorative.
- Aim for skeuomorphism in icon design.
- Rely upon existing semiotic conventions to ease comprehension.

General Aesthetics

Prioritise Ease of Reading

The specific fonts chosen as part of a game can be problematic, and font choice can greatly impact on readability. Arial, Helvetica, Verdana, and Open Sans are generally considered solid choices for assisting those with dyslexia.

- Use san serif text where possible.
- Use darker text on a lighter background to ease the cognitive load of reading.
- Avoid text ornamentation except for genuine emphasis. Use bold for this when possible.
- Avoid underlines and italics in larger blocks of text.
- Avoid text in block capitals outside of headings.
- Make headings large and bold.
- Avoid dense paragraphs – shorter, punchier text tends to be more readable.

Give People Reminders of Probability and Composition

Sometimes a game relies heavily on knowing the chance of something happening. Sometimes this is knowing the 'sweet spot' in a dice pool (knowing for example that 2d6 is more likely to produce 6, 7, and 8 than it is to produce 2 or 12). Sometimes it is what proportion of a deck is made up of cards that satisfy a condition (knowing the chance of drawing an ace versus drawing a heart). This stresses numeracy and memory, and this burden can be reduced in the design of components.

- Provide reminders on cards as to deck composition, showing how many of each type of card are present at the start of play.
- Indicate the desirability or otherwise of ranges of numbers with colour codes or symbols.
- Use aesthetic design to indicate especially desirable regions of a board.
- If tiles or cards have scoring opportunities associated with them, provide some visual indicator as their desirability and the appropriate mechanism.

Rules

Limit Context Shifting during Play

Part of the way the mind works is through firing up neurons to prep them for a task that is presumed to be forthcoming. If someone is talking about their cat, for example, the neurons associated with your dog get warmed up ready for use. When we rapidly shift from one context to another, our brains take a little time to catch up. That's true of everyone, but it is most impactful on those with cognitive impairments. It's especially problematic when the shift is temporary – for example, when playing a card means we play an additional card as part of its action, and then return to where we were in executing the actions of the first card. Whether a context shift is short term or long term, relying on recollection of earlier context is cognitively expensive.

- Limit 'context shifts' where game actions are broken up by the execution of other actions. Instead, make them sequential – queue them up to be handled at the end of the current action.
- Provide token reminders for pending actions that are yet to be resolved.
- Within free-form games with evolving historical context (storytelling games, for example), provide a mechanism for offering a recap to the table at certain choke points of the game. Explicitly support this in the rules if necessary or provide game components for recording it.

Limit the Need for Real World Knowledge

Certain games rely on knowledge of the real world to play correctly – not necessarily the kind of embodied knowledge associated with dexterity games but rather historical or theoretical knowledge that offers a gameplay advantage. Trivia games, for example, or games where popular cultural references inform play. Some games stress real-world skills, such as pantomime, improvisation, or rhetoric. Others use real-world references suggestively, such as in a theme. A war-game making use of tanks for example often communicates implicitly to players the typical use-case of a tank even if it's not explicitly encoded in rules.

- Avoid a reliance on general knowledge or trivia.
- When communicating gameplay through thematic resonance, also explicitly define the relationship between the theme and the game.

- Where real-world skillsets are required, consider providing alternatives that can be employed in their stead or allow players to choose which real-world skill they wish to demonstrate.

Limit the Need to Remember Special Cases

One of the most problematic issues that exist in executing upon rules is 'special cases'. These situations almost always make up complex gameplay – 'an attack with a sword may do damage, **unless** the target is immune to being slashed'. 'If the attack is fire, then reflect d6 damage on the caster'. In individual cases, this can often be fine – the problem is most exhibited in compound conditions or if almost everything comes with its own special case.

- Ensure rules are consistent throughout the game so they behave the same in all circumstances.
- Limit the number of exceptions and 'if this then that otherwise' style rules.
- When special cases must be encoded into the game, then clearly indicate them in game material.

Game Layout and Experience

Clearly Represent Everything with Tokens and Components

There is a lot of implicit information in playing a game. Remembering who picked the blue pawn, or who is the current player, or what the actual goal of play may be. 'Oh, is it my turn?' is a thing that we've all heard during a gameplay session or ten. 'Whose meeple is that?' is another. Make the implicit explicit through the use of current player tokens, visible goals, and formal links between playing pieces and piece owners.

- Make sure all game state is represented in the play area with tokens and cards. Don't rely on people to remember.
- Provide players with a formal way to separate elements that have been used versus those still to be used: rotating cards at angles, flipping tokens, and so on.
- When providing 'once-per-turn' actions and activities, provide a way to track whether they've been used.
- Allow the game to be played solely on the basis of the information available at that moment, without players having to recall past events or information.
- Permit players to investigate spent cards or tokens to remind themselves of previous actions or probabilities.
- Avoid systems that involve obscuring game state with other game state, such as moving units on top of information-bearing board elements.
- Avoid where possible components that may serve multiple uses, especially those that are double-sided. Try to ensure each component has one well-defined use.

Game and Player Boards

Provide Reminders of Rules and Objectives

To maximise cognitive accessibility, big-picture information should be available directly on the board rather than hidden in the manual. This doesn't need to be written, or even necessarily explicit, but if someone is confused about what they are trying to do, they should be able to look at what's on the table and find indicators. They should be able to answer questions such as 'Who you are?' 'What are you doing?' 'How you gain points?' and 'How do you win?'. Players should rarely have to check the manual to understand the context of what's going on.

- Break setup into numbered sections, each linking to annotations on a diagram at the start of the manual, and contextualised against game mechanisms.
- Include a table of components, with photos, with the name used for each. Situate this before any reference to the component in the rules.
- Show players what the area in front of them should look like at the start of the game and how that relates to the shared game state.
- Permit players to see a reminder of key objectives somewhere on the game board or their player mat.
- Provide worked examples of how turns should progress in the manual, with explicit linking to the game components involved.
- Where appropriate start with basics. Begin with the minimum needed to play, and gradually introduce complexity through the layering of additional rules.
- Provide a summary of scoring and rules on the board or player aids.
- Duplicate all content contained in external instructional sources (such as video tutorials) within manuals.
- Offer simple board layouts that can be used and then destroyed or act as overlays on top of a board. Randomised paper boards can also substitute for games with long setup time.

Meeples and Miniatures

Give People a Reminder as to Which Pieces Are Theirs

Sometimes players have a philosophy of which pieces on the board represent them ('I always play blue'). Others pick pieces more situationally. If a game doesn't formally link player role (such as medic) to player colour (such as the medic being the blue pieces), it's easy to forget who is who if there is no explicit reminder. Even if someone remembers which colour or form factor is theirs, they may not remember it for everyone.

- Provide a formal link between selected miniature and owner – colour, symbol, or miniature silhouette that is reflected on a player mat or equivalent.
- Ensure that ownership of pieces can be clearly determined by each player **for** each player.

Dice and Randomisation

Show People when They Have Exhausted Their Options

If left to their own devices, people will mentally spend the same resources over and over again. Partitioning available goods versus spend is cognitively complex unless it is translated into a less expensive process. This can be through clear instructions regarding discard decks and discard dice or by allowing players to do a preliminary assignment of dice and tokens as to where they are planned to be spent.

- If dice are 'used up' during play, ensure that there is a part of the game board where they can be discarded or temporarily allocated.
- Put slots or sockets on player cards and player boards to allow players to see how they spend their budget before they commit to it.
- Explicitly permit, within the rules, experimentation with the outcome of different resource allocations until such time as the game state changes.

General Component Design

Ease the Management of Turn and Phase Order

It's easy to forget phases and the order of activities within a turn if it is made up of several steps. Clearly communicate to all players what the procedure is, including when turn order markers should be passed along or at which stage components are gathered or spent. Critical here is also consistency – the hobby-wide inconsistency between the terms 'turn', 'phase', 'action', and 'round' is a problem, but the best you as an individual can do is ensure the terms have robust meaning in your own games.

- Explicitly indicate what you mean by round, turn, action, phase, and any other sequence-based terminology. Be consistent with the use throughout your manual and game.
- Allow players to indicate through markers at which stage in a multi-step turn they are. Provide clear sequencing of this in rules and player aids.
- If players have a pool of action points, provide spendable tokens to indicate this.
- If a game permits temporary or passive bonuses, provide reminder tokens for these and explicitly note in the game sequence when they should be returned to the supply.
- When providing lots of different actions that can be activated once or several times in a round, provide a formal way of tracking the state of such activation.
- Provide tokens for tracking 'charges' in mechanisms with a limited number of uses.

Provide Reference Aids

The lack of a player aid **for each player** is one of the easiest ways to mess up cognitive accessibility. This should be a separate handout, and ideally **not** double-sided with different information on the obverse. The most common kind of player aid is a rules and scoring reference, but other games may require other forms of player aid to limit the need for recollection. One player aid printed on the back of the manual is insufficient. Forcing people to turn over their player aid to access other information is sub-optimal. In particular, player aids on the back of player boards (upon which may place components and pieces) are not appropriate. It requires sliding everything off and back on every time you want to check the contents.

- Provide reference cards and summary sheets for each.
- Consider using a 'standard' and 'advanced' manual system to reduce the amount of reading needed of players.
- If players are expected to remember role-specific information, give a player aid for that too.
- Provide a brief summary of the main rules and objectives for quick reference during play.
- Player aids should also define scoring options and win conditions, as well as perhaps some simple advice for play if there is room.
- Avoid placing information on the back of a reference aid – provide a separate aid for each set of information. This may not be an issue if the back of a reference aid refers to a different game mode.

Make Calculation as Easy as Possible

Many games involve spending accumulated currency against a goal. 'Spend 5 red tokens to get 2 points'. It is more cognitively accessible to change the sum of this into a visual representation, such as a set of empty squares into which cubes can be placed at which point you take two other cubes off of a different track. It's the same mechanism; it just translates arithmetic into a less cognitively problematic matching exercise.

- Visually represent, where possible, the outcomes of calculations and their modifiers.
- Try to limit the need for players to work out number and types of dice and tokens.
- Translate complex cognitive tasks into simpler visual and physical manipulation.

Miscellaneous

Show How to Use Your Insert

One unexpected puzzle players often encounter is how to pack a game away into a custom plastic insert. Many gamers, myself included, will throw out a bad insert and replace it with plastic bags in a bare box. However, a publisher going to the trouble of making a custom insert is rarely doing so with the intention of it being discarded. If you have lots of components, all of which are expected to fit neatly into vacuum-packed plastic, provide a diagram that shows how it's supposed to work.

- Provide a visual guide to how your box insert works, if it's complex.
- Provide a guide as to in what order components should be replaced in the insert.
- Visually indicate on the insert where different tokens should go.
- Provide some flex in the space made available for components to make manipulation easier.

Note

1. Seriation is the ability to sort objects based on differences in dimensions. For example, putting numbers in order or sorting objects by size. Classification is the ability to group objects based on similarities in dimensions.

BIBLIOGRAPHY

Bory, P. (2019). Deep new: The shifting narratives of artificial intelligence from Deep Blue to AlphaGo. *Convergence*, *25*(4), 627–642.

Box, G. E. Editor(s): Robert L. Launer, Graham N. Wilkinson. (1979). Robustness in the strategy of scientific model building. In *Robustness in statistics* (pp. 201–236). Elsevier.

Cattell, R. B. (1963). Theory of fluid and crystallized intelligence: A critical experiment. *Journal of Educational Psychology*, *54*(1), 1.

Cowan, N. (2008). What are the differences between long-term, short-term, and working memory? *Progress in Brain Research*, *169*, 323–338.

Gourville, J. T., & Soman, D. (2005). Overchoice and assortment type: When and why variety backfires. *Marketing Science*, *24*(3), 382–395.

Heron, M. J., & Belford, P. H. (2015). All of your co-workers are gone: Story, substance, and the empathic puzzler. *Journal of Games Criticism*, *2*(1).

Horn, J. L., & Cattell, R. B. (1967). Age differences in fluid and crystallized intelligence. *Acta Psychologica*, *26*, 107–129.

Kieras, D. E., & Bovair, S. (1984). The role of a mental model in learning to operate a device. *Cognitive Science*, *8*(3), 255–273.

Norman, D. A. (1999). Affordance, conventions, and design. *Interactions*, *6*(3), 38–43.

Parizet, E., Guyader, E., & Nosulenko, V. (2008). Analysis of car door closing sound quality. *Applied Acoustics*, *69*(1), 12–22.

Salthouse, T. A. (2009). When does age-related cognitive decline begin? *Neurobiology of Aging*, *30*(4), 507–514.

Van de Pol, J., Volman, M., & Beishuizen, J. (2010). Scaffolding in teacher–student interaction: A decade of research. *Educational Psychology Review*, *22*, 271–296.

Williamson, A. M., & Feyer, A.-M. (2000). Moderate sleep deprivation produces impairments in cognitive and motor performance equivalent to legally prescribed levels of alcohol intoxication. *Occupational and Environmental Medicine*, *57*(10), 649–655.

5

Physical Accessibility

Many board games are unashamedly intellectual exercises. Few games exemplify this more than **chess** (1475) – an abstraction of war played out largely in the minds of its players. The lexicon around **chess** emphasises this aspect. 'Thinking ten moves ahead', for example. BoardGameGeek (BGG) – the pre-eminent website of cardboard nerds everywhere – has a massive database of crowdsourced data points sourced from its admirably diligent audience. One of those data points is a sense of 'weight', which is a loose measure of how difficult it is to learn a game[1]. Of the top ten games of all time listed on BGG (at the time of writing), their average weight is 3.7 out of 5, which classifies as *medium* to *medium-heavy*. **Monopoly** (1935) gets a 1.63 in this scale, **chess** gets 3.66, and **Go** (-2356) gets 3.93.

That is to say – of the ten best rated board games ever, the average game is considered to be as intellectually taxing as chess. Many of them are regarded as weightier than Go – the phenomenally deep and complex game that bested all the greatest artificial intelligence routines long after chess had its first grand-master bend the knee to cold, unfeeling silicon. It was around 2015 before AlphaGo won the first ever game of Go against a professional.

All these heavy duty games stress strategy and deep thinking in their design. As such, the physical requirements of play associated with a board game often receive scant attention. Aside from a few explicitly dexterity-based offerings, we tend to assume that we play games in the mind. Where the body is involved in board games, it is often merely as a taxi for our brains.

Except ... not really. It turns out that yes, we can play a lot of games in our mind. But reflecting what's in our mind onto a board is a different story.

Before we dig too deeply into that, as is now customary we need to spend a little time outlining what we mean by physical impairment and how it manifests. And in this, we're going to make use of the concept of *motor control* or specifically control over our *motor neurons*. Humans have around 150,000 *motor neurons* which act in concert to handle the contraction and relaxation of approximately 600 separate muscles. Specific combinations of these neurons must fire together to manipulate *muscle groups* to produce the right kind of movement at the right time. The neural architecture involved in this process is mind-bogglingly complex. Our nervous systems have to work out – autonomically and often without our conscious thought – the specific combination of factors that must be satisfied to accomplish a goal.

Consider the complexity involved in simply catching a ball that has been unexpectedly thrown to us. We must move a hand to intersect a predicted path of movement, from what may be a sub-optimal staring point, in a specific window of time, with a current configuration of muscles which may not be in alignment with our goal. We don't calculate any of this consciously. We just will our hand to be where it needs to be and our nervous system does the rest. And our nervous system – fittingly named when you consider how

DOI: 10.1201/9781003415435-5

much responsibility it has to bear – has to contend with multiple possible trajectories of movement, noise in the synaptic systems, the physical delay of muscle contraction, inferences regarding external signals, secondary impact of reactive forces elsewhere in the body, and the fact that not every muscle can be operated linearly. Our bodies do all of this, without our brains offering much in the way of guidance.

In fact, our conscious attention often just makes things worse. If you want to see that in action, just ask someone who is happily wandering past you 'in what order do your muscles activate when you walk?' Directing mental attention to these autonomic processes is like pushing a stick into the wheel of a bicycle. It all ends in disaster. In fact, this is a phenomenon that is a formal part of the psychology of certain activities, like sports. It's often called 'The Yips' – when the biochemical aspects of an activity find themselves in competition with other factors … like human psychology.

We're going to take all of that largely as read and simply concern ourselves with how to discuss impairment in this complex and phenomenally powerful system. To do that, we're going to collapse all this sophisticated architecture into two broad categories – *gross motor control* and *fine-grained motor control*. Gross not as in disgusting – although for some of us, myself included, that might be an accurate label. Gross as in the Latin **grossus**, which means 'coarse'.

Gross motor control relates to large-scale motion, executed through groupings of our larger muscles. The muscles in our arms, our legs, and our torsos fall into this category. *Gross motor skills* are what drive our ability to walk, to run, or to cycle. They handle balance and co-ordination. Sitting down and standing up are controlled by these muscles, as are climbing and throwing. Our general everyday locomotion is an act of *gross motor control*.

Fine-grained motor skills, or simply *fine motor skills*, are reflected in the control exerted over smaller muscles and grouping of muscles to bring about precise movements. These cover things like holding items and manipulating them with exactness. Typing a message on a phone, putting a key into a lock, tying shoelaces, and buttoning clothes – all of these are examples of *fine-grained motor control*.

There's a third aspect to all of this – the human body is complex enough that few processes are truly embodied completely in any one part of our physiology. It's not just our ability to voluntarily contract and relax muscles to achieve large and small goals that matters – often we must do this in conjunction with the processing of visual information. *Hand-eye co-ordination* is what comes into play here. When we need to synchronise physical activity against a visual benchmark, our eyes and muscles all must play their part in relaying the right information to the right places at the right time. Impairments in the eyes can impact on these processes, resulting in miscommunication of depth and placement. It is possible, in other words, for a visual impairment to have primarily physical consequences. We see similar thing when information is incorrectly processed in the brain – the observable impact might be in how the body engages with its nervous system.

But wait, there's more! Let's not forget the role that your **ear** has in all of this.

Our *vestibular system* – located primarily in the inner ear – is what drives our sense of balance. It's essentially like an accelerometer inside your skull, constantly updating information regarding the relative motion of your head alongside awareness of your spatial context. If there's an upset in your *vestibular system*, it can throw off all other motor skills. The system is made up of *canals*, which pick up on rotations, and *otoliths* which pick up on acceleration. All of your movement is co-ordinated with this system, making sure that you are where you think you are relative to where you've been before.

A disruption in any part of this – or in any of the other parts that make up the complex architecture of our physicality – can result in situational, temporary, or permanent impairment.

A few years ago, I had a profound bout of *vertigo* caused by an issue with my inner ear. Calcium crystals inside the ear canals are used by our vestibular system to help detect movement, and every so often these crystals can detach or fracture. This disrupts the connection between actual movement and perceived movement. This is a common condition – called *benign paroxysmal positional vertigo* – and often goes away on its own. If it doesn't, there's a procedure called the *Epley Manoeuvre* that takes you through a series of head movements designed to send a fractured crystal safely out of your ear canal so that it no longer impacts on perception. It often requires numerous applications – particularly if done by an untrained muppet like myself. As I'm often forced to say to people, 'I'm not **that kind** of doctor. Sure, I can take a look at your rash but I can't do more than say "hey, nice rash" in reply'.

I spent about a week with vertigo which switched on and off largely at random and for unpredictable periods of time. It really communicated to me how temporary vertigo is simultaneously hilarious and **absolutely no joke**. I have never experienced quite such a debilitating condition in my life. When it activates, it feels like you have become unmoored from the world, vision spinning and your stomach lurching as if you'd just been placed – without consent – on the world's more dangerous and least regulated rollercoaster. If it hit me while I was traveling somewhere, I'd be almost unable to make my way on and off of buses or ferries. If I had been driving – I live in Gothenburg and there's no need to own a car here – I can't imagine how dangerous it would have been. In other words, a condition manifesting in my ear hugely impacted on motor control – all from a tiny piece of calcium being where it wasn't expected.

Impairments in this category – like in any category – may exhibit in multiple forms. At one extreme, there is absence of capability – after amputation, for example. A similar effect may be seen in paralysis. However, it is not as simple as identifying that an activity cannot be performed by a digit or limb – the nervous system may rebalance itself, or not, unreliably around compensation for absent capacity. However, impairments can also result in restrictions with regards to degree of freedom in movement. They might manifest through tremors – either persistent or intermittent. They may be pain-related, where it is not the ability to perform an action that is in question but rather than physical discomfort that must be paid as a cost. Most of our motor control system is based on voluntary triggering of motor neurons, but impairments may result in occasional involuntary triggers. As with all conditions, they may modulate in severity.

We always need to be nuanced in how we consider the issue, as well as discount any stereotypes we may have built up through cultural expectation. Someone in a wheelchair, for example, may well be capable of walking – at least, short distances. The wheelchair does not indicate a complete absence of ability – rather, it represents the solution that offers the greatest quality of life impact for its user. This may be as much to do with sustainability of gross-motor functions as it is with precision.

Our system of movement is extremely complex, extremely sensitive, and extremely impactful. It's only fair really that it should also be extremely important when it comes to making games playable. It's relevant when moving pieces – reaching over a board (*gross motor skill*) and manipulating a token (*fine motor control* along with *hand-eye co-ordination*). It can relate to simply observing a board from multiple perspectives (*gross motor skill*) or in some cases walking around the table to see everything from the other side (*gross motor skill* again). Some games emphasise flicking pieces (*hand-eye co-ordination* and *fine-grained motor control*) or placing pieces atop others through balance and careful acts of precise positioning (*fine-grained motor control, gross motor control, hand-eye co-ordination*, and the *vestibular system*). We mustn't forget too that board games are tactile experiences – all those thick cards and pleasant wooden figures – touching and feeling them is a part of what it means to play. Simply engaging physically with nice components is a joyful activity. Games are played using almost all of our senses.

However, some games let us engage physically with them more easily than others ….

Problematic Physical Design

Many of the games that are most problematic in this category of accessibility are those that are explicitly indicated as dexterity games – games where physical precision is the primary mechanism through which one might play. We can broadly categorise these into two main groups: **stacking games**, in which pieces are placed on top of pieces, and **flicking** (or **pushing**) **games**, in which pieces are propelled against other pieces.

Within a stacking game, we're usually placing components – shaped for maximum inconvenience – atop other pieces shaped for minimal solidity. Sometimes the pieces are artificially weighted to make them more troublesome. Some games, such as **Meeple Circus** (2017, Figure 5.1) and **Junk Art** (2016, Figure 5.2), are explicit about showing skill in this endeavour – points are awarded for the complexity and sophisticated of how pieces are arranged. **Meeple Circus** for example awards points for the highest position you've placed acrobats or how many things you've stacked onto the strongmen. Camels balancing seals balancing balls – all of these can yield rich rewards in terms of points. The care you take in accomplishing these often difficult and occasionally contradictory scoring goals is what determines success. High levels of both *fine-grained* and

FIGURE 5.1   Stacking pieces atop others in Meeple Circus. (Photograph by the author.)

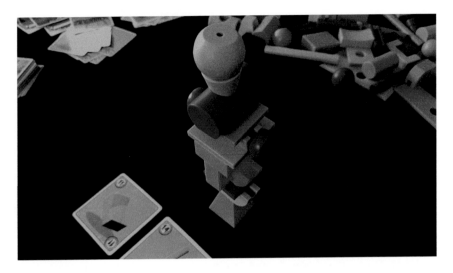

FIGURE 5.2   The complex constructions of Junk Ark. (Photograph by the author.)

gross motor controls are important here, especially as you get to the end rounds of the game where you make your arrangements under the watchful eye of every other player at the table. Often a player will stand up to access higher parts of the structure from a more advantageous angle – if, of course, that's something they can actually do. **Meeple Circus** is not, as you might imagine, a game that is optimal for someone in a wheelchair.

Junk Art is a similar style of game. It has a number of mini-modes that allow you to flavour the experience. The Monaco variant, for example, works by having players flip over cards at random and then search for the piece the card revealed so they can add it to their growing structure. The first one to get through their whole stack wins and gets points based on the pieces placed. If someone knocks over their edifice, they need to rebuild it – in the correct order – before they can move on to the next piece. Again, these structures can become big and unwieldy and often the best place to manipulate them is from above. All your motor skills come into contention here. The exact blend of skills needed will shift over time – *fine-grained* in the beginning, with *gross motor control* becoming more important as you are forced to live with the consequences of early decisions.

Oh, and both of these games are real-time games where the speed at which you do something is a factor in your eventual success.

The problem here, from an accessibility perspective, is two-fold. One is the difficulty associated with fitting things together precisely when they were not meant to precisely fit together. The other is that the difficulty of that is multiplied by the pressure put on players with the time limit – whether that's enforced by 'fastest wins' (**Junk Art**) or the duration of the musical circus track employed in **Meeple Circus**.

But **Meeple Circus** also adds in a third fold – that the final round of the game is a genuine performance. For the first few rounds, everyone builds their arrangement simultaneously so there's limited time for anyone to gawk at anyone else. The final round requires you to do this under the gaze of your friends. There is a neuroscientific concept called the *action observation network*, which governs how we 'mentalise' how we might perform purposeful actions that we have previously observed. There's some early work to suggest that being watched closely can interrupt how parts of this system communicate, creating a sense of *performance anxiety*. In other words, you can fail to perform tasks you know well simply by knowing other people are paying attention. Anyone who has ever watched me type on a keyboard during a lecture will have seen this happen with distressing frequency.

Flicking (or pushing) games offer a different, but related proposition – employ physical dexterity to impart force to one component with the intention of effecting change at a distance. Or, less pompously – flick a thing at another thing for good times. Cue sports, such as **Snooker**, **Pool**, and **Billiards**, could be argued to fall into this general category – the primary distinction being the use of an intermediate tool rather than direct manipulation by the hands. We'll leave them out of this discussion since they're not quite what we think of as 'board games'. As a short-hand though for what impact gross-motor control may have in a board game, just imagine the pool-hall hustler stalking around the table for the optimal angle of attack. As the kids say, it really do be like that sometimes.

Games in this category may involve flicking pieces, such as **Cube Quest** (2013), **ICECOOL** (2016), **ICECOOL 2** (2018), **Crokinole** (1876), and **Pitchcar** (1995). They may instead involve pushing pieces, such as **Shuffleboard** (1930). What changes in all of these different incarnations of the game form is the specific accessibility profile required of players. A game which involves pushing makes more use of joint movement at the wrist with correspondingly less on micro-positioning at the fingers.

A flicking game may put restrictions on what counts as a flick – for example, using a thumb to build up pressure before releasing it is often prohibited. In general, they require the ability to use one finger to strike a piece (often oddly weighted and proportioned) at a direction and force compatible with having it trace a predicted line, or arc, to a target or target zone. Traditionally, this stresses the ability to assess and action a plan in the Z axis, rotated around some reliably accessible strike point. Skilled players may also take into account the X and Y axes – making use of angled shots, top and bottom spin or its equivalent, or perhaps even making use of the ability to have a piece leave the physical confines of the board. Most of this stresses fine-grained control. Trick shots in **ICECOOL** (2016) for example allow a player to leap over the walls of the board or trace a curve through doors. **Pitchcar** (1995) by comparison explicitly punishes players who have a piece leave the track of the race. Most games though do acknowledge real-world complexity by allowing repositioning of pieces when certain criteria are met. The laws of physics are not constrained by the rules we may choose to write about them.

There is also a considerable degree of pressure put on gross motor skills in these games. The game board may be large (**Shuffleboard**, Figure 5.3; **Crokinole**, Figure 5.4), or it may sprawl in complex ways (**Pitchcar**) or have physical walls within the wider borders of play (**ICECOOL**). Even in games where that isn't true (such as **Cube Quest**), it is rare that one can get a good angle on a piece from the same sitting position from which one might start play.

Dexterity games then – as a broad category they do not cohere well with an agenda that focuses on improving physical accessibility. It is easy though to make the claim that dexterity games are inaccessible to people with physical impairments. It's too easy a target even if it is an entirely fair assessment. The problems that we see in board games with regards to physical inaccessibility are more common than that.

Take from a starting point that someone is unable to easily reach over and interact with parts of a large game board. In such circumstances, it's common for someone to

FIGURE 5.3   A full-sized Shuffleboard in its natural environment. (Photograph by the author.)

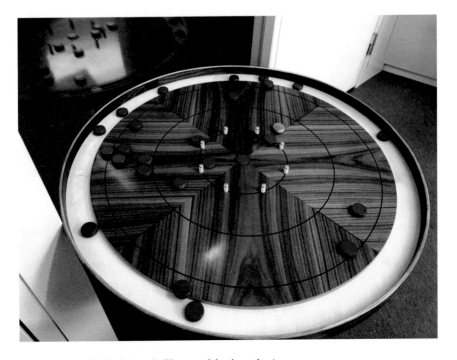

FIGURE 5.4   A Crokinole board. (Photograph by the author.)

verbalise an instruction for someone else to execute. 'Please move my piece ten spaces along the track', or 'Could you build me a track from London to Paris?' This *verbalisation* is an important compensatory strategy when dealing with many categories of physical impairment.

Consider **Kingdom Builder** (2011). A player will place down houses according to particular placement rules indicated by a card that they draw from a deck. Drawing the card isn't a problem – someone else can enact the physical portion of that activity. Verbalising intention is the problem.

How easily can someone describe where they might want to put a house down on the board in Figure 5.5? It's not impossible – if I say 'Place my house in the forest on the bottom row of the bottom right quadrant next to the placed house', probably everyone can agree on where that is. If not, a supporting player pointing to different matching regions will allow someone to say 'Yes, there' eventually. Placement can be a little more complex than that, though. Let's zoom in on the bottom left (Figure 5.6).

Let's say you drew a paddock card (green). You have to place your house adjacent to one of your existing houses on the board, and if there are no matching locations for subsequent houses, you can then start into a terrain with no adjacent houses. You're playing the uncoloured pieces in the top right. You want to place your first house in the only matching hex, and then taking advantage of there being no other matching places, you want to leapfrog the existing settlements of the player with the black pieces and start building on the other side. You need to articulate your starting point, which green field, which direction, and perhaps more depending on the complexity of the board state. There's a lot of descriptive work that goes into providing unambiguous referencing of action and that can greatly impact on the flow of play. **Kingdom Builder** makes use of four board sections that slot together randomly – it's not even as if you can learn the board.

Even the issues discussed above with regards to *fine-grained* positioning aren't unique to dexterity games – verbalisation is a strategy only insofar as it doesn't lose something essential in the game. Consider **Potion Explosion** (2015, Figure 5.7) in which players

FIGURE 5.5   The full board of Kingdom Builder. (Photograph by the author.)

FIGURE 5.6   A close up on a quadrant of the Kingdom Builder board. (Photograph by the author.)

must take marbles out of dispenser tracks so as to collect the components that allow them to make potions.

Here, it's not that verbalisation isn't possible. 'Pick the blue marble between the two yellows in the first track'. The problem is that a large part of **Potion Explosion** is in the simple joy of manipulating marbles. The same game using colour tokens would not – I suspect – be remotely as enjoyable to play. Sometimes things are just enjoyably tactile and even if someone can execute an action on behalf of another player, it's not at all the same thing. Similarly for **Takenoko** (2011, Figure 5.8). Some of its fun is found in just physically growing a garden.

FIGURE 5.7   The marble dispensers of Potion Explosion. (Photograph by the author.)

FIGURE 5.8   Takenoko and its bespoke pieces. (Photograph by the author.)

We've spent a lot of time here looking at the board of games, but that's not the only place we see physical accessibility issues. Many games require players to secretly hold a hand of cards that act on the game state, and this can be another source of physical difficulty. A common solution to this is to use a card holder – a plastic strip into which cards can be made visible without being held. However, there are different kinds of card holders (opaque versus transparent), with many different sizes. Not all of them work well for every game. **Dixit** has huge cards that only work in a transparent holder, so you need a few of them to hold your hand of six. Figure 5.9 shows a standard transparent holder that can hold only three **Dixit** cards at a time. Since the contents of your hand must

FIGURE 5.9   Dixit cards in a transparent card holder. (Photograph by the author.)

FIGURE 5.10 A selection of the information dense cards from Star Trek: Frontiers. (Photograph by the author.)

remain secret, there are additional complications when it comes to how these holders should be angled.

Ticket to Ride (2004) is a game that encourages hoarding of cards, as well as building sets of these cards in hand – for example, grouping up all the cards of a specific colour. There is so much in-hand management – over so many cards – that even if the game is playable with a card holder, it is so inconvenient to do so that many players simply won't bother. Some cards don't 'compress' well into a holder either. For **Ticket to Ride**, all that's needed is a sliver of the card to show its colour. Other games require the full face of the card to be visible in order to convey important game information. **Dixit** is one of these games. The only solution in these situations is to use a massive card holder or several. Consider the content of a card in **Star Trek: Frontiers** (2016, Figure 5.10).

You couldn't overlap these cards in a holder. Not only do you need to see the full spectrum left to right (they have different icons in different top corners), they have top and bottom parts too. Also problematic are cards that technically speaking could easily enough be overlapped except that they have different information on different edges. This is also a problem for 'handedness', as the way in which one might splay cards differs depending on whether one prefers a left-handed fan or a right-handed fan. For some games, the choice changes the information profile. **Oh My Goods** (2015, Figure 5.11) shows the combination of all these problems. It has a seven card limit with cards that have key data that would be obscured in an opaque card holder. They have information that requires the full face to be seen and different information on the left- and right-hand side so that even if none of that was true, you still couldn't overlap them without information loss.

Games with large numbers of cards have additional problems, such as when it comes to shuffling. Small, non-standard sizes are difficult for anyone to shuffle, but especially problematic for someone with physical impairments. They may have access to a card shuffler (an electronic device that will do the job for them), but those tend to be built around the assumption of a standard-sized poker deck. They can be ineffective when dealing with other shaped cards and can even damage the cards in the attempt.

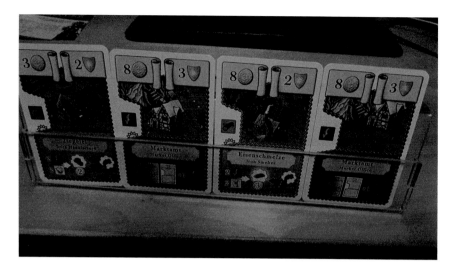

FIGURE 5.11   Oh My Goods cards, as shown in a transparent card holder. (Photograph by the author.)

Huge decks of cards usually require multiple passes of shuffling or the adoption of less effective shuffling techniques such as a wash shuffle. Non-standard card stock in non-standard card proportions can cause difficulty, and that difficulty is proportionate to how much shuffling is likely to be needed. Deckbuilder games, which involve exhausting a deck and shuffling the discard pile, may require lots of uncomfortable shuffling many times per game. Shuffling, like many physical activities, is an interaction cost for which we often fail to account in design. Even picking up a card from a glossy table can be a challenge.

Some games require simultaneous performing of an action. **Rock, Paper, Wizard** (2016) is a game of casting spells by forming particular hand gestures. The problem is probably already apparent, but like in a game of **Rock, Paper, Scissors**, both players must reveal their choice at the same time to prevent another changing their mind in response to what they see. **Rock, Paper, Wizard** requires *fine-grained motor control*, with *gross-motor control*, linked into a temporal window that must sync up with another player.

Other games suffer simply because they are made up of complex boards with lots of pieces in place or that they require pieces to be moved around physical obstacles. **Colt Express** (2014, Figure 5.12) shows both of these things in action.

A player here is often reaching into the interior of a train to move pieces and pick up loot. Angle of approach is important, as is the density of the internal state of each carriage. More than this, the nature of the game removes the ability of players to predict what's going to happen on their turn. By the time you go in to pick up the one piece of loot from the carriage you were in at the start of the round, you might be on a roof-top with three other people. Or, sometimes such as (again) **Takenoko**, you might find physically placing components challenging because of the relative fragility of their placement. The tactility associated with growing a garden is enjoyable – physical joy, like in **Potion Explosion**, is a feature of play. But it comes at a cost. And, given these tiles just nestle against each other, even adding a new tile to the board has a risk of upsetting the neat arrangement of everything else.

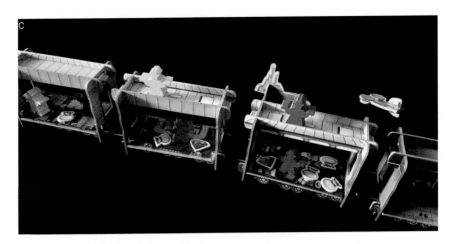

FIGURE 5.12   The 3D train that is the playing area for Colt Express. (Photograph by the author.)

We also have the classic example of **Terraforming Mars** (2016) where the meaning of currency cubes depends on their position on your player mat (Figure 5.13), and the rate of acquisition of each of those currencies is indicated by a single plastic cube on a very low-friction surface. All it takes is for someone to sneeze, and the entire game state gets randomised. Simply spending some of your money in Terraforming Mars is an act of considerable delicacy. Having another player enact these kind of administrative tasks

FIGURE 5.13   The low-friction player mat of Terraforming Mars. (Photograph by the author.)

on behalf of a physically impaired player is a common compensatory strategy, but it's not feasible in Terraforming Mars. A loose t-shirt sleeve can accidentally and instantly turn someone into the richest – or poorest – player around the table. This is not a game where you want to encourage people to lean over to make changes.

But as usual, there's smooth in with the rough ….

Games with Good Physical Design

We spoke earlier about the problems of physical accessibility when it comes to dexterity games, but we also have to acknowledge there's a second side of that coin. I mean, all coins have a second side but you know what I mean. The thing that makes the games we've spoken about problematic is quite simple – they're more fun when you're doing **well.** There is though a class of games I refer to as 'inevitable catastrophe' games, and these work a different way – they're most fun when you **fail.** Or, more accurately – they're most fun when you fail at the right time.

Consider the perennial classic **Jenga** (1983) – a game of creating a stack of wooden blocks that successive players push out of place before replacing atop an increasingly rickety tower. **Jenga**, if flawlessly played by skilled players, would be a sad thing indeed. A sombre experience. So lacking in fun and whimsy that you could play it without concern at a funeral. The game equivalent of solemnly saying 'I am sorry for your loss'.

We don't play **Jenga** for the tower. We play it for the **collapse.** The game needs to go on just long enough that everyone feels invested in the result. We all want to see the tower fail; we just don't want to be the one who makes it fail. Accessibility problems are greatly reduced here because it is the fall that is the thing – as long as it doesn't happen too late, everyone gets the fun payload. The **funload.** Everyone is sharing a game state in which each player is creating inevitable complications for the next. For this, we can look at **Rhino Hero: Super Battle** (2017, Figure 5.14) as an excellent example – a game

FIGURE 5.14   Rhino Hero: Super Battle. Not yet part of the Marvel Cinematic Universe but it's surely just a matter of time. (Photograph by the author.)

of placing floors on top of rickety walls and moving weighted super heroes around the edifice with the intention of making the next person's life harder.

This is not to say these games are physically accessible – manifestly they are not. But they can be enjoyed at a much lower level of physical dexterity because of the arc of the game experience. It's easy to play in the beginning, harder to play as time goes by, and it only needs a few rounds of building for the fall to be cathartic. Both the 'demonstrated skill' and 'inevitable catastrophe' styles of game require assessing structure solidity and manoeuvring pieces in and out of a dangerously unstable construction. They're both *hand-eye* challenges stressing all factors of physical dexterity. The inevitable catastrophe just doesn't sting at the fall.

This isn't a solution to physical accessibility issues. It's just an interesting way to change the ethos of a game to accommodate differing skill levels more equitably. I mean, I say it's interesting but I'm an academic and as such interesting may not mean the same thing to me as it does to people who are, pardon the pun, better balanced.

We have already talked about verbalisation as a solution to physical accessibility issues – the ability to issue instructions to other players for them to enact on your behalf. It's sometimes impossible (such as in dexterity games). It's sometimes sub-optimal (such as in games where the tactility is part of the experience). In many games, though, it is a general-purpose solution to a general-purpose problem – telling someone something about the board in a way that seamlessly translates into game information.

If we want to see a solution to the issue of verbalisation, then we can really look back in time to **chess** (Figure 5.15). The notation system that we all have come to love and admire solves a problem shared by many games – it makes it trivial to indicate a square meant because it provides a row identifier and a column identifier.

Chess' notation system allows for completely unambiguous representation of not just game state, but gameplay.

It doesn't have to be anything as stark as having squares indicated as A4 or F5. It can be as simple (and thematic) as providing names for landmarks that people can reference.

FIGURE 5.15   A good old-fashioned chess board. (Photograph by the author.)

FIGURE 5.16   A good old-fashioned set of playing cards. (Photograph by the author.)

Parks (2019) for example gives each of the locations along the board a descriptor. Each of the national parks you can visit has its name prominently indicated. 'Move my hiker from the trailhead to the lookout so I can buy the Grand Canyon National Park card'. Imagine if **Kingdom Builder**, as we discussed above, had a name for each of its regions. 'Place my house next to the Sadlands, left of the Plains of Oblivion'. Not only does the game become more accessible but it also becomes more **thematic.** Accessibility design changes are not always a trade-off.

The issue we discussed regarding card holders and the difficulties of overlapping them have long been solved by another relic from antiquity – the everyday pack of playing cards. These have a design that is optimally accessible in this regard. Consider Figure 5.16.

A playing card works no matter what way you overlap it. They replicate the face information in each of the corners. They also mirror themselves in the vertical axis – a card can be read upside down without having to do any mental gymnastics. Games that draw from this design will always score highly in the accessibility of their cards, as we can see in **Arboretum** (2015, Figure 5.17).

If we want to solve the issue of a game board that is difficult to keep together and lined up (as in **Takenoko**), we can borrow a convention from modern iterations of **Catan** (1995), which slot the hexes of the board into a neat frame (Figure 5.18) that is resistant to nudging.

Sagrada (2017) solves the Terraforming Mars problem of randomisable player state by ensuring everything is firmly locked into place through sockets on the board (Figure 5.19).

Understanding physical inaccessibility is about abandoning our often unintentional disregard of what our bodies can usually do and think about what happens if they are not available to us. Playing a game where we may not touch our board, but others may touch it on our behalf, exposes many of the assumptions we make during play. Similarly, playing a game where we expect that a significant bang of the table might happen clarifies the consequences of unexpected physical disruption. Those of us without significant

FIGURE 5.17   The playing card inspired layout of Arboretum. (Photograph by the author.)

physical impairments may often forget how often we're relying on everyone around us to be capable of doing a whole bunch of things of which we are not consciously aware.

Games with Especially Interesting Physical Design

A pair of games that are relatively interesting from the perspectives we've discussed in this chapter are **ICECOOL** (2016) and **ICECOOL 2** (2018) – flicking games that take an approach to their accessibility that solves a problem we have otherwise not really

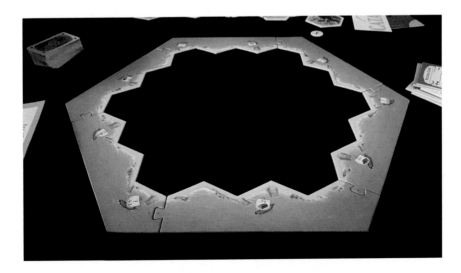

FIGURE 5.18   The frame into which Catan tiles are held. (Photograph by the author.)

FIGURE 5.19   A player board in Sagrada. Note the sockets it has for dice. (Photograph by the author.)

discussed in this chapter – specifically, the assumption that we even have table space to play flicking games.

One of the aspirational items often associated with the tabletop hobby is a 'game table' – this is a luxury piece of furniture with a removable top, which reveals a recessed and often felt surface beneath. This makes it more convenient to play games of all kinds – the felt surface makes it easier to manipulate cards and pieces, and the border of the table puts physical limits on play that ensure things don't fall onto the floor. The relative elevation of players gives a better view of what's happening. And when it's time for dinner, the top can usually be replaced, preserving the state of a game in play in a way that allows it to be resumed later.

One common physical accessibility issue relates to simply keeping pieces on the table. Small, awkwardly shaped components can ping out of fingers, or be dropped and bounce off the table surface and under a cabinet. Dice can be rolled onto the floor. Cards when imperfectly shuffled can go cascading everywhere. We've all played the game **52 Pickup** at one point.

ICECOOL is not an accessible dexterity game – in my experience, no such thing exists. But it is an interesting dexterity game in that it constructs its playing area from the box itself. The larger box of these games contains a series of smaller boxes arranged like nesting dolls. These clip together using provided connectors, and this is the arena around which pieces are flicked. This strikes me as an accessibility feature because it turns any table into a **gaming** table – the walls of the box prevent pieces from sailing off the side and into unknown territory. It still requires skill and precision to play, but the cost of lacking it is not quite so large.

We've spoken before about how games should use their inserts as part of their user interface and that few do. I feel games that use their box as a board (and as one that solves accessibility issues in the process) is a similarly under-explored innovation.

Guidelines for Physical Accessibility

- *Games to look to for inspiration*:
  - Funemployed, Blank, Skull, Port Royal, Codenames, Arboretum, Wits and Wagers, and Love Letter.
- *Games to look to as cautionary tales*:
  - Galaxy Trucker, Terror in Meeple City, Rhino Hero: Super Battle, Terraforming Mars, Pit, and Escape: The Curse of the Temple.

Icons

Limit the Need for People to Move in Order to See Game State

The everyday movement that many people take for granted can be a problem when someone is experiencing a physical impairment – even lifting up from a seat to get a better view may not be feasible. Icon design should take this into account, as should expectations as to the orientation at which people may view the board.

- Ensure icons can be differentiated at a distance.
- Make sure icons can be read clearly at all different orientations.

General Aesthetics

Ensure the Readability of Information when using a Card Holder

A card holder is a common way for someone with physical impairments to ease in-hand management of cards. These come in different forms – curved and straight, opaque and transparent, and long and short. Bear in mind that cards might be placed in a card holder and where possible adapt the design accordingly.

- Avoid putting game information such as victory points/purchase requirements on the lower edge or corners of cards. If information must be obscured, make it the information with the lowest impact and the least frequent applicability.
- Make sure when cards overlap, either left or right, they don't obscure key game information.
- Where this is not possible, provide a reference chart for all cards and encode some clear identifier on the card itself.

Aim for Board Visibility at Fixed Angles

Not being able to adjust viewing angle easily means that players are at the mercy of everything from the gloss of a board or the angle of the sun through a window. Consider how a game's information profile may change over time within this frame.

- Avoid too much reflectivity in boards, tokens, and card decoration.
- Avoid 'magic-eye' style game systems or those where a viewing angle is assumed.
- Limit the need for perspective or binocularity in game mechanisms.
- Ensure the board itself is readable from multiple orientations.

Rules

Include Only Those Physical Game Mechanisms Mandatory for the Game

Obviously some games are built on physical engagement – we've seen plenty of examples of that in this chapter. Where games don't **require** physical engagement for gameplay, providing alternate forms of interaction can reduce inaccessibility. Sometimes these are just a matter of convention – 'raise your thumb to indicate which of you are betrayers' and sometimes they represent different phases of a game such as moving from verbal descriptions to pantomimed descriptions. Look for these, and consider where they can be replaced with non-physical alternatives.

- If covert actions or stealth are required, adopt a system or provide a variation where this can be performed by players with restricted movement.
- Avoid, as far as is possible, the requirement that players operate under a physical restriction such as 'one hand behind their back' or 'blindfolded'. If such mechanisms are core, then consider additional supporting roles where participation with restriction is not required.
- Eliminate, as far as possible, physicality in rule systems. Don't require players to indicate or change game state with physical gestures without providing a non-physical alternative.
- Avoid or provide alternatives to very high fine motor requirements, such as flicking or throwing pieces to a specific location.
- Avoid the need for components to be worn, placed, or balanced on a player's body.
- Avoid the need for players to initiate or maintain physical contact with other players.
- Limit, or eliminate, the need for players to write or draw. Allow any writing to be handled digitally.
- Avoid the need for large amounts of physical activity if that is not the main focus of the game. This might include switching seats, changing places with other players, long periods of standing, or continuous movement.

Alleviate the Discomfort of Cards and Manuals

Large hand limits can make holding cards difficult, especially if said cards require some in-hand management to put them into sets or sequences.

Similarly, shuffling is required to randomise a deck. When this is a single shared deck at the start of the game, it isn't a problem. It can become an issue if there's a lot of shuffling of a personal player deck, such as in a Deckbuilder. Tools used to make this more comfortable, such as automatic card shufflers, often assume playing card dimensions and won't function correctly with other form factors.

Additionally, sometimes creative manual design can be a problem – manuals that open like maps or make use of spiral bounding can create interaction difficulties.

- Limit the number of cards a player has to hold in their hand at any one time.
- Limit the number of cards a player must personally search through.

- Limit the amount of shuffling needed in general.
- Ensure that cards can easily be used left or right handed.
- Make it easy for people to shuffle a deck on behalf of another.
- As far as is possible, use standard playing card dimensions for cards so as to enable supporting accessibility equipment.
- Make rulebooks comfortable and convenient to hold. Limit page count as much as is possible. Avoid large fold-out posters or pamphlets.

Minimise the Impact of Real-Time Mechanisms

Real-time mechanisms are a problem, pardon the pun, across the board. They create time pressures that can complicate – or even, completely undermine – efforts to enact accessibility compensation techniques. They should be used as sparingly as possible or co-exist with non-real-time and relatively accessible variants.

- Provide alternatives to timer-based gameplay.
- Provide turn-based alternatives to games where fast actions and responses are required.
- Avoid or provide alternatives to timers.
- When racing other players in real-time to an outcome, minimise the penalty to the slower players.

Game Layout and Experience

Permit Accessible Alternative Components

When using standard game components (dice and meeples) in non-standard ways, consider what this might mean for those making use of alternate, accessible components such as larger dice or accessible tokens. Where possible, make it easy for people to swap in their own accessible game components or make use of digital tools.

- Support alternative game pieces, such as a digital dice/number generators.
- Consider offering alternate, accessible designs of components or as downloadable models for home 3D printing.

Aim for Comfort of Play

Consider the 'zone of interaction' around each player – which is to say, how much they need to access the game state at any one time. Consider too the comfort of those who may wish to make changes on the behalf of a physically impaired players. Try to 'cache' interactions so that the most common ones happen closest to the player's physical location. Try to avoid assuming a full range of movements is feasible for all players.

- Have the majority of component movement for a player happen within easy reach.
- Try to avoid the need for players to move around a board to assess game state from different angles.

- Avoid the necessity of disturbing elements of game state to reach other elements.
- Limit, as far as is possible, the distribution of different kinds of tokens across a wide area of a game.
- Consider alternative accessible ways to represent game state – sliders on cards versus tokens, as an example.

Game Boards and Player Aids

Facilitate Verbal Descriptions of Game Areas and Actions

When describing an action to be performed on someone's behalf, it is important to be able to do that quickly and clearly. The more difficult or cumbersome this is, the more cognitively taxing it is and the greater the negative impact on game flow. We can think of most game actions as being a thing, that happens to another thing, at a location indicated by a third thing. 'Move my blue meeple to the north square', for example. Ensuring that every part of an instruction can be described means that a game becomes much more playable for those that require assistance.

- Ensure that all game actions can be verbally described without ambiguity.
- Ensure that all game components can be verbally described without ambiguity.
- Ensure that all player pieces can be verbally described and unambiguously related to its owner.
- Ensure that all parts of the board can be unambiguously referenced with grid co-ordinates or named landmarks.
- When making use of directions, provide an unambiguous anchor point on the board in the form of a compass or similar.

Provide Generous Proportions on Boards

Board with small spaces can require a greater degree of *fine-grained* and *gross motor control* than is reasonable to expect of a physically impaired player. Moving a piece under these circumstances may result in nudging and adjusting others, perhaps with an impact on game state. Similarly, spaces on a board that are crowded by too many components make it difficult to move things around, especially if they must move as collections (a piece and the tokens that describe the condition of that piece).

- Give room for imprecision in game interaction through spacing on the board.
- Limit, as far as is possible, the busyness of the board. Small areas containing too many tokens are a problem here.

Make Game State Resistant to Disruption

A lot can disrupt game state during play: a sneeze, a gust of wind, an excitable pet, and someone unexpectedly disrupting the table upon which a game is being played – all common circumstances we all experience. The physical dimensions of wheelchairs and other accessibility aids can intensify this unless the playing area is specifically adapted towards accessibility. The game state is going to be disrupted, in other words, and it's accessible to design it around that likelihood.

- Make use of more frictive boards to reduce the risk their contents are disrupted during play.
- Avoid the need for neat stacking or ordering of game tokens.
- Consider a frame for game boards that are made up of tiles that otherwise would simply nestle together. Consider too jigsaw-style connectors.
- Consider slotted and socketed boards so as to hold pieces firmly in place even when there are disruptions.
- If providing sockets for gameplay elements that will be changed around repeatedly during the game, make them slightly larger and looser than the peg.
- Where slots and sockets cannot feasibly be provided as part of the standard game, make overlays available as purchasable extras or downloadable models for home 3D printing.
- Limit the extent to which nudging a game component can change game state – people won't always notice it's happened.
- Ensure correctability of board game disruption by making it clear where a misplaced piece likely originated. For example, provide generous distance between action spaces.

Let People Put Components where They Are Comfortable

A hallmark of many modern games is that they come with multiple boards and game components. While the rulebook may outline a recommended layout, in the end it is up to the players to decide what is maximally comfortable for everyone. Make use, as far as is possible, of the opportunity to decouple regions of the board from a monolithic design. That way, things can go where they are most easily reached rather than requiring players to reach over to where they are not.

- Make use of modular boards and discontinuous player areas if possible to permit players to define their own radius of interaction.
- If making use of modular boards, consider a frame that permits players to set formal constraints on sprawl. Jigsaw-style snapping can be used to limit the amount of alignment shock when the game is nudged.
- For snappable components in a modular board, consider the use of sturdier plastics or perhaps magnets in the base to keep them secured.
- Provide player screens as a valuable method for providing privacy for players to consider hidden game state in a convenient and comfortable way.

Tokens and Currency

Use Anything Except Paper Money for Currency

Paper money, as we have discussed before, is an accessibility nightmare. Avoid it at all costs! For one thing, it's difficult to deal and count out, resistant to the usual compensatory regimes, and easily disrupted. There are also additional complexities when it comes to how well it interacts with accessibility equipment. For example, light materials such as paper money may blow away when looked at by people using nasal ventilator masks.

- Avoid the use of paper money.
- Where paper money cannot be avoided, aim for heavier paper stock or plastic alternatives.
- When deciding on denominations for money, use those in most common usage in real life so as to allow people to swap in alternatives.

Meeples and Miniatures

Make Miniatures Easy to Build

Pre-assembled miniatures are a common feature of board gaming, but in other areas of the hobby, it is common for complex figures to come in sprues which must be snipped before the figure is put together, IKEA style. It is the detail and complexity of models that define the feasibility of pre-assembly, but where assembly can be avoided it should be.

- If miniatures are to be provided, provide them pre-assembled.
- If miniatures cannot be provided pre-assembled, don't require fine-grained movement for players to construct them. Make their elements push-fit.
- Try to avoid presenting miniatures for assembly on sprues as these usually need additional tools not provided in the box.
- Avoid spikes and sharp edges on miniature elements that must be repeatedly handled.
- When spikes and sharp edges cannot be avoided, ensure they are not located where pressure must be applied during assembly.
- Clearly indicate on buyer-facing packaging the difficulty level associated with assembling any non-assembled miniatures.

Put Predictable Constraints on the Sprawl of Miniature-based Gameplay

The space a miniatures game will take up is often decided by the scale of the figures – smaller miniatures imply smaller playing areas and vice versa. The more sprawl, the more movement required to engage with the game.

- For miniature-based games, consider the units you're using for movement, the distance which units may travel, and the implication this has for game sprawl.
- For ease of using alternative accessible figures and measuring tools, ensure your scale conforms to set external standards.
- Give some indication on buyer-facing packaging as to the expected table space required for comfortable play.

Dice and Randomisation

Use Randomness that Doesn't Permit Peeking

Some games make use of randomness that comes from cards or bags – such as drawing a random token from a pouch of possibilities. However, it is possible – unintentionally or otherwise – for someone to see what is coming up in a way that others at the table may not. Design components and processes to mitigate this possibility, especially in circumstances where someone may be acting on behalf of another player. When rolling a die, players can't 'fudge' it in the same way they might be able to with a token draw.

- Ensure that there is no opportunity for a player acting on behalf of another to benefit from accessibility-based asymmetric information as to the future.
- Provide guidance as to a resolution mechanism for if someone mistakenly reveals future game state.

Insert Design

Limit Sprawl with Insert Design

We have seen some examples of games that use their insert as a way to create a more elegant user interface for play. Consider that an insert may have a role not only as storage for a game when put away but also as a convenient way to store 'supply' components for a game in progress.

- Consider an insert design that reduces the need for component sprawl during play.
- Permit some degree of give in insert spaces so as to ease the removal and insertion of game tokens.

General Component Design

Use Good Quality, Well-weighted Materials

The cheaper the materials used, the less accessible they tend to be. For example, thin card is harder to pick up off of a table than thick card. Counting cardboard tokens is harder than counting plastic counters. Light plastic meeples are more easily dislodged than wooden ones. There is obviously an economic trade-off that has to be made here, but aim for the highest quality components that can be afforded.

- Make sure pieces are as easy as possible to pick up, especially from everyday surfaces.
- If requiring players to collect precise enumerations of components, make those components as chunky as is reasonably possible.
- Consider providing containers for small game components and ensuring the walls of these containers are styled to permit ease of collection.
- Aim for bottom-heavy, reasonably chunky physical pieces.
- Avoid the use of rounded components that easily roll when they are knocked over, dropped, or dislodged.

Avoid Physically Awkward Game Components

Not all components are as easy to use as others, so consider the link between physical method and physical impairment. Consider whether there are easier ways to accomplish a game goal without sacrificing game intention.

- Avoid as far as is possible the use of dials and other such state identifiers unless they are designed with ease of manipulation in mind.
- If these must be used, consider suggesting alternate homebrew solutions in the manual or making alternatives available as downloadable 3D models.

Avoid Obscuring Game State

Large, bulky components may hide parts of the game state – easily resolved if one has full physical mobility but less convenient for those that don't. As far as is possible, limit the extent to which anyone will be blocked from seeing parts of the board or game state unless that is a stated game goal of the component.

- Avoid tall or extra wide meeples or other components that block viewing of the board when placed.
- Avoid the use of extra-large cardboard standees, as these too may block viewing of the board.
- Where large components must block game state when placed, consider if transparency is a possibility.
- Limit the need for players to cover up important gameplay information with other components, especially if that information may need to be referenced again.

Permit People to Use Their Own Accessibility Tools

Remember that those with accessibility needs will often have preferred solutions in mind, and working with these rather than against can solve many problems before they occur. Home 3D printing is increasingly feasible too, as is having something 3D printed at a local business. However, simply accepting a player's right to use their own preferred tools is an ideal way to support them in play.

- Make use of standard card sizes where possible, to allow for the use of card shufflers and card holders.
- If using egg-timers or other analogue timing systems, make it clear what the expected duration is so alternative timers may be used.
- Document, in general, the dimensions of components that a player may reasonably desire to replace with alternatives.
- When existing standards for components, miniatures, boards, boxes, and such are available, then conform to these as much as possible.
- If bespoke accessibility components are possible but not economically feasible to distribute in the box, consider whether they can be provided as downloadable 3D models.

Make First-Play Setup as Physically Convenient as Possible

The initial setup of a game is a time-consuming process, and some games make this more difficult by requiring a 'first-setup' phase where components are annotated and separated for play. We're all familiar with the ritual of 'punching out' the cardboard for a game, and this in itself can take up a significant amount of time. Other games add to this by – for example – adding stickers to pieces (perhaps many pieces), separating out multiple decks of cards, and folding and assembling cardboard furniture. While some of this is unavoidable, where possible the game should be manufactured in a way that takes the physical labour out of setup.

- If requiring the affixing of stickers to game components, strive to make these optional.
- Avoid implementing key game mechanisms through components that may be difficult to assemble.
- If possible, design punch-out components so that they can be punched out in a just-in-time fashion – for example, by locating all the currency tokens together on the same board.
- Provide an outline of what components are needed per player for a game session so as to allow players to stop punching out components once they have enough for their current needs.

Note

1. https://boardgamegeek.com/wiki/page/Weight

BIBLIOGRAPHY

Clarke, P., Sheffield, D., & Akehurst, S. (2015). The yips in sport: A systematic review. *International Review of Sport and Exercise Psychology, 8*(1), 156–184.

Heron, M. J. (2023). Computer supported accessible dexterity board games. *The International Journal of Games and Social Impact, 1(2),* 98–118.

Kim, J.-S., & Zee, D. S. (2014). Benign paroxysmal positional vertigo. *New England Journal of Medicine, 370*(12), 1138–1147.

Mesagno, C., & Beckmann, J. (2017). Choking under pressure: Theoretical models and interventions. *Current Opinion in Psychology, 16,* 170–175.

Rosenbaum, D. A. (2009). *Human motor control.* Academic press.

Yoshie, M., Nagai, Y., Critchley, H. D., & Harrison, N. A. (2016). Why I tense up when you watch me: Inferior parietal cortex mediates an audience's influence on motor performance. *Scientific Reports, 6*(1), 19305.

6

Emotional Accessibility

Our exploration of this topic to date has covered territory that is reasonably well-accepted as within the 'catchment area' of accessibility. There are deniers out there, but most would agree that visual impairments, cognitive impairments, and physical impairments are 'well within scope' for a book of this nature. As we go on, we're going to begin progressing through some more controversial inclusions.

As we discussed back in our first chapter, the problem domain of gaming is different from almost any other. The need to find a balance between design goals and accessibility is one that is difficult to satisfy. The verisimilitude of interface choices adds complexity. And – the most challenging and ineffable consideration – people need to **enjoy** individual interactions **and** the overall experience of play. There's an almost chemical consequence to all of this – as these elements come together, they create new and exciting compounds that don't exist in simpler contexts. One of those, I argue, is that there is an **emotional** aspect to accessibility that games must address.

We all have experience of bad winners and poor losers. We know the kind of games we might be willing to play with them and the ones we'll avoid. We also know what it's like to have someone who is getting sulkier and sulkier in proportion to their bad fortune during a game. It can be corrosive, eating away at the fun of everyone else at the table. Someone having a perceivable negative emotional reaction is patient-zero for an unpleasant time. Emotions can be contagious. Almost in a blink of an eye, everyone can find out – retrospectively – that they signed up for a stressful, unpleasant evening of watching someone ruin everyone's fun. Conversation dries up. Everyone starts planning their exit strategy. The game becomes a trial to endure when it was supposed to be a treat to enjoy.

Some physical conditions exacerbate this – dialling everything up to eleven due to a churning cocktail of brain chemistry. Some game design decisions make things better … or make things worse. Sometimes the problem is in the wider perception that culture has of the merit of certain activities. And sometimes people have just been conditioned by their past traumas to react with intense negativity to relatively benign stimuli.

One of the clinical terms used to describe this is *emotional dysregulation*. It refers to an emotional output that is – generally speaking – outside the bounds of what would be considered proportional to the *triggering* input. The word *triggering* is one that is commonly used in online discourse, but it's part of the lexicon of the areas which we are discussing here and it's in that frame we use it. There is an event, a *trigger*, which leads to a response. We are all *triggered* by all kinds of things, big and small, good and bad. These triggers are sometimes linked to biology, sometimes to the presence of social relations, but also often linked to experience. I cannot hear the song **Spanish Sahara** by the Foals without feeling myself tear up because it is forever associated for me with the end of the video game Life is Strange[1]. The horrific electronic screech associated with the ZX Spectrum computer loading data from tape … that sound makes me so nostalgic that for

DOI: 10.1201/9781003415435-6

a brief time it was the ringtone on my mobile phone. We're all a tapestry of experiences which interact with our body chemistry at erratic moments. *Involuntary autobiographical memory* is how the literature often phrases it. Marigold Linton, referred to surprising and pleasant involuntary memories as 'precious fragments', citied Marcel Proust's story of how eating a particular kind of cake dipped in a particular kind of tea triggered an overpowering sense of nostalgia through the sensation of taste.

Not all of these memories are 'precious' though. They may relate to childhood trauma – particularly those events that were most formative in the development of personality. They may relate to periods of neglect or mistreatment. They may be formed through a constant reinforcement of invalidation – when people feel themselves being regularly rejected, judged, or undervalued. Our minds are not always on our side. They often feel like they're playing for the away team rather than the home side. All you need to do is let your mind wander during a sleepless night to wonder where its allegiances actually lie.

The neurochemistry involved here is complex, but there is compelling research to suggest that these negative events, experienced repeatedly or with intensity, impact on the effectiveness of the neural architecture that regulates emotion. This can result in an over-sensitive *fight or flight response* – specifically, we are more likely to feel anger or fear in response to elevated norepinephrine levels in the brain. This is known medically as the *acute stress response*. It can happen quickly, in response to an immediate threat. It can also build slowly over time, as in general stress. The *fight or flight* response is an accelerator on your brain chemistry, but when the threat has passed, the brain is supposed to hit the brake. *Fight or flight* should be answered with 'rest and digest' when the triggering stimuli has passed into irrelevance. With long-term conditions of *emotional dysregulation*, the brakes on one's emotions just aren't working properly.

We can see this very clearly in conditions such as *post-traumatic stress disorder* (PTSD), which can develop when someone experiences – first, or second-hand – a traumatic event of life-threatening intensity. *Involuntary autobiographical memory* associated with that event can regularly *trigger* recall of that event, which in turn causes the body to kick into overdrive. Your heart beats faster. Your brain offloads some of its higher-level processes onto autonomic systems. Senses become sharper as the lungs expand to bring more oxygen to the brain. Nutrients flood the bloodstream, offering a short, intense burst of energy to all parts of the body. Adrenaline floods the system. All of this happens so quickly that people sometimes don't even know it's happening until it has happened. The body is in a heightened state of awareness until cortisol levels fall and the brakes kick in.

In life-threatening situations, these responses are a powerful evolutionary survival mechanism. In everyday life, they can be debilitating – especially since *triggers* are not consciously selected. They can be specific to the details of an event, or they can be contextual. Watching your best friend killed in a car accident might be a constantly reoccurring *involuntary memory* triggered by a sunny day simply because the sun was shining when it happened. Moreover, this can impact on the ability to form emotionally proportional responses to external context. That's not surprising, given the laundry list of effects that PTSD and other severe emotional reactions can have: intrusive thoughts, nightmares, anxiety, spiralling negativity, disassociation, and emotional deadening.

All of this is to say that it might not be the game itself that triggered an outburst at the table. It might be that the click of a plastic tile subconsciously reminded someone of the footsteps of an approaching attacker. They themselves may not even be aware of what's happening and might likewise be unable to pinpoint the *trigger*. Sometimes when people say 'Nothing is wrong', they're actually reporting authentically on their emotional state as they consciously understand it.

Not all emotional control impairments are related to autobiographical trauma. Brain injury, especially to the frontal lobe, can have severe impact on emotions and their proportionality. Mental health issues too, whether persistent or situational, are a common source of *dysregulation*. The *American Psychiatric Association* (APA) defines a mental health disorder as a form of medical problem – one which causes distress or problems while functioning in social, work, or family activities through significant changes in thinking. The medicalisation of several of these conditions, autism in particular, is seen as a problematic framing by other advocacy groups. Many prefer to categorise these conditions as differences rather than deficiencies. Often this gets framed as *neurotypicality* (the baseline), and *neuroatypicality* (different from the baseline), and *neurodivergence*. The latter is a broad catchall that covers cognitive profiles that are significantly at variance with the larger population.

I, for example, am *aphantasic* – I cannot form mental imagery and I consider it a super-power that anyone can. This has no perceivable impact on my ability to function in society. Indeed, I didn't even know mental imagery was a thing until I was about 40 years old – every time I heard someone say 'picture this', I assumed it was a mere figure of speech. My brain just processes information in a different way. It would be misleading to label it a disorder or to medicalise it as a problem. Many feel the same way about their own distinctive cognitive architecture. After all, the definition of a disability is inextricably bound to how it makes life more difficult for a person through limitation on their activities or on their participation in wider society. If there is no perceived difficulty, then there is no perceived disability.

However, *emotional regulation* can be impaired in many conditions linked to *neurodivergence*: attention deficit hyperactivity disorder (ADHD), autism spectrum disorders (ASD), borderline personality disorder (BPD), bipolar disorders, obsessive compulsive disorder (OCD), and more – all of these are associated with impairments in emotional control to some degree, in some people. As with every condition of impairment, there is so much intra-category variance that it is impossible to say anything definitively.

What matters, from our perspective, is how all of this impacts on the experience of play in a game – and there are many manifestations that are relevant:

- Minor incidents receiving major emotional responses.
- A difficulty in supressing what seems like impulsive behaviours.
- Unpredictable outbursts.
- A tendency towards catastrophising.
- Anxiety.
- Moments of intense frustration.
- Extreme perfectionism.
- Interpersonal conflict.
- Escalating tension with an inability to self-regulate emotion.
- An overfocus on the negative.
- Lashing out at others.

You can imagine ways in which all of this can make for a fraught experience at game night. Extreme perfectionism for example might lead into analysis paralysis. Blocking a player from a resource they had wanted might result in an explosive outburst. The sense of being judged on performance might result in anxiety, which can be masked through interpersonal conflict.

There's a secondary aspect to all of this too, which is that **recognising** emotional context is a skillset all of its own. Neuroatypicality is often associated with reduced capacity for lying, for improvisation, for detecting social manipulation, and for identifying emotional context in oneself or others. There may be symptoms of reduced empathy or difficulties in interpreting posture and body language. *Empathic accuracy*, in more clinical terms, may be low. We all engage in a kind of 'everyday mind reading' as part of understanding the people around us. Impairments in this faculty not only have real-life impact but also make a number of games virtually unplayable.

Much of this is about brain chemistry and cognitive architecture, but that's not to say that game designers don't have a role here. In fact, considering games are largely systems for manipulating our brains, it's not surprising that we have a lot to talk about as we unpack how to design emotionally accessible game experiences.

Problematic Emotional Designs

First of all, let's talk about the obvious area this tends to be an issue – in what it means to win and what it means to lose. In this, we have no better example than **chess** and the cultural short-hand it represents. It's a game of steely eyed intellectuals, locked in a tense battle of wits. Moves are made on the board: feints, ripostes, traps laid, and then avoided. The game is fully deterministic – no dice, no randomness. The only unknowable quantity is what's in the mind of each player.

Then, suddenly, there's a dramatic flick of the wrist as a piece is moved. One player leans back, satisfied, in their chair. 'Checkmate', they say, demonstrating for all observers their superior grasp of the game and, as a consequence, their superior intellect. They may perhaps steeple their fingers in front of them.

'Plays chess well' is a very common short-hand trope in literature for 'Is very smart'. So, imagine how it feels to play a game of chess and get absolutely destroyed by your opponent. Centuries of fiction have built this connection between intellect and chess skill into the fabric of culture. By the transitive property, 'beats you at chess' can transmute in some minds to 'is smarter than you'. And often people don't react well to that suggestion.

Scrabble (1948) demonstrates some similar features. Picture this (if you can – hello fellow aphants!) – you're playing **Scrabble**. Your opponent looks at their rack and plays out 'Effervescent', making use of some tiles already on the board and a triple-word tile in the corner. Eleven billion points. You look at your rack, and the best you can manage is 'Dog' for four points. Your opponent then thinks for a moment and turns your 'Dog' into 'Dogmatically', spending all their tiles, making three other words in the process, and earning another 8 billion points.

It's hard not to feel as if you've fallen short of some basic intellectual capacity when the skill difference is so large, and in a domain where skill is considered a reasonable proxy for knowledge. Smart people play chess well. Verbally dexterous people should be able to excel at Scrabble. Look at you – you poor chump. Can't think good and can't speak no good neither.

One thing that Scrabble does that chess doesn't though is offer an explicit frame of comparison. **Point differentials** describe the difference between the highest and lowest scores in a game. A game with median differentials that are quite small can feel tight and like everyone in play had a chance to win at any time. The larger the differential, and the earlier that differential becomes apparent during a game, the more disconnected players may become from their turns. 'What's the point? I can't win any more'.

I play **Scrabble** well – it's one of the few games where I do genuinely care about winning. My view though is that **Scrabble** is not a word game. It's a war game. It's territory control and mastering the terrain, occasionally burning bits of it to the ground so nobody else can have it. As such, I use all the two- and three-letter words that people hate. I aim for maximising the value of each tile, not the size of each word. As such, if I play against someone equally annoying, I can usually count on a small difference in points. If I play against others who don't take it so seriously, I might end up with double their score without really trying. I know the tricks for getting reliable seven-letter words (and thus the 50 point bonus associated). On average, I play out about two-and-half bingo words per game. More casual players may not see a bingo in a dozen games. Chess has informal conventions about piece value (the queen is worth nine points, rooks five, pawns one, and so on), but it never explicitly concretises that score at the end. You win or lose chess. In Scrabble, you can lose or you can **lose.** Point differentials matter in how it **feels** to lose.

Patchwork (2014) makes this even worse by allowing players to end with a negative balance (Figure 6.1). You get buttons (which are the game's currency) through play. You spend those buttons to buy patches, and you use those patches to cover the blank tiles on your player board. Your score is your button total minus two points per uncovered space. It's possible for one player to have a score of 50 and for you to have negative 20. There's something especially galling about that negative sign even if in reality the difference between winner and losing would be the same if it was 70 to 0 instead.

FIGURE 6.1   Patchwork, in which it is common to finish with a negative score. (Photograph by the author.)

We are **loss averse** as a species. In rough terms – we feel the loss of something twice as intensely as we feel the gain of its equivalent. If I find a 20-pound note, it feels like I found a 20-pound note. If I **lose** a 20-pound note, it **feels** like I'm 40 pounds less well off. This phenomenon tells you a lot about human beings, and why daylight savings time feels like such a perpetual long con. Psychologically speaking, they're stealing an hour a year from us.

It's reasonable, in other words, to come away from games of this nature with a profoundly depressed sense of ego. I've been there – I play **chess** like someone rammed a railroad spike into the reasoning centre of my brain. There is a special sting that comes with losing games where real-world capability is embedded into the game systems.

There are certain categories of games that exhibit this feature, and they tend to belong to the family where there is no randomness to hide behind (deterministic games). **Hive** (2001, Figure 6.2) is a game that borrows some of the DNA from chess – fixed pieces, two-player, deterministic game state. Its pieces move differently, its board is more febrile, but these are design evolutions rather than revolutions.

Hive, by virtue of its design lineage, inherits some of the features of intellectualism from **chess**. The chain of inference is reasonably clear. Everyone knows the rules, and everyone knows the state of the board. The game is perfect information; thus, there are no surprises. The game is therefore won by the person best able to manipulate game state through the application of rules. That person is thus better at information processing, and therefore that person is smarter.

This is a story people can tell themselves about why they lost a game – or indeed, why they won it. It's not a true story – some of the links in that chain are flimsy at best. It's a story of which people can convince themselves. At this point, *cognitive dissonance* can take hold. This is the psychological principle that a person cannot hold two contradictory pieces of information in mind at once and believe them both. So, 'I am smart', and 'This game shows I am not smart'. That tension has to be resolved in some way, and what often happens is the brain finds a resolution that breaks the incompatibility. The stronger

FIGURE 6.2 Hive, which shares some features of 'a game for smart people' with chess.

the belief, the less likely it is to change. In some circumstances, someone might change their self-perception so that they are no longer a smart person. More likely, it will be resolved in a way that deals with the implication that playing the game well is the same as being smart.

That's healthy, provided the resolution is 'There are aspects of skill here that are not merely products of intelligence'. Familiarity with this specific game and familiarity with games in general. 'I am bad at this game, but I can get better'. That's a healthy resolution of *cognitive dissonance*.

For others though, it comes out in a more negative fashion. 'This game is stupid/ unfair/boring!', 'you cheated!', 'games are for chumps!' Flipping over the board, storming out of the house, having a good ol' stew in your own fury – all of these stem in part from badly resolved *cognitive dissonance*. Games with semi-deterministic states can offer additional pathways for the dissonance to discharge itself. Or sometimes, overly developed *cognitive consonance* (a state of congruence between our beliefs, behaviours, and values) can result in unbearable gloating or fatalistic acceptance. Consider the player who believes that winning is important, and winning reflects skill or ability. That can give a nice, warm, fuzzy glow. But if they also have the dissonant belief that someone else is otherwise smarter or more accomplished than they, that particular combination can lead to a kind of 'Ha, not so smart now are you?' response.

That's not to say that you can solve the problem just by adding randomness or nondeterministic game systems. As discussed in the introduction to this chapter – it's not as if our minds are on our side. There are additional emotional *triggers* when someone feels as if victory has been snatched from their hands by the roll of a die or the draw of a card. We're too complicated as a species to be predictable in how we respond to anything.

Catan (1995) is my go to example of a game that is pitched at exactly the right combination of frequencies to shatter my self-control like glass. I say to people it's a game I will only play on a mobile device because nobody else gets hurt if I throw my phone against a wall. For those that haven't had the pleasure, Catan is a game of building houses around resource-bearing tiles. Each of those tiles has a number on it. Two dice get rolled at the start of each turn, and everyone who has a building adjacent to a tile bearing that number gets matching resources. That is, unless the robber is on the tile – a rolled seven allows the player to move the robber somewhere on the board and steal a resource from another player. And also, when that happens, anyone with more than seven cards in their hand has to discard down to half.

My experience of Catan is playing a round and not being able to do anything because I don't have the needed resources. Already I'm not having fun because 'I guess I pass' is not a satisfying way to conclude your turn. Maybe though I just need someone to roll a six and I get to have fun next time. And they do! They roll a six, and now I have enough resources to build a city – I got the stone I needed to pay the cost. And then someone rolls an eight, and I have more than enough resources! I have extra sheep now. And then the player before me rolls a seven, moves the robber to my stone-bearing tile, and steals the stone I got before. I offer up my additional sheep in trade. 'A sheep for some stone?' I whine. But I have the most points in the game – I'm closest to winning – so nobody is willing to trade.

'I guess I pass again' is all I can say.

Yeah, that's phone against the wall territory right there.

Sometimes luck gives people a reason for failing that they can live with. 'Ah, the dice just weren't on my side tonight'. It's not a fault in them; it's a fault in the stars.

Sometimes that excuse transmutes into blame. It's sometimes said that luck is probability taken personally. Overly weighting individual die rolls or card pulls can be exciting – risking everything on the turn of fate. It can be equally exciting to lose under those circumstances because it was a brave swing and a noble miss. Or, if you've built a lot of your sense of self into winning … it feels like the universe itself is coming together to undermine you.

Catan has other features too that create a problematic combination for emotional accessibility. It's a game that someone wins when they pass a certain point threshold – many of those points are visible on the board, but others are held secretly in hand. Everyone is incentivised to pull the player that is furthest ahead down into the centre of the pack. Crab mentality comes into play. This is a term referenced in many places, referring to the anecdotal behaviour of crabs in a bucket. When one crab starts to climb out, the others will pull it back into the interior. Colloquially, 'If I can't have it, then nobody can have it'. **Catan** encourages this by letting players shut the lead player out of trade, but again – infuriatingly! – the perceived lead player is not necessarily the **actual** lead player. The player seemingly in last place may have enough secret points to achieve sudden victory. Many games have this 'punish the leader' design. Essentially it is a kind of mechanistic bullying – one person made to suffer at the collective whim of the rest of the group. If it's hard to accept failure because the dice didn't go your way, it can be worse to know you were kept from winning by the people you thought were friends.

In normal circumstances, most of us can clearly differentiate what happens in a game from what happens in real life. The concept of the *magic circle* comes into scope here – that we are all capable of understanding that life is complex enough to permit for moral discontinuity within particular domains. Consider a boxing ring. In day-to-day life, we consider it problematic for two people to beat each other up until one falls down. We'd gasp. We'd intervene. We'd attempt to de-escalate. The fighting is incompatible with society.

Within a boxing ring, it's the other way around. Intervening is incompatible with the sport. If you tried to separate two boxers in the middle of a match, **you** would be the one at fault. We throw a *magic circle* around the boxing ring and say 'What happens in there is not judged by the standards of what happens out here'. Games occupy these *magic circles* – most of us can separate what happens in a game from what happens outside.

When other people get involved though, that *magic circle* starts to look awfully porous. When your significant other promises to aid in battle, and then the next turn betrays you to join up with your rival … it's part of the game, right? Right?

Right. Sometimes it doesn't feel that way. The *magic circle* has holes in it. The real world can leak past the magic circle too. Consider the alternate scenario, when two players in a romantic relationship spend the entire game helping each other for no justifiable tactical or strategic aim. It's easy to get aggravated there too.

We can see games that stress social mechanisms as being a particularly problematic category of games from this perspective. Consider **the Resistance** (2009) – a wonderful game of espionage and deception. Around the table, some people are courageous freedom fighters. Others represent the sinister dystopian government. Only the government agents – the infiltrators – know each other. Everyone else has no idea where any other loyalties lie. The game is played over a set of rounds in which a mission must be accomplished. The current leader puts together a team to perform the mission, and everyone else votes the team forward or down. The noble freedom fighters secretly submit 'success' cards. The government infiltrators can play success **or** fail. The cards are collected up, shuffled, and if there are the requisite number of fails, the mission fails. Three failed missions and the government wins; three successes and the resistance wins.

It's simple and straightforward and a lot of fun. But that fun comes from being able to elicit information from other people and meaningfully interpret their trustworthiness. There's a lot of reading facial expressions, identifying contradictory information, and slinging accusations. But more than this, it's a game that relies on the ability to wield rhetoric. Cold facts don't impress anyone when you're trying to explain why someone is a government agent, especially when their confederates are doing everything they can to discredit **you.** *Empathic accuracy* comes heavily into play, but so does the ability to convince other people. **The Resistance** is also a game when your best friend might suddenly turn against you and spend the entire game explaining why you're not to be trusted. The *magic circle* can buckle under assaults like this. It can also collapse entirely, especially if the evidence for your untrustworthiness draws from shared external experience. 'Michael once stole a chocolate bar out of his nephew's Halloween haul – we definitely can't trust him!'

Or consider **Shifty Eyed Spies** (2017) in which much of the game is spent making intense, intimate eye contact with other players. I once got a group of computing students to make a paper prototype of this and they described it as 'the single most uncomfortable experience' they ever had playing a game. Computing students – of course – famously not noted for their ease in social environments.

Reiner Knizia, a famous and well-regarded board game designer, once said, 'The goal of playing a game is to win, but it is the goal that is important: not the winning'. That is part of the informal contract we all form when we sit down at the table. That we will all try to win, and not take the winning too seriously. We shake hands, say 'good game', and then leave the *magic circle*. Residue is often left behind though as we breach its barrier, in both directions. As such, care must be taken with the game design to ensure as little residue as possible remains.

We have other problematic elements to take into account – such as theme or content. There's a kind of cultural war being fought over 'content warnings' or 'trigger warnings'. It's fair to say these can often be taken to extremes. Literally anything **can** be a trigger – we discussed why above. Certain topics or terms though are disproportionately **likely** to trigger emotional distress because they are reflective **of** emotional distress. Trigger warnings don't necessarily serve to signpost content to be avoided – rather, they are to indicate trouble ahead so someone can prepare themselves for when it is encountered.

So, let's talk about **Cards Against Humanity** (2009), henceforth **CAH** – a game so intentionally, unremittingly transgressive that simply sitting down to play it has to be interpreted as you clicking the 'I waive all my contractual rights' button on an especially over-reaching software user agreement. The makers of the game have made some attempts of late to sanitise the content. This a futile endeavour, in reality. Much of the most aggressively offensive content in the game comes from the juxtaposition of the relatively mundane. I'd show you some examples, but this isn't really that kind of book. Drop me an email, and I'll send you some photos.

For those that have managed to avoid it, **CAH** is a game where you get dealt a hand of distressingly horrifying phrases, memes, and social references. Each round, a judge plays out a question, such as 'The last time I ever threw up was _____'. Everyone picks the card from their hand that best answers the question, and then the judge votes on which was best. Usually the 'best' is the one that is most comically offensive although more subtle forms of the game exist.

The problem with **CAH** in this frame is that you cannot possibly avoid content that others would prefer you did not address, and drawing attention to it is almost like a red rag to a bull. If you let a table of **CAH** players know there are references you'd prefer nobody made, you might have deescalated a situation or you might have just signposted the best way for everyone to get points. It's **CAH**. Everything goes, right? At its best, **CAH** is about ritualistically exorcising the cultural power of taboo. But that's only at its best.

More than this, **CAH** has what I call 'emotional splash damage'. You don't always opt-in to being exposed to its content. It just needs someone else in the same room to be playing. You won't be able to escape the laughing or the ritualistic chanting of especially good combinations. The opting-in part is vital here – it's the consensual agreement between the player and the game that 'we're cool here'. For this reason, when running a game night, I don't ban **CAH** but I do ask people to play it somewhere away from the main group.

A slightly more sophisticated example of this problem can be seen in the game **Billionaire Banshee** (2014, Figure 6.3) in which players are each presented with a fictional person they might take on a date. Prospective romantic partners are made up of a perk (a reason you might want to date them) and a quirk (a reason that you might not). They're a fashion designer and they can get you free clothes! But they're a cult leader and believe that medicine is evil. They can transform into an all-terrain vehicle! But they are also super clingy! The traits range from the perfectly innocent to the practically pornographic – we'll come back to that in the next section.

Everyone votes on whether the current player would date that person, the answer is revealed, and then you have a laugh about it.

It's much cleverer than **CAH**, and much more restrained in how it plays around with Not Safe For Work (NSFW) content. But also, it can cut close to the bone. Imagine a particular quirk or flaw is brought up and all your friends are laughing about how that's a massive dealbreaker. To have that perceived flaw autopsied by their friends might be

FIGURE 6.3 Billionaire Banshee, in which you might have to secretly endure your friends making fun of you. (Photograph by the author.)

FIGURE 6.4 I believe Secret Hitler is intentionally transgressive in its theme and design. Reasonable people can disagree though. (Photograph by the author.)

very uncomfortable. And it's not like you can just turn and say 'Hey, you're talking about me here' because that's going to draw attention your way in a likely unflattering manner.

Then we have games like **Secret Hitler** (2016, Figure 6.4) which manage a double whammy of requiring relatively complex social skills within a theme that is likely to genuinely upset people on mere utterance of its name. In its defence, I think **Secret Hitler** requires its transgressive title to really sell the message embedded in its mechanisms[2] but also it's not a game I'm going to immediately propose when I have Jewish friends around to visit. In fact, a Jewish anti-defamation league in Australia directly condemned any store selling it.

> "What's next? A board game set in the gas chambers and ovens of Auschwitz?" charged ADC chairman, Dvir Abramovich.[3]

That game exists, by the way. It's called **Train** (2009). It's by Brenda Romero, and it's an attempt to communicate morality through game mechanisms. It is also not exactly something that I would consider to be emotionally accessible.

There are other factors to be considered when it comes to emotional accessibility.

What about 'take that' mechanisms, where players can be deprived of game progress through special abilities that often have no feasible counter? Open ballots in games with voting, where people are forced to defend their choices in front of the collective. Player versus Player (PvP) actions in general are likely to transgress aspects of the *magic circle*, and even if they don't, they can feel unpleasantly non-consensual.

Even without all of this, some games just lend themselves to making careless mistakes. Having to ask the table for permission to 'take back' a move can be uncomfortable, especially if it's likely to be denied by one or more of the stricter players at the table.

And let's not forget the old favourite, player elimination. That's when you lose a game so badly you're ejected from it mid-session and all you get to do is watch the rest of your friends continue to have fun. Or not, in the case of **Monopoly**. Sometimes an emotional inaccessibility can turn out to contain a mercy.

Games with Good Emotional Design

If that's a taster of some of the problems – what counter-examples do we have of things done well? Let's begin by returning to **Billionaire Banshee**, which we discussed in the previous section. While it does have a challenging framing, it also neatly accommodates consent by prominently noting the category of offence to which each card belongs. If you want the vanilla, safe for work version – just build the deck from those cards. If you're okay with fantastical content, include the cards with the unicorn on the back. If sexual content is fine, the bear with the whip should be included.

You get to build – to a certain extent – the game around the themes you find most comfortable for the comfort of the current group. That doesn't even need to be a group where emotional impairment is likely to be involved – I wouldn't want to be discussing issues of consent in sadomasochism when playing a game like this with my mother, for example.

The issue with explicit targeting in PvP games is neatly dealt with in both **Cosmic Encounter** (2008) and in **7 Wonders** (2010). Both games involve explicit mechanics that disadvantage other players, but they move responsibility from targeting from the player onto the game mechanics. **7 Wonders** (Figure 6.5) places you in perpetual war with the players to your left and to your right, and there is no choice as to the target of aggression otherwise. In such circumstances where you dominate an opponent, it's not because you explicitly chose to target them. That fact removes the consequences of targeting from the player onto the mechanisms. Similarly when it comes to offering certain gameplay advantages, seat position, rather than social context, determines who can be involved.

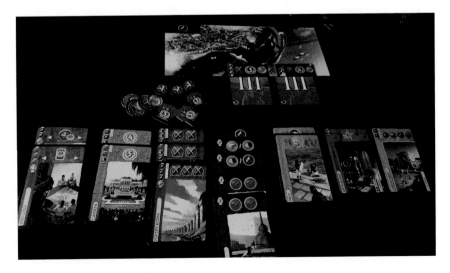

FIGURE 6.5   Seven Wonders takes the politics out of aggression. (Photograph by the author.)

Cosmic Encounter makes the target of aggression the outcome of card draw – it doesn't matter who you **want** to invade. The negotiation about who is going to help with invasion can still be fraught and set up interesting interplays of tension, but you never have to answer the dreaded question, 'Why me?' The cards said so, buddy! It's all out of my hands!

For games where randomness can be the difference between having fun and **not** having fun, some games introduce a formal catch-up mechanism – if you haven't had anything good happen to you for a while, a good thing will happen for free! **Catan** has this in some versions of its rules – if you don't get a resource for a certain number of rolls, you can pick a resource of your choice from the supply. **Isle of Skye** (2015) gives everyone but the leader free money at the beginning of every turn.

These systems don't even need to be this explicit – **Isle of Trains** (2014) puts limits on how many contracts a player can be working with at a time, giving a player who is behind a chance to pick the easiest cards while someone is otherwise distracted by their current obligations. **Flamme Rouge** (2016, Figure 6.6) gives a movement bonus to everyone who can position themselves correctly behind a player ahead of them. It's encoded as a slip-stream effect in the game mechanics, and it's simultaneously why the game is so much fun and why it also feels surprisingly fair. It's a catch-up mechanism that requires skill to use.

One way to mitigate the problem of arbitrary dice rolls is by switching to a probabilistically balanced number deck. In **Catan**'s deck – available as an optional extra – each number from 2 to 12 is proportionally present within the cards. Instead of rolling the dice on your turn, you draw a card instead. The result is that you get a statistically smooth distribution of numbers you can rely upon rather than a completely random set of numbers that might take ten games before they start to smooth into the expected distribution curve.

FIGURE 6.6   Flamme Rouge, which encodes a clever catch-up mechanisms into its design. (Photograph by the author.)

Sometimes the solution lies in how you pitch the game. Consider family game nights when you were young, where your relatives screamed at each other over **Pictionary** (1985), bitterly complaining about every cat that is drawn more like a camel. It's to do with the pressure of having spectators, along with having to do a complex task requiring real-world skill, at speed, in real-time, in an act of collaborative interpretation. It's all stressful. Pictionary is a lot more fun when you can draw because that skill reduces the stress and also improves the odds of success.

Telestrations (2009) on the other hand is more fun when you **can't draw.** It's a simple design for a game – the artistic equivalent of whispering a phrase into someone else's ear for them to transmit to someone else and so on. You get a thing to draw. You draw it (badly, usually) and then pass your 'drawing' on to the next player. They look at it. They look at you. You look away. They look back at the thing. They sigh, and flip over to the next page of the drawing pad and write a description of what they think you drew.

They pass that description on to the next person.

They look at it. They look at the person that just passed it their way. That person shrugs. The poor soul then has to draw what was described, and that gets passed on. This continues until all the pages of the book are full and then you all reveal the sequence of guesses and draws to the general amusement of the table. If there's someone with talent in the group, you might get something like Figure 6.7 to describe.

FIGURE 6.7   My talented colleague Sofia Vales at Chalmers University of Technology drew this wonderful picture during a round of Telestrations. (Photograph by the author, used with permission.)

FIGURE 6.8   This Telestrations picture was drawn by the distinctly untalented me. (Photograph by the author.)

It's Ace Attorney! You'll guess 'lawyer' because of course you will. If you know the game series, you can't possibly fail to get the meaning. It's a work of art, put together in mere moments in a fast moving game of clumsy people drawing clumsy things. This is an outlier though. It's far more likely you'll get Figure 6.8 passed your way instead.

It's a haunted house, okay? It is. **It is.**

But the cool thing about **Telestrations** is that it's impressive if you can draw well – everyone will say 'Oh wow that is exactly what that ridiculous thing you were asked to draw would look like', and you'll get to bask in the appreciation of the table. But it's **funny** when you **can't** draw and that's what's going to consistently achieve the best response. If it is emotionally problematic to ask people to demonstrate skills they may not have, then you can mitigate that by getting them to comically fail in a way that makes laughter the core payload of the experience. **Rhino Hero: Super Battle**, as we discussed in Chapter 5 on physical accessibility, has a similar feature – building the structure is part of the fun, but the real pay dirt is to be found in the **collapse.**

Once Upon a Time (2012) is a game of storytelling drawing from the tropes of fairy tales. And you know what? Fairy tales are **dark.** I have been more genuinely disturbed by 'children's stories' than I have in even the worse round of **CAH. Once Upon a Time** gives everyone the opportunity to explore all the most worrying contours of the human experience, while still making it completely inclusive for children. It's a remarkable design, allowing cultural context to subtly communicate what shock horror can only shout. It also has a wonderful sensibility in that when someone is pulled up for breaching the game rules, it's done to chants of 'Silly!' or similarly non-threatening terminology.

For games where it's difficult for someone to make their point because a whole bunch of people are screaming at cross purposes, **Deception: Murder in Hong Kong** (2014) offers much of the same model of deduction and cross-interrogation as we see in **the Resistance.** What it also does is build natural points into the game where people are permitted to talk unchallenged. It turns a riot into a court-room and gives people a chance to compose themselves and put forward their case clearly without contradiction. Obviously people can still interject, but they're breaking the rules in that case and can be quietened on that basis.

Being a villager in **One Night Ultimate Werewolf** (2014) – another social deductive game – comes with no powers, no secret information, and no additional responsibilities. It's ideal for someone who wants to play but doesn't want a role that draws attention. You don't get to choose to be a villager though – it is thrust upon you and perhaps you'll end up with a role that is far more complex or pivotal. The opposite might also be true – you might want to take an important role and yet end up with no such thing. **Mafia de Cuba** (2015) solves this problem by allowing players to choose which role they want out of a box that gets passed around all the players. It also allows players to choose just how important they're going to be to the argument – they can also steal a number of gems from the box as it comes their way. This way, people get to opt-in to their optimal level of comfort. Given how rounds of **Mafia de Cuba** are reasonably short, they can also modify that level of comfort on a round-by-round basis.

Finally, if the problem is that the competition in a game is too fierce, games can solve that problem by instead setting a difficult shared task that must be completed **alongside** other players. **Pandemic** (2008), **Forbidden Island** (2010), **Forbidden Desert** (2013), and **Forbidden Sky** (2018) all offer different takes on the same basic concept of people spending action points to stop something terrible happening. You all win together, or you fail together. **Flash Point: Fire Rescue** (2011) is a game we discussed in an earlier chapter and offers a similar experience – fighting fire together to save a building and the people within it. **Spirit Island** (2017) is a much heavier, more challenging game of anti-colonialism where players take on the form of island spirits chasing off the invading forces. There's a wide range of challenge, and variety in scenarios, that people can face together.

Some games blend competitive and co-operative elements, allowing for a one versus many experience. The most skilled player can be made to face off against everyone else, allowing for a more evenly balanced game than might otherwise be possible.

That's of course not to say that co-operative games solve emotional inaccessibility problems entirely. Important in the design is that there has to be a challenge, and thus failure should be a more likely outcome than success for most groups. That's a challenging task if you also want to make it fun. More importantly though, failure has to be an accumulation of small factors – no one of which being decisive – so that nobody can point to the single player that lost them the game. Consider the penalty kickout in football – all that focus on one person, carrying the hopes of winning the match. They're taking that kick in the penalty box because of what happened over the entire game. Everyone played a part in them being there. Miss the penalty though and they'll still individually bear the fury of the fans since they are seen as the person who lost them the match.

Games with Interesting Emotional Design

Let's finish up our discussion here by looking at some games that offer themselves up as interesting – occasionally even courageous – examples of emotional impact in board gaming. This they do through both design and storytelling, but their primary contribution is in how they blend the two together. This offers an opportunity for a kind of 'sociological storytelling' where the actions you take in a game carry a narrative weight. Sometimes this is only obvious through a close reading of interpretation. We'll only talk about two games here, but they are both well worth checking out for the ways in which they blend real-life themes, game mechanics heavy with implication, and potentially troublesome real-world resonances.

Before we get into them though, it's worth contextualising this a little. There are people who believe games inherently trivialise serious topics. I don't buy that.

Secret Hitler, if you believe games can tell stories through their mechanisms, is actually a powerfully compelling deconstruction of the way that adversarial politics can create the breeding ground for fascism. It contains an important message – liberty dies bit by bit, not all at once. Many believe though that the rise of Hitler is not a topic suitable for a game. The video game **That Dragon: Cancer** (2016) is an emotional interactive retelling of a couple raising a terminally ill child. It was lambasted by some for 'cashing in' on tragedy even though it is clear that couldn't be further from the intention. Brenda Romero's 'The Mechanic is the Message' series explores everything from the slave trade (**The New World**, 2008) to immigrant labour practices (**Mexican Kitchen Workers**, in development).

These are **inaccessible themes**, but they are inaccessible in a way that is compatible with we discussed in the first chapter. They are **intentionally** transgressive and it's important to approach them on that basis. The discomfort felt by players is part of the experience and cannot be designed away.

With that in mind, let's talk about **Holding On: The Troubled Life of Billy Kerr** (2018). The framing of this game is that an old man is admitted to a hospital. He's dying – that much is clear – but it's also clear that he has a story to tell. Managing his health is critical, but so too is making time for simply recognising his dignity as a human being. It's about keeping him alive while building trust. You play the medical staff of the hospital, who already have too much to do and too little time to do it. It's a game built on the 'five fires, four buckets' style of design. There are always more calls on your time than you have capacity to deal with, and everything you don't deal with is going to make the future more difficult. It is a brutal satire of the UK's historical underfunding of the National Health System. It's also a touching exploration of what it means to deal with stretched resources in a job that is largely about having the bandwidth to **care.**

The story is gradually revealed through vague memories (Figure 6.9) that must be brought into clarity (Figure 6.10) through repeated gentle interrogation of a recalcitrant

FIGURE 6.9 Fuzzy memories in the game of Holding On: The Troubled Life of Billy Kerr. (Photograph by the author.)

FIGURE 6.10   A fuzzy memory in Holding On becoming clear. (Photograph by the author.)

Billy Kerr. Each time you're delving into his past though you're not improving staff wellbeing or proactively intervening in future medical emergencies. Every single shift in the hospital, in other words, involves making difficult choices between which mandatory actions you'll perform. Sometimes you spend whole days in the game just watching Billy's health deteriorate as he accelerates towards death.

The game effectively handles these themes and has an emotional resonance that is far out of proportion with the fact you are, in the end, just moving pawns and cards around a board. But what I personally found most painful in play was how it constantly reminded me of my father, and how we watched him die from a cancer that was almost Blitzkrieg like in its brutality[4]. I had experienced the flaws in the care economy first hand, and every time we played Holding On, it triggered *involuntary autobiographical memory* in the form of distinctly **unprecious** fragments.

My father died on my 21st birthday. I haven't celebrated a birthday since. And Holding On, sitting on my shelves, was like an open wound that I had placed in my game collection. Every time I saw the box, it brought me back to the mental imagery of my father's last few hours.

In the end, I gave the game away. It was too raw a reminder. I wasn't going to play it again – or at least, certainly not for fun. But that doesn't change the fact that **Holding On: The Troubled Life of Billy Kerr** is a meaningful and important board game that does something few other games do or even attempt to do. Anyone who is interested in the design of games for emotional impact should study it. It is **intentionally** raw – its inaccessibility is a core part of the message it communicates.

Fog of Love (2017) has a much more approachable framing. It makes use of real-world elements, within a roleplaying context, to explore the nature of relationships and what it means to succeed within one.

My experience of playing (and watching) **Fog of Love** (Figure 6.11) is what compelled me to describe it as 'Awkward Conversations: The Board Game'. In it, two players take on the roles of partners in a (usually) romantic entanglement. They each have different features that define their starting personalities, and each has a set of personal traits

FIGURE 6.11   Fog of Love, or 'Awkward Conversations: The Board Game'. (Photograph by the author.)

that represent a set of 'hidden goals' with regards to the person they want to become. Each also has a hand of destiny cards, which represent a life goal that they are working towards. Someone may wish to be dominant in their relationship while another may simply want to be happy. Someone may be looking for a face-saving exit from the their partner, and another may be unconditionally in love with the other. He's a royal heir; she's a teacher. They fight crime!

The game is played through scenes which offer one or both players a choice to make. Scenes may be relatively trivial, such as 'Where should we go for dinner' or 'What do we need to get from IKEA?' They may become serious, such as how to best deal with relatives who disapprove of the relationship. They are sometimes explicitly sexual, and more often revolve around proper, adult decisions like 'I'm pregnant – what do we do?'.

What makes this interesting though is that the game is unquestionably about playing the part of a character, and all your choices can be constrained within the *magic circle* of that framing. In theory. Many of these scenes invite conversation around the choices made – that's natural and a big part of the fun. Some of these scenes though may crowbar open conversational topics that veer dangerously towards the occult barriers constructed around the gameplay. I often use the example of playing Fog of Love with a prospective romantic partner. 'Oh, your character said here that you want to get married and have kids. That's interesting. We've never had that discussion. Is that how you feel in real life? Is that what you want from us?'

It's roleplaying closer to couples' therapy than it is to Dungeons and Dragons.

In other words, whether you wanted the 'Should we have kids' conversation during game night, you're having it now because the game brought the topic into scope. Infidelity is part of the game, and it's entirely possible that a couple may have an incident of that in their past or, indeed, their present. Maybe they've grown past it, but much as with **Holding On** and my father's death, we don't get to choose when we have an emotional response to an *involuntary autobiographical memory*. The game cleaves very closely to common experiences in a relationship, and as such playing might pick at a few scars.

That's going to vary from person to person of course, but the risk is always there. That's what makes **Fog of Love** such an absorbing design for a game. It is explicitly framed as a romantic comedy in a box, but in my experience, it can just as often become a romantic tragedy with real-world resonance. Again, this is a game that I recommend that anyone interested in handling emotional themes in a tabletop game should study.

Our final topic in this section relates to the social contract of modern gaming. It's another area where we could learn from classical games like **chess** and **poker**. Specifically, one of the easiest ways to make a game emotionally inaccessible is to force people to play when they are having no fun. It is generally part of the default expectation of hobbyist gaming that everyone has to grind it out to the end because to do otherwise is to spoil the enjoyment of those in contention for a winner's trophy. **Chess** however has a mechanism that allows someone to resign when they know their position is untenable, and it is considered to be the height of etiquette to concede victory rather than force someone to mechanically execute upon an incontestable strategy. **Poker** permits players to fold when they decide that the risk of their position outweighs the perceived benefit.

We rarely see mechanisms of this nature in board games, and it strikes me as a missed opportunity. To be fair, many modern games are incompatible with this ethos in that their fun comes from laying the groundwork for the endgame. Their design also may not benefit from what is essentially 'consensual player elimination' if it means an eliminated player must simply watch other people have fun for a couple of hours. If well implemented though, resignation systems allow for players to remove themselves from what might be a triggering situation in a way that is respectful of the skill other players have demonstrated. A timely resignation can be a mark of a gracious loser, allowing someone to transfer what would be future emotional distress into positive social capital. If implemented into the rules, a resignation system allows for an opportunity to formally state what should happen with regards to accumulated territory, cards, or resources. Resignation can be absorbed cleanly into the game experience. Players who resign can be offered other optional roles in play during long, extended sessions. All of this is much better than forcing someone to metaphorically (or physically) 'flip the table' as the only way to alleviate their distress.

Formal resignation rules also offer great opportunity in alleviating modulating discomfort for players – when a condition flares up to an intensity that wasn't present at the start of play. Resignation may offer physical relief in circumstances where someone may otherwise feel obligated to see a session through to the bitter end.

Guidelines for Emotional Accessibility

- *Games to look to for inspiration*:
    - Welcome To, Barenpark, Potion Explosion, Kingdom Builder, and Telestrations.
- *Games to look to as cautionary tales*:
    - Star Fluxx, CAH, The Estates, Arboretum, Holding On – The Troubled Life of Billy Kerr, Imhotep, Innovation, Tigris and Euphrates, Merchants and Marauders, Survive—Escape from Atlantis, and Scrabble.

Text

Include Trigger Warnings for Content that is Commonly Perceived to Be Traumatic

If challenging content is provided as part of the game, consider how it might be received by a person with trauma. When making use of potentially controversial or triggering content, provide appropriate content warnings in game documentation and on the box.

- Include content warnings on game packaging, to aid buyers in decision making.
- Include specific content warnings linked to the location the triggering content is encountered in game.
- Where possible, support triggering content being removed from play by annotating the back of cards and components.

Rules

Limit the Need for Stressful Social Interaction

Many of the most significant emotional inaccessibilities in this category are associated with the performative aspects of combative social interaction. Some games require this to function, but ideally games are also flexible enough to permit people to self-select the degree of involvement, and the social skills needed, in an argument.

- Minimise the need for mandatory bluffing, argumentation, or lying.
- If roles involve being the centre of attention under stressful circumstances, consider alternate roles that minimise this for individual players.
- Limit or eliminate the need for eye contact, physical contact, or other uncomfortably intimate gestures.
- Limit, as far as is possible, the need for adversarial discussion. Allow mechanisms and roles that permit players to opt-out of arguments.
- If a player can be interrupted in their turn for prevarication or hesitation, make the interrupt as thematic and non-judgemental as possible.
- If players must ballot for game decisions, try to aim for hidden ballots. Where hidden balloting is not possible, consider systems that permit ambiguity of motivation.

Avoid Opportunities for Bullying

Games that encourage groups to gang up on a leading player are always going to bring with them connotations of bullying, as do games that offer the ability to inflict an unpleasantness that cannot be countered. Some games are explicitly confrontation in that they include prominent PvP mechanisms. These can be problematic unless that PvP is consensual. 'I challenge you to a duel – do you accept?' versus 'I burn down all your houses and all you can do is watch'.

Other problematic game design decisions focus around control and domination, such as when one player is permitted to unilaterally act on behalf of another as may be the case when a character is charmed or possessed.

Remember here too that simply choosing a target of aggression is as much an act of potential bullying as the act itself.

- Eliminate, as far as is possible, the ability for players to gang up on others at the table. Where it cannot be eliminated, limited the benefit.
- Consider mechanisms that remove the benefit of targeting the same player more than once.
- Be wary of having too many 'take that' mechanics with no ability to counteract.
- Consider limiting the number of opportunities players have to undo the work of another player.
- Where appropriate, aim for PvP activities to be consensual (flee mechanics, negotiations, etc.)
- Avoid players being able to dictate the actions of other players at the table.
- Offer, if possible, ways for targeting to be made non-personal.
- Avoid putting the tools for alleviating a player's game disadvantage into the hands of other players.

Let Players Recover from Mistakes

Few things can cause someone to stew over their circumstances more than knowing they made a mistake and being unable to undo it because of resistance at the table or because of the broader etiquette of the culture of play. It's not always reasonable to undo a mistake – for example, if one chooses to get rid of all the cards from a marketplace only to find the new marketplace is even worse, few would say that an 'undo' mechanism would be fair or balanced. At least until the game state changes, it improves accessibility to allow people to undo their actions.

- Provide explicit options for players to 'take back' moves and outline the circumstances under which this may be permitted.
- Permit for game mechanisms that allow players to compensate for earlier mistakes.
- Consider the use of catch-up mechanisms.
- Evaluate your game for positive-feedback loops in which a player in the stronger position will inevitably get stronger or when a player in a weaker position will inevitably get weaker.

Make Sure Everyone Gets to Have Fun

It stands to reason that, unless a game is tremendously good as a spectator sport, it is better to be playing than it is to not be playing. Similarly, it is more fun to be playing with the possibility of winning than it is to go through the motions of play when victory is out of reach. Resignation in chess is a system for a reason.

- Avoid non-consensual player elimination, whether formally or de facto.
- If player elimination is necessary, make it either a short game or give an eliminated player something fun to do when they are removed from the main game.
- Offer players a way to honourably resign from play when they are in a position of no longer being able to compete.

Leave People Feeling like They Were Always a Contender

As discussed above, if it feels bad to lose, it feels **worse** to be dominated in a way that shows how infeasible victory really was. Large point differentials emphasise this, but so too do runaway leader problems where the player in the lead gets advantages as a result of being in the lead. Consider rubber-banding mechanics (that reduce lead player advantages) and catch-up mechanisms (that improve the chances of players in last place) as a way to keep everyone in with a chance.

- Aim for a scenario where score differentials are small, or not directly comparable.
- Ensure that everyone around the table gets an approximately equal chance to have fun on their turn. Make sure there's always something someone can do to progress towards their objective.
- Provide catch-up mechanics that ensure nobody falls out of contention.
- Consider the provision of alternate achievements for those who do not win the game, so as to cushion the cost of loss.
- Avoid situations where the winner is clear during the game. Use end of game scoring where relevant to help make the outcome less predictable.

Don't Leave Things Entirely up to Chance

Chance is a risky tool – it can make a game exciting, but it can also disconnect players from a sense of accomplishment. It can permit a degree of face-saving ambiguity as to the reasons for a loss, but it can also enrage people when it comes to denying them a win. One way to mitigate this is to allow some way to control randomness, either strategically or with explicit management tools.

- Don't rely too much on pure randomness – permit randomness to be mitigated with skilful play.
- Try to scale the amount of randomness to the length of a game.
- For short games, consider explicitly endorsing a tournament style model of gameplay to mitigate win and loss impact.
- Consider the use of techniques that allow some control over the dice – limited rerolls, spendable modifiers, control over the order in which rolls are made, and so on.

Offer a Healthy Co-operative Experience

Competitive games are often an inaccessible prospect from the start – some players simply don't want to be adversarial. For a game to offer a winner, it must also have a loser. As such, if you can add co-operative elements or variants to a game, it becomes more accessible to a much wider range of people.

- Consider offering co-op variants if your game does not have a co-op mode.
- With co-op games, give each character their own agenda that can be achieved alongside the main objective.

- In co-operative games, try to avoid having a point of the game where failure can be uniquely linked to particular players. Failure should be a property of the group.
- In competitive games, consider systems that permit for multiple players to win together if they choose to co-operate.

Aim for Satisfying Failure

Many games are fun when you are winning. Great games are also fun when you are **losing.** Sometimes that comes from finding yourself in what's known as the 'zone of proximal development'. That's the region where learning is most effective because the gap between capability and challenge is small enough to be breached without assistance. Games are essentially engines for learning, and learning itself can be fun. Tools for managing difficulty can help with this, as can offering alternate win conditions that allow people to find their own individual fun at right angles to other players.

- When designing a game around the idea of likely failure, provide ways to influence the challenge of the scenario at setup.
- When designing a game around the likely outcome of failure, consider tiered win conditions that permit for some degree of victory to be claimed under most circumstances.
- Avoid game systems that can result in an unwinnable game state from setup. Provide bailout points in the rules to prevent it.
- Make failure states interesting and entertaining.
- Avoid players ending up with negative scores at the end of game.
- Avoid circumstances where a game has many winners and one loser.

Notes

1. Bae before bay, always.
2. https://www.meeplelikeus.co.uk/secret-hitler-2016/
3. https://www.australianjewishnews.com/game-shame/
4. I won't talk about it too deeply in this book, but if you are curious about how Holding On affected me, you can read a fuller account here: https://www.meeplelikeus.co.uk/holding-on-the-troubled-life-of-billy-kerr-2018/

BIBLIOGRAPHY

Berntsen, D. (1996). Involuntary autobiographical memories. *Applied Cognitive Psychology,* *10*(5), 435–454.

Berntsen, D. (2010). The unbidden past: Involuntary autobiographical memories as a basic mode of remembering. *Current Directions in Psychological Science, 19*(3), 138–142.

Bracha, H. S. (2004). Freeze, flight, fight, fright, faint: Adaptationist perspectives on the acute stress response spectrum. *CNS Spectrums, 9*(9), 679–685.

Brathwaite, B., & Sharp, J. (2010). The mechanic is the message: A post mortem in progress. In *Ethics and game design: Teaching values through play* (pp. 311–329). Edited by Schrier, Karen, Gibson, David. IGI Global.

Cuff, B. M., Brown, S. J., Taylor, L., & Howat, D. J. (2016). Empathy: A review of the concept. *Emotion Review, 8*(2), 144–153.

Harmon-Jones, E., & Mills, J. (2019). An introduction to cognitive dissonance theory and an overview of current perspectives on the theory. In E. Harmon-Jones (Ed.), *Cognitive dissonance: Reexamining a pivotal theory in psychology* (pp. 3–24). American Psychological Association. https://doi.org/10.1037/0000135-001

Heron, M., & Belford, P. (2014). 'It's only a game'—Ethics, empathy and identification in game morality systems. *The Computer Games Journal, 3*, 34–53.

Heron, M. J., & Belford, P. H. (2014). Do you feel like a hero yet? *Journal of Games Criticism, 1*(2).

Hofmann, S. G., Sawyer, A. T., Fang, A., & Asnaani, A. (2012). Emotion dysregulation model of mood and anxiety disorders. *Depression and Anxiety, 29*(5), 409–416.

Koster, R. (2013). *Theory of fun for game design*. O'Reilly Media, Inc.

Linton, M. (1986). Ways of searching and the contents of memory. In D. C. Rubin (Ed.), *Autobiographical memory* (pp. 50–67). Cambridge: Cambridge University Press. https://doi.org/10.1017/CBO9780511558313.007

McFarlane, A. C., Atchison, M., & Yehuda, R. (1997). The acute stress response following motor vehicle accidents and its relation to PTSD. *Annals of the New York Academy of Sciences-Paper Edition, 821*, 437–441.

McLeod, S. (2019). *Vygotsky's zone of proximal development and scaffolding*. Simply psychology.

Schmidt, U., & Zank, H. (2005). What is loss aversion? *Journal of Risk and Uncertainty, 30*, 157–167.

7

Socioeconomic Accessibility

Emotional aspects as we discussed in the previous chapter are not traditionally considered one of the problem domains of accessibility. Hopefully, this book has managed to convince you that it's a key consideration in the design of games. In a similar vein, I would like to make a case as to why socioeconomic factors are also a key accessibility domain and why accessible design must be mindful of the sociological and economic context in which they function.

First of all, let's put a definition to these vague terms. When we talk here about 'sociological accessibility', we can usefully (if somewhat inaccurately) think of these as **perceived** obstacles in front of someone and a goal. They don't represent fundamental interaction barriers – if someone wants to play a game, they still can. There's nothing physically stopping them – no impairment that prevents engagement. The perceived obstacle exists farther back in the decision chain. It's good if someone can play a game if they want to, but sometimes aspects of a design prevent that **want** from manifesting. As ever, these may be an intentional part of the design. You'd perhaps be hard pressed to get your lovely church-going grandmother to play **Cards Against Humanity**. It's just too off-putting a pitch for people who don't see themselves as 'horrible people', as in the game's tagline. Part of the pitch of **CAH** is linked to its branding.

But as usual, this can also be an unintentional issue that emerges accidentally. There exists a cognitive effect called the 'people like me' bias or the *similarity bias* depending on who you talk to. This is the tendency for it to be easier to identify with people that have similar experiences, appearances, outlooks, and capabilities. This also extends to design – it's easier to design for people who are similar to us because there is a lot of assumed common ground. It's not necessarily a conscious choice – the things with which we are most familiar tend to leak into the things we create unless we take intentional action to avoid it.

In the process, there is a natural effect that we may exclude other perspectives because we simply never think to do otherwise. We may embed our own prejudices in wording and in mechanics and in aesthetic choices. We may encode cultural stereotypes into stories or representation. We assume knowledge that we perhaps shouldn't or rely upon a level of game literacy that is outside of cultural norms. Those inaccessibilities have an impact on how broadly the hobby can reach outside of its existing devotees.

I often say there are few sights more off-putting to a young woman entering a board game shop than the shelves themselves. Imagine looking around to see a bunch of stern-faced middle-aged white men staring back. What better way to say, through the often unconscious choices of designers and artists, that this is a hobby for middle-aged white men? What better way to make that same young woman feel like she should have gone with her instincts when the only woman character she can pick in a game is basically dressed in lingerie while the men are fully decked out in plate armour?

DOI: 10.1201/9781003415435-7

The problem for us is that the world is complicated, and people are even more so, and the sociological context in which we function makes it almost impossible to 'do right' in this. It might be obvious to say 'Don't sexualise women in art', but there are plenty of women who enjoy playing as sexy women just as there are men who enjoy playing as sexy men. As we discussed when we talked about *identity-* versus *person-first language* – it's inappropriate to assume that any group of people believes any one thing. People are too varied for easy answers. Mostly we address this topic as a conversation that designers must have with themselves and their audiences. We can think of this as defining a set of what were previously implicit inclusion and exclusion criteria – who am I unintentionally including in this design, and who am I unintentionally excluding?

Those implicit criteria get communicated everywhere through the game's design. Men tend to have more time for leisure than women, and that time tends to be easier to allocate in blocks. As such, if you're asking players to sit at a table for four hours to play an epic game of emerging strategy, you will likely find that the design – through no intentional choice of your own – favours men over women. You can't fix the societal maladies that create this time disparity – or at least, you can't outside the context of your own life – but you can accidentally build the inequity into what you are asking of your players.

The truth is that board gaming is, by and large, a luxury hobby. It is **expensive** to be a board gamer. The problem with that 'truth' though is that it changes its value depending on how you frame the concept of 'expense'.

Let's start with the obvious one – cash money. Opponents of the position that board gaming is a luxury hobby will often use the cinema as an example. In 2021, the average price of a UK cinema ticket was £7.70 before family discounts and promotions are taken into account. That's a decent baseline. Let's say you want to spend an evening with your friends, and you decide to go see the newest Marvel movie. The one released this week as opposed to the one released the week before or the week before that.

(There are **a lot** of Marvel movies is what I'm saying. Too many, right? Right?)

Four of you decide to go, putting the ticket cost at £30.80. Already that's more than the cost of some genuinely excellent board games, and we're only really getting started. A regular soft drink in a UK cinema might cost £3.25 (price correct as of 2023) and a regular popcorn £4.90. Let's say everyone gets a drink and a snack. That's £13 for drinks and £19.60 for popcorn. That's a total of £63.40 for maybe two hours worth of entertainment, and you don't even get to keep the movie. We're not even factoring in travel costs, parking, babysitters, and what have you. In terms of 'cost per hour per person', that's about £8 an hour and you need to pay the same if you want to watch the movie again. There are a whole lot of board games that cost less than that, support more players, for longer **and** you get to keep them once you're done!

In terms of 'cost per hour per player', board games represent truly excellent value. You only need to play them a few times before that metric is down to a trivial outlay compared to going to the cinema.

But this comparison – common as it is – isn't quite like for like. A more apt comparison would be watching a movie at home, using store-bought snacks and streaming something off of Netflix. The financial outlay of most 'at-home' activities is basically negligible. And in that frame, we start to see the issue of economic inaccessibility emerge.

Monopoly, for good or ill (it's mostly ill), remains the baseline comparator most people have when the words 'board game' are said to them. It's the one they remember, the one they've probably played, and the one they see on every supermarket shelf.

There's a psychological principle that's important here, and it's called **anchoring**. Essentially, we set the mental value of something in comparison to other things (the anchor). Strack and Mussweiler demonstrated this back in 1997 with a simple experiment they conducted with 60 university students (male and female). Half of them were asked if Gandhi was older or younger than nine years old when he died, the other half if he was older or younger than 140. After answering the first question, they were asked to estimate Gandhi's age at death.

The first question served as the anchor – to create the reference point at either 9 or 140 years old. Those in the first condition estimated Gandhi's age at death as an average of 50. The other group estimated his death age at an average of 67. There were no other changeable factors in the study (in technical terms, the first question was the only independent variable). The initial anchor set the context for the estimate to follow.

Monopoly is the anchor of board games. We might not like it, but it's true. Monopoly is what sets the template for what most people think of when they try to imagine a board game, imagine its players, or imagine its price.

Monopoly costs £23 at the time of writing. Using BoardGameGeek as a baseline for comparison, the average Amazon price of the games in the BGG Top 10 is approximately £58.30, again at the time of writing. Several are on pretty hefty temporary discounts. When it comes to the cost of a hobbyist board game, there is a very meaningful sticker shock for the average **potential** player. Sure, there are plenty of excellent games available cheaply, but you need to know what they are to seek them out. There's plenty of strong argumentation to be made that hobbyist board games are actually **unsustainably cheap**, given the production value and personal cost that go into them. Even with that implicit subsidy, they are still **way too expensive** for most people. Every time I visit my mother and bring a new game for her to play, she will – without fail – ask how much it cost. Usually in a tone people reserve for worried inquiries into the drinking habits of a suspected alcoholic.

In a tight economic climate or within the context of the median income of any country you choose to name … buying **Frosthaven** (2023) at £189.95 is an absolute non-starter. A sputtering, incredulous, 'HOW MUCH??' kind of non-starter. The original Milton Bradley version of **Hero Quest** (1989) was £25, which is about £38 when adjusted for inflation. The newly released edition (2022) costs £110 at retail. The production value is much higher, and the costs of raw material are greater. There are reasons behind the inflated sticker price. That doesn't change the cold, hard arithmetic of a parent working out how to keep the kids maximally happy for minimal financial outlay. Even I – a committed board game addict – look at the current prices in game stores and most often think 'Too rich for my blood'.

However, economic factors go deeper into games than simply how much you pay for the box of stuff. Increasingly games are built around a philosophy of ongoing monetisation – that buying the box is only a down-payment on buying the game. As such, there is often a mismatch between buyer expectations (I have bought a game and now I can have fun) and business reality (you have bought a taster of the game, and the actual game is still £100 of further purchases down the line).

Board gaming isn't perceived as an affordable hobby for most people, and anchors used by hobbyists for judging value aren't the ones used by the general public. Until that disparity is resolved, it's difficult for board games to genuinely break into the mainstream in the way that they have threatened to do for years. The ones that do make it are usually the ones that are most economically viable or the ones that are most sociologically accessible.

There are other factors of luxury that we also need to take into account – the luxury of space, the luxury of time, and the luxury of social capital. These bridge between socio-logical and economic factors.

Space is the one most obviously linked to economic factors because it relates to whether or not you even have room to **play** a game. Simply having a table you can dedicate to a game for hours is a luxury for many – not everyone can afford a separate gaming room or single-purpose furniture like a dining table. Space expectations vary from country to country, but certainly within Europe, the average house or flat is consid-erably smaller than is considered acceptable within America. According to the research website Shrink That Footprint[1], the average house in the United States is 2,164 ft^2. In Sweden, it is 893 ft^2. The UK manages 818 ft^2, and in Hong Kong, it is a diminutive 484 ft^2. Australia manages 2,303 ft^2, and in Canada, it is 1,948 ft^2. In China, it is 646 ft^2, and in Russia, it is 614 ft^2. These are the 2023 figures.

Simply having a place where a group of people can gather uninterrupted for hours at a time is an unimaginable luxury for many people. Consider when many of us abruptly had to start working from home during the coronavirus pandemic – some were fortu-nate enough to have dedicated home offices. Others had to find a corner of an already cramped kitchen and constantly fend off interruptions from family members. Games that need tables are already asking a lot of their players, and the more they sprawl, the more they ask.

Then there is the issue of time, which we've already touched upon. Some games aren't just casual play – they're a **commitment.** Consider the rise of legacy games, where each play session is connected to the next through the imposition of accumulated con-sequence. **Pandemic Legacy Season 1** (2015) takes the vanilla **Pandemic** co-operative game (2008) and adds a 12-mission campaign. Maybe in your first session you let London fall to the disease, and in the next session you find its resources and routes are permanently unavailable from that point on. It makes for a rich, detailed, and person-alised game experience – but it needs a whole group of people to commit to 12 sessions, each of which are an hour (or more, most likely), where you all play much the same game again and again. Technically speaking, it doesn't have to be the same group of people every time, but it's hard to feel ownership over the evolution of a game when you had no hand in the decisions that led to its current state.

For context, many of us can probably relate to the difficulties associated with being adults with real-life responsibilities. For those with children, those responsibilities are both unavoidable and often unpredictable. Sure, you may know that little Suzie takes her extra-credit programming classes on a Wednesday evening. You don't know though when a parent will send their child to school with nits, necessitating serious life adjust-ments for everyone with whom their child came into contact. Simply allocating an eve-ning to leisure is just not going to happen for many people – and when they do find the time, it's always written in the faintest pencil in their calendar. Parents can't say, 'Yeah – sure my kid is sick but I'm still coming to play **Pandemic'**. In the hierarchy of calls on our time, leisure is the one most easily and most consistently sacrificed.

Many of you reading will already be nodding your heads, but I bet I can get you to nod your heads clean off if you've ever tried to arrange a **Dungeons and Dragons** (or system of your choice) campaign amongst your adult friends. You are all **super keen** on the idea because few things are as pleasant as spending an evening simply enjoying the creativ-ity of the people you care about. But you **all** need to be available at the same time, on a regular basis, for several intense hours. Maybe you can occasionally absorb a missing person by having their character 'go on a side adventure'. Maybe you can handle a few last minute reschedules without it becoming a chore for everyone. What's more likely to happen is that every knock to the routine puts a permanent dent in the sustainability of the endeavour. Enough dents, and the thing breaks. It becomes, 'Let's just skip this session and pick up with the next session', which them becomes, 'I think we need to skip this week, so I'll put out a poll to reschedule', to everyone 'putting a pin in it until things are quieter'. Those pins are often permanent.

It's nobody's fault. It's just that **time is a luxury** and games ask a lot of it. I have owned **Star Wars: Rebellion** (2016) for seven years now. I haven't even taken it out of the box because the playtime is estimated at three to four hours. Even within the confines of my own romantic relationship where no children are involved … I can think of vanishingly few evenings where both of us had four hours in a row free at the same time. And when we did, there were plenty of other things we could be doing that didn't need us to have the mental bandwidth to master a 20-page manual.

Almost every part of this hobby also relies on the luxury of **social capital** – specifically having people willing to spend time with you, and **also** willing for that time to be playing a board game. Truthfully, those people are unlikely to be your friends – they have their own things they are into, and what interest are you paying to **their** obsessions?

There's a truism in the board game hobby that it's harder to turn friends into gamers than it is to turn gamers into friends. Some of that is the time issue we've discussed above, but a lot of it is that many people just aren't interested in playing board games. Again, we can probably see **Monopoly** as the anchoring point here.

This is a point made several times before, but it's important – when you say 'board games' to most people they think '**Monopoly, Scrabble, Cluedo**, and **Risk**'. If you're lucky, they might have heard of **Catan** or **Carcassonne**, but realistically – probably not. So when you say to a friend 'Can we play a board game?' they are going to look at you with the same puzzled incredulity you'd get as an adult asking someone to playfight with action figures. The anchor most people have is 'board games are for children'.

You can invest your time trying to change their mind. 'No!' you might say. 'Board games are amazing now'! You might talk about the current golden age – the cardboard renaissance – explaining the rich variety of joy to be found out there. They'll probably listen politely as you explain the rules and the systems and oh my, the fun you'll have. I've been there. Oh buddy, have I been there. And I will say that the response I get is most similar to what happens when you try to tell someone about your dreams – a fixed rictus smile that endures just long enough for the other person to make a face-saving exit. That's only natural. Games don't exist in the rules. They exist in the experience, and by definition you can't experience that which you avoid. I will say though that it is far easier to convince people to play when it looks like the games have been designed with them in mind.

Money, space, time, and people – you need all four of these to align harmoniously for board gaming to really be possible. Or at least, you need a strategy for managing their absence. You can borrow games. You can meet at public places. You can say no to other calls on your time and jealously protect the spaces you carve out. You can go to public game meetups and play with strangers.

This is why we talk about this as a socioeconomic issue – you can spend money to save time. You can use time to build social capital. You can spend social capital to save money. But games can also make things easier, or harder, as a result of how they are designed.

Problematic Socioeconomic Designs

Let's start with something (relatively) straightforward here – representation. Overt racism, sexism, homophobia, or transphobia is relatively rare in board games. What's far more likely to be observed are subtler biases – erasure of ethnicity, gendered assumptions, heteronormative game mechanics, and negatively coded language. In fact, there is only one game that I have looked at where I would consider it to be explicitly 'phobic' in its framing. That's **Tales of the Arabian Nights** (2009), where the modern edition is both explicitly heterosexual in its framing and insulting in its depictions of gender identity. This is a game of fantasy storytelling, where players encounter scenarios and decide what do from a set of options. It's **remarkably** flexible in how it deals with player choice – adjectives intersect with reactive responses within a matrix, which directs players to a passage that outlines the consequence of their actions. You can honour a lovesick lion or rob it. You can bargain with a vengeful hag or question a terrifying djinn. Each time you take an action, it's from a menu of seven context-dependant choices and the game will simply roll with it. So, it's strange a game that is so otherwise accommodating of player agency explicitly outlawing any hint of homosexuality (Figure 7.1).

Note the exclamation mark which does a pretty good job of underlining how unacceptably transgressive such a thing may be. It also enforces this in reaction choices, when a player chooses to – for example – seduce someone of the same sex. We see similar author-insert judgements in how the game talks about sex change as something inherently disgusting. Figure 7.2 talks about a 'horrifying transformation' which is – one might argue – at odds with how many people see their gender identity.

Tales of the Arabian Nights does two other notable things here. The first is that it 'defaults to masculinity', which is to say it is written as if 'he' is sufficiently encompassing to also count for 'she' (Figure 7.3). We also see this issue in play when art in games defaults to showing men more than women. We see it too in the title of some games. **King of Tokyo** (2011), **Lords of Waterdeep** (2012), **Kingdomino** (2016), and its sister

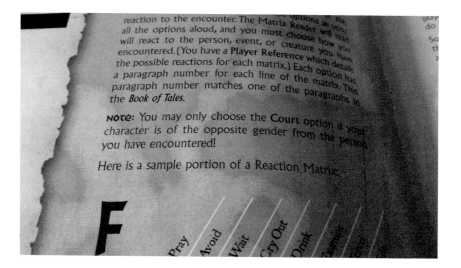

reaction to the encounter. The Matrix Reader will read all the options aloud, and you must choose how you will react to the person, event, or creature you have encountered. (You have a Player Reference which details the possible reactions for each matrix.) Each option has a paragraph number for each line of the matrix. This paragraph number matches one of the paragraphs in the *Book of Tales*.

NOTE: You may only choose the Court option if your character is of the opposite gender from the person you have encountered!

Here is a sample portion of a Reaction Matrix:

FIGURE 7.1   An extract of the manual from Tales of the Arabian Nights. (Photograph by the author.)

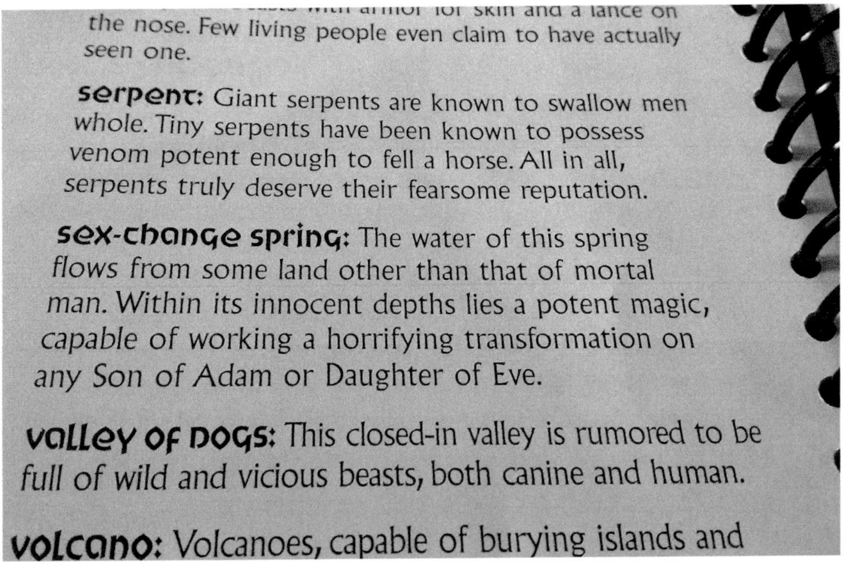

the nose. Few living people even claim to have actually seen one.

serpent: Giant serpents are known to swallow men whole. Tiny serpents have been known to possess venom potent enough to fell a horse. All in all, serpents truly deserve their fearsome reputation.

sex-change spring: The water of this spring flows from some land other than that of mortal man. Within its innocent depths lies a potent magic, capable of working a horrifying transformation on any Son of Adam or Daughter of Eve.

valley of dogs: This closed-in valley is rumored to be full of wild and vicious beasts, both canine and human.

volcano: Volcanoes, capable of burying islands and

FIGURE 7.2 Another extract of the manual from Tales of the Arabian Nights. (Photograph by the author.)

outes leading to it.

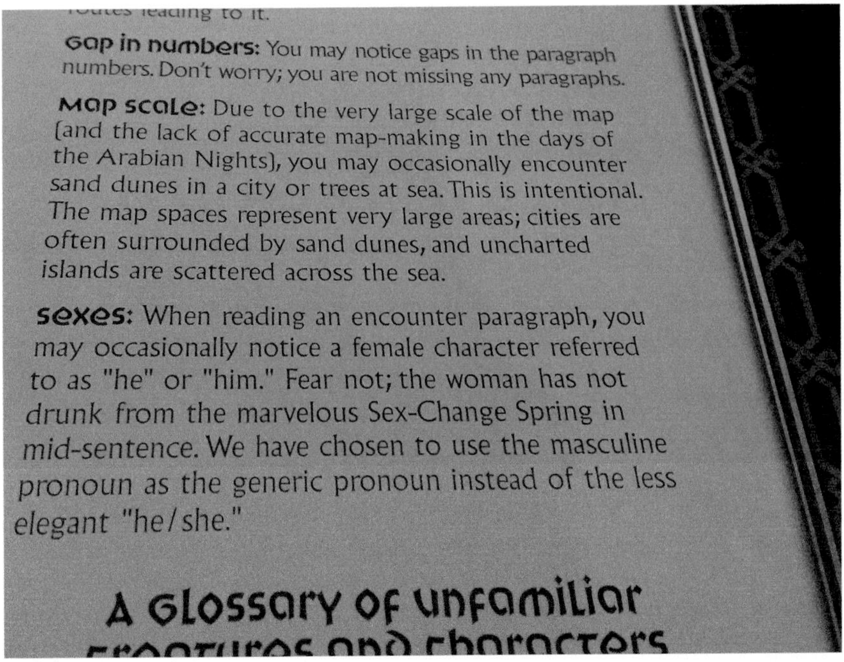

Gap in numbers: You may notice gaps in the paragraph numbers. Don't worry; you are not missing any paragraphs.

Map scale: Due to the very large scale of the map (and the lack of accurate map-making in the days of the Arabian Nights), you may occasionally encounter sand dunes in a city or trees at sea. This is intentional. The map spaces represent very large areas; cities are often surrounded by sand dunes, and uncharted islands are scattered across the sea.

sexes: When reading an encounter paragraph, you may occasionally notice a female character referred to as "he" or "him." Fear not; the woman has not drunk from the marvelous Sex-Change Spring in mid-sentence. We have chosen to use the masculine pronoun as the generic pronoun instead of the less elegant "he/she."

A Glossary of unfamiliar creatures and characters

FIGURE 7.3 Fear not, this shows the fallacy of the 'generic pronoun' as expressed in Tales of the Arabian Nights. (Photograph by the author.)

game **Queendomino** (2017). A gendered title may not be enough to put someone off a game, but it's part of the invisible language of assumptions made about for whom games are actually for.

Suffice to say, the idea that there is a 'generic pronoun' is an off-putting assumption. He/she may not be as elegant, but there are gender-neutral forms that are both grammatically appropriate and inclusive. Similarly, it's always possible to use 'the player' or provide second-person perspective text such as 'You take the card and pay the money' rather than 'He takes the card and pays the money'. **Tales of the Arabian Nights** is far from an isolated example though – games that assume their players are male are innumerable. That's been getting better in recent years, but it still remains an ongoing, persistent, and utterly correctible problem of exclusionary language.

There's a problem with regards to defaulting to female pronouns and characters too. **One Deck Dungeon** (2016) made the conscious choice to only have female characters playable in the game. Given the number of games that skew the other way, that's certainly a somewhat admirable way to address the imbalance. The problem is that inaccessibility remains even if its intentional – if there is a substantial population of women who want to play female characters, there is an equivalent population of men who want to play male characters. Exclusion in favour of either sex is still exclusion. As one review on Amazon put it, 'My boys and I have no interest in playing female characters'[2]. Denying players roles they can identify with – even through relatively noble motivations of addressing a historical imbalance – is a sociological inaccessibility. If players don't see a character they can identify with, they may choose instead to not play. It doesn't need to be male or female characters, of course – consider the number of people who identify with the car or the wee Scottie dug (as it should be written in proper Scots) in **Monopoly**. Denying people options is to deny yourself players.

Most games aren't quite so bad as to offer no options, but they do almost always set being a woman as the minority position – three male characters to one female character isn't an uncommon ratio. **Sheriff of Nottingham** (2014) as an example has six characters, and only one is a woman. And of course, she's the character associated with the 'hot pink' colour scheme.

The default 'background player' in much game art is a man, and most often a white man. But more than that, there's often a reflected power disparity. Judges, warriors, mages, scholars – men. When you see women, it is often in the context of caregiving – mothers and nurses – or they're temptresses and witches. **Kingdom Builder** (2011) actually does a better job of this than many games, as we can see in Figure 7.4. Women are citizens or they are discoverers. Everyone else is a man. But at least women get some agency – some of them get to go out exploring.

7 Wonders (2010, Figure 7.5) has a baths card which adopts the traditionally titillating 'hand-bra' pose for the women whereas the men are in positions of authority and power.

Then we have the many games where women are explicitly set up as sexualised figures for the male gaze. The original version of **Spyfall** (2014) drew on old-fashioned, misogynist cliches of double agents to explicitly objectify the women it portrays. Figure 7.6 shows four examples of this.

There are plenty of common offenses in board game representation: women who eschew sensible armour choices to show off the contours of their body, for example. We see that in lots of fantasy-themed games. Men go into the darkness encased in full-plate armour. The women, if they're lucky, get a leather bodice that leaves their vulnerable torso exposed.

FIGURE 7.4 Cards in Kingdom Builder. (Photograph by the author.)

The problem isn't sexualisation in and of itself – it's about the disparity in how characters are portrayed. Sculpted abs and naked torsos are perhaps fine if it's an aesthetic decision applied with equity. The problem lies in the old observation that 'Male characters are designed for male wish fulfilment. Female characters are also designed for male wish fulfilment'. The audience for a game is, or should be, broader than that. Remember wishes come in all different forms, from all different kinds of people.

Before we move on to the economic side of game design, let's first discuss two common responses to sociological accessibility issues in gaming. The first of these is **realism** – specifically that it's not realistic, for example, to have women Lords or

FIGURE 7.5 Cards from 7 Wonders. Note the card on the far left. (Photograph by the author.)

FIGURE 7.6   The timewarp sexism of Spyfall. (Photograph by the author.)

dark-skinned people in a medieval European context. I once described **Once Upon a Time (OUaT** 2012) as being 'aggressively white' because it has few, if any, non-white faces in its art – see Figure 7.7 for a small sampling. Someone objected – not unreasonably – on the grounds that the base game of **OUaT** is set in the context of European fairy tales and the art reflects that. The argument was it is realistic to have it represent what is largely a monoculture.

There are two problems though with this line of reasoning. The first is that historical records and contemporary art show that Europe was considerably more cosmopolitan than our white-washed histories may suggest. A deeper study of that is well outside the

FIGURE 7.7   A selection of the cards in Once Upon a Time. (Photograph by the author.)

scope of this book, but the interested scholar can find abundant evidence elsewhere. The bibliography for this chapter contains some starting resources. That point though is largely subservient to the second, more important, observation which is that **fairy tales aren't real**, and neither are the games based upon them.

For 'realism' to be a convincing defence against allegations of white-washing or gender bias, there needs to be a credible case made that the work is notably more realistic as a consequence. Games are abstractions. They're simplifications. For realism to carry weight, it must apply consistently to all levels of that abstraction. **Memoir 44** (2004) is a game of tactical warfare set during World War II, and historical fidelity to the theme is expressed in everything from the cards to the wider campaign. You can realistically say that **Memoir 44** takes its setting seriously and is trying to communicate something important about war in its design. At the level of abstraction through which it observes World War II, I think it's fair that women are not well represented in the gameplay mechanisms. However, that still represents a distortion of the truth. World War 2 had plenty of women as active combatants, particularly on the Russian front. *The Unwomanly Face of War* is a **must-read** treatment of the topic. The 'Night Witches' were an all-woman regiment of female military aviators. Women served in the Army Nurses Corps on the front lines as part of the US war effort. Germany marshalled around 500,000 uniformed women auxiliaries. Britain employed women extensively in the scenario testing that eventually won the Tonnage war. Women were a big, important part of World War II but not within the areas with which **Memoir 44** tends to occupy itself. Its fidelity to its abstraction is high. Its exclusion of women is, arguably, defensible.

Without that, realism is an unconvincing explanation because designers pick and choose what is important and what is not. Consider **Tales of the Arabian Nights** again – it states explicitly, as we see in Figure 7.8, that liberties were taken with the game's theme to change the historical tone for a more contemporary one when it comes to women.

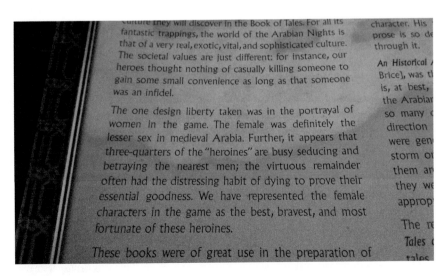

FIGURE 7.8 Tales of the Arabian Nights again. If you are willing to update or editorialise aspects for a modern audience, what does that say about the things for which you didn't do that? (Photograph by the author.)

Conan (2020) from Monolith did a similar thing when it came to Conan's typical ene-
mies – it smoothed over some portrayals that would in modern times count as intensely
problematic proxies for explicit racism. The problem is that the selectivity of these edits
shows that fidelity to the setting is not pre-eminent, and it casts an unfortunate contrast
on those elements that **weren't** altered for a modern audience. **Tales of the Arabian
Nights** remains homophobic and transphobic and worryingly keen on the 'inspiration
porn' of highlighting people with disabilities as being especially noble. **Conan** retains
the misogyny of the setting, with women frequently being little more than objects to be
carried around a game board. If 'truthiness' is to be honoured, you can't simply pick and
choose. And if it's not to be honoured, then what you choose **not** to change is as telling
as what you choose **to** change.

The second objection is that we can't judge old games by modern standards, and that
is genuinely fair. It would be easy to criticise games from the 1940s and 1950s in terms
of their portrayal of women and differing ethnicities. It wouldn't offer us any new insight
into design for a modern audience. The thing is though - every single game that gets
referenced in this book was widely available for purchase, in the edition in which it was
analysed, within the five years previous to the date of publication. These are not historical artefacts. These are games you can, by and large, purchase now and play now. Their
continued presence as commercial outputs indicates a degree of implicit support for
their content. Sometimes new editions come along and address some of these problems,
and that's great. Not all games and not all new editions are improvements.

Finally in this section, we're going to talk about business models and how they can
create inaccessibilities. We've already introduced the topic of 'gee whizz, games are
expensive', but that can manifest in different ways. The **X-Wing Miniatures Game**
(second edition, 2018) is a genuinely wonderful miniatures-based tabletop experience.
It takes all the excitement of X-Wings duelling TIE fighters and converts it almost loss-
lessly into a game of plastic and cards. And it certainly looks **sort of** affordable. The
'standalone' box is £43 on Amazon, which puts it well below the average at which we
already boggled earlier in this chapter.

The problem is that you don't buy the game with the standalone box. You buy a taste of
it. A sampler. The core box contains one single X-Wing figure and two TIE fighters. It's
not so much an epic battle between good and evil as it is a pub-brawl in a supermarket
car-park. There's no Millenium Falcon, no Slave-1, and no imperial destroyer – none of
the ships you might want to field in a battle. You can **get** them, sure – but be prepared
to dig deep into what may already be a wallet that is screaming. It's another £44 to
bring Han Solo's ship into the battle, £32 if you're a Boba Fett fan, and £100 if you want
to bring the massive Tantive IV into play. Individual ships (A-Wings, B-Wings, and
experimental TIE fighters and bombers) are often £15 each. Really, to have a chance at
a satisfying X-Wing battle, you need a **minimum** of two standalone sets. You can incrementally buy into an expensive game over time but don't expect to see the game actually
unveil itself until you've gone way beyond the cost of the starter set.

That's a common thing in all miniatures games, but it's a business model that has
become more common in games that don't have 'expensive plastic' as a reason for their
eye-watering cost. Consider as another example the **Arkham Horror Card Game**
(2016), which has a core set that costs £62 at time of writing. This is a genuinely excellent game of deckbuilding fun – you may remember deckbuilding from our chapter on
cognitive accessibility – where you build characters through cards and then send them
off to combat eldritch horrors within unsettling locales.

The problem is that this game employs a business model that, to me, is almost indistinguishable from a long con. The original version of the core set only supported two players, and if you wanted four, you'd need to buy a second box to give yourself enough cards and components. The revised version comes with enough cards for four players, with a notably steeper buy-in price. But that's not even where the problem is – it's that you don't even get a full story in the box. This is a game of horror, and horror thrives in the unexpected and the unanticipated. Sure, you can play through the scenarios provided many times (as in common in such games), but you'll find them becoming less and less effective because you'll know all the story beats and the horrifying revelations. You are almost required to keep buying expansions and story packs to keep experiencing the 'high'. If you'd bought the first iteration of the **Dunwich Legacy** 'deluxe' expansion (£30 in 2016), you'd get two new scenarios and would have to buy an additional six as separate purchases. The new Dunwich expansion does at least come with all of the story packs, but it costs a correspondingly eye-watering £70 for eight scenarios. Each will give – if you're lucky – about two hours of exciting fresh horror.

This isn't a mandatory feature of these kind of living card games (LCGs) though. **Game of Thrones: The Card Game** (2015) is perfectly replayable dozens of times using only the base set because it's not a game where a large part of the experience lies in the unknown. It makes further buy-in genuinely optional – you continue based on intentional desire. I would argue that the **Arkham Horror Card Game** is designed around a relationship model that you only really see in catfishing on social media.

The problem here, from an accessibility perspective, isn't really in how much the game costs. It's how **opaque** the **real** cost of a game can be. It's one thing to say 'It's £60 but at least we can play this a hundred times', and 'It's £60 and now that I have bought it I know that all it takes is £200 more to have fun with it'!

We're not quite done here though with troublesome socioeconomic factors. Player counts are an issue because the design of most games is often at odds with what is feasibly available for any given game night. The standard two to four players is fine for an engineered games evening for two couples, but it suffers in circumstances where larger families may wish to play together, especially extended families. A specific player count with no variation can make social events fragile. Games that require large numbers of players likewise ask a lot of social capital and space, and we've already discussed how these are luxuries. **Telestrations** (2009) is a game that really only works at six players and only gets really good at eight. That's a player count that basically means it can only be played at larger game nights, and it needs **eight people** to want to play it **at the same time.**

Sometimes when you buy a game you're just purchasing the frustration of never being able to play it. The more flexible a player count, the more easily it slips into the sociological context of complex lives. It's entirely possible to have hundreds of games available and yet nothing that you can play with the people who are here with you right now.

These issues, as we have discussed, interleave and interconnect – as do the manifestations of the problem. Consider for example how much of the positive diversity represented in modern Star Wars is often locked away in game expansions. The original trilogy wasn't exactly a shining example of inclusion, so it rankles a little when you need to buy a £40 expansion to include 'people like me' in the roster of available choices. It makes sense from a structural perspective of monetising a property, especially one built around a franchise that has only recently started to become inclusive in its outlook. It's still a problem that some groups of people need to spend more to unlock opportunities for identification.

One final socioeconomic inaccessibility to be discussed here is in the environmental cost of certain games. To be fair, board games are basically a rounding error in this category of consumerism. Gamers, overall, treat their board games tremendously well and in a lot of ways the hobby is a poster child for the circular economy. The environmental cost of a board game comes from its creation and shipping and then largely dips to zero. Games are kept for a long time, and when it's time for them to go, it's usually through a transfer of ownership. Board games retain their value on the secondary market very well – some even increase in value as they move out of regular production and become sought-after collectibles. A board game that cannot be sold is more likely to be stripped for spare parts (meeples, dice, cubes, and so on) than it is to be thrown out. As such, it's rare when the destiny of a board game is in a landfill.

That said, it's not as if there aren't improvements that can be made. Board game boxes are regularly much larger than they need to be – often mostly what a game box holds is air. That's a waste of materials, normally as a consequence of games needing to battle for consumer attention on the shelves of a game shop. It's a shipping inefficiency, requiring more pallets, more containers, and more fuel. Many games contain lots of cardboard tokens that need to be punched out, and the leftover frames are usually discarded. There's more shrink-wrap involved in game production than there should be. And probably no-one other than a drug dealer is likely to have so many plastic baggies within easy reach as your average board gamer – that's another related environmental cost.

Within this framing of 'upfront environmental cost and then largely carbon neutral', we then have things like the **Exit** series of board games. They're designed as explicitly 'one-play' escape rooms, where part of the game requires the destruction of game components. Sometimes this is so solutions can be revealed – for example, poking a pin through one page of a booklet to identify an area of interest underneath or folding sheets of paper in particular ways to reveal new information. Sometimes cards are ripped up. Sometimes components are explicitly cut with scissors so they become puzzle pieces for another part of the room. You play through these games once and then you throw them out. This permits for the design of some genuinely innovative puzzles. When you compare though **Exit** versus the similar **Unlock** games – which can be played and then passed along, fully intact – it does seem alarmingly wasteful.

We can see a similar trend in Legacy games, where each session results in a change for all games to follow. You might annotate a board with stickers or open mystery boxes to add new components. Often you'll be asked to permanently destroy cards, or write on player aids, or change the manual.

In both of these examples, once the game is finished you're left with a choice of what happens next. Sometimes people frame the boards of their legacy games and turn them into wall art. Sometimes they just throw out the box. These games have no secondary market value because they are not complete, transferable experiences. The best have purchasable 'recharge kits' that allow for a modified game to be returned to its original state, but only a handful offer this. Otherwise, nobody wants to play a defaced copy of a game when all the juice has been sucked out of it. It's like trying to 'solve' a completed crossword puzzle in a second-hand newspaper.

Games with Good Socioeconomic Design

If those are some of the problems, what are some of the good examples that we'd recommend people look to?

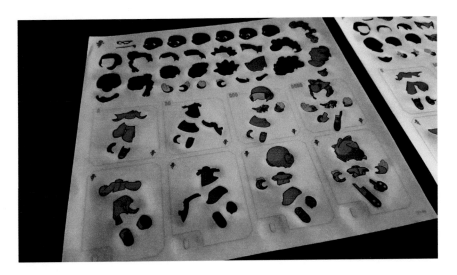

FIGURE 7.9 Stickers from Prisma Arena. (Photograph by the author.)

There's a game which – as far as I'm concerned – basically solved the inclusion problem the minute you open the box. It's **Prisma Arena** (2020) and it works by putting representation directly into the hands of the players. Instead of giving you some pre-defined characters and asking you to choose, it gives you a locker room and a bunch of stickers and invites you to make the character you want to be. It's fantastic – it's like they transplanted the character creator from the Sims into a board game (Figure 7.9).

You choose outfits, hair styles, and accessories and whatever else are provided. One of the issues with 'top down' choices when it comes to representation is the combinatorial explosion it implies. It's one thing for players to be able to choose from a selection representing different sexes, different genders, and different skin colours. What about the combination of these? It's awesome if there's a character in a wheelchair, but what if I want to see that character in other manifestations? The stickers of Prisma Arena are a genius solution, and they're also infinitely flexible. If there's something missing, release a new sticker pack. I did complain in the previous section about representation being hidden behind additional costs but I think that's mostly an issue when you need to spend £40 to see someone like you in a game. It'd be different if you could buy a pack of stickers for a couple of quid.

For games that can't, or won't, go this far, there are other options. Consider the flippable player board that shows men on one side and women on the other. **Fog of Love** (2017) does this, and it takes what could be a fraught issue of representation and instantly reframes what could be unpleasantly heteronormative. The blue card shows a man. The pink card shows a woman. That's a problem until you realise if you flip them you'll get a blue woman and a pink man. It's still not ideal because it's a binary that doesn't accommodate other personal identities, but it's still better than making a fixed choice in design and expecting players to be happy with it. **Oh My Goods** (2015) similarly allows you to flip your worker and apprentice cards from men to women, and the player boards in **Roll Player** (2016) are likewise double-sided. While it doesn't give the flexibility of stickers, it gives **some** flexibility and we shouldn't allow perfect to become the enemy of the good.

The Resistance (2009) and **Coup** (2012, Figure 7.10) – games which are broadly set in the same dystopian universe – go a step further with representation in that they make

FIGURE 7.10   Diversity as storytelling in Coup. (Photograph by the author.)

everyone, regardless of what role they play in the game, look **absolutely bad-ass** while also reflecting a diverse makeup.

Diversity is sometimes implemented in games as a kind of tokenism – a change of skin tone here, a few feminising features there. **Coup** and **The Resistance** are excellent examples of a much better approach – diversity **as storytelling.** The world which these characters inhabit is clearly globalised, clearly one in which women are skilled and of high stature, and one in which high society fashions are excitingly othering. It would be much easier to portray the future as being full of white billionaires, but the setting becomes meaningfully less vibrant as a result. Attaining diverse representation isn't, or shouldn't, be an exercise in compliance. It's an opportunity to reflect the interesting variety of the world as it genuinely **is** or as it genuinely **would be.**

For those looking to the past for inspiration, it's a way to counteract the often literal whitewashing of the historical record. In the middle ages, it was common for ancient paintings of – for example – dark-skinned magi to be retouched so they were instead light-skinned. That shouldn't be a surprise – enhancing or diminishing racial characteristics still happens through the power of Photoshop. If you're aiming for realism in an aesthetic, then make sure what you are reflecting is genuinely real and not a result of historical revisionism. Your games will be much cooler as a result.

When it comes to business models, really the only thing that works is to keep the price down into an affordable frame while ensuring that the cost implications are transparent. Some business models rely on a degree of game literacy to carry the emphasis to the buyer. If one starts playing a collectible card game (CCG) like **Magic**, one should assume that it comes with ongoing costs through buying booster packs until you find the cards you need. LCGs on the other hand are expected to be fuelled through the regular purchasing of fixed update packs. That's something you know going in if you are aware of the vocabulary.

That's often used as a dismissal of those who find the financial outlay to be out of scale with their expectations – 'you should have done your research'. However, to argue that is to dismiss a very significant proportion of the population who might become gamers provided they don't feel burned in the process of exploring their options. And it also omits the vast audience of people 'buying games for other people'.

The other option that designers and publishers have is offering a sliding scale of **quality**. Some publishers will make their games available as print and play versions, asking nothing of their players other than some of their time. **Secret Hitler** (2016), **Funemployed** (2013), **Cards Against Humanity** (2009), **Tiny Epic Galaxies** (2015), and more come with official print and play downloads. These let people play a low-fidelity version of the game that they can later convert into a full purchase when they see the need. You can't argue with 'free' as a price point. **Thousand Year Old Vampire** (2020), a solo journaling Role-Playing Game (RPG), makes its PDF available through a 'pay what you like' model that also explicitly includes 'free if you want it'.

Scaling what is in the box to price can also help too – it's always great to get a handful of custom metal coins and nice figurines in a box, but often cardboard counters and tokens would be just as effective. The others can be offered as additional 'bling' or kept as part of a deluxe edition. The collectors in the community will still pay for things at the highest price points, but it opens up a whole bunch of consumers at the lower level. Even better if they're available as deluxe upgrades rather than only available as a separate purchase.

Games with Interesting Socioeconomic Design

As usual, let's wind up the broader discussion here with some hopefully interesting examples of games that don't fit neatly into the dynamic of 'this is good' and 'this is bad'. We'll start with some of the art from **Five Tribes** (2014, Figure 7.11).

I think this is interesting because any perceived objectification can be defended from multiple perspectives. It's a bit like the video game character Bayonetta, a witch who

FIGURE 7.11 The bottom left corner of the Five Tribes box. (Photograph by the author.)

uses her hair for magic and for clothing and so when she casts spells she ends up partially nudifying herself. For many, that's objectifying and Bayonetta is a problematic character as a result. For others, it's clear that she is absolutely in her element with it and they perceive it instead as empoweringly provocative. That debate rages on.

Whether any particular element of portrayal is likely to be problematic varies from person to person, but one useful rule of thumb relates to 'what is the portrayal supposed to communicate to the person that sees it'. Everything about this kind of art should be part of how a story is told – it's about depth of characterisation. A woman who is half-naked on a cover for no obvious reason is clearly an issue. If she's half-naked in a way that deepens your understanding of the character, the situation becomes less stark. We can see with **Five Tribes** that we're dealing with an assassin or similar warrior type, and as such her outfit could certainly be seen as character building. 'She uses her sensuality to get close to her victims'. You can close your eyes and visualise how she insinuates herself into a position of what seems like vulnerability before she dispatches her target with ruthless efficiency. You can see a steely resolve in her eyes and a firm determination in the set of her jaw. Is her portrayal objectification or is it characterisation? It's not for me to say in the end, but this is a guiding principle to bear in mind – all of your aesthetic choices should be part of telling the story you want to tell. If you find that your characterisation relies on secondary assumptions regarding sex, gender, or ethnicity – that's a red flag.

Some of you may have an obvious objection to suggestions regarding the objectification present in **Five Tribes**. 'Yeah, but it's the desert and the desert is hot'. That is a fair point and we should never lose sight of context. If that was the reason for the outfit though, we need to ask why the man beside her is in a full beard and robe. He must be boiling. If there is no deeper message being told in this kind of representation, it comes back to the topic of parity – if the women are portrayed half-dressed and sensual, the men should be too.

This is why so many people balk at, for example, Figure 7.12. I picked this image specifically because it is not an outlier or particularly extreme. Rather it underlines the

FIGURE 7.12   An unwise choice of armour in Legend of Drizzt. (Photograph by the author.)

FIGURE 7.13 A sampling of women characters in Mage Wars: Arena. (Photograph by the author.)

larger point of what portrayal means for storytelling. What actual purpose, other than objectification, does it serve an archer to leave her most vulnerable midsection unarmoured? Why would she leave a space in the armour between her breasts (what we often call 'the cleavage window') for an arrow, sword, or dagger to more easily slip in?

All this adds to the story of who this person may be is 'she certainly don't know what armour is for'. Everything from the almost ubiquitous 'boob plate' to 'battle panties' and the many examples of armour that is interchangeable with lingerie – they undercut characterisation; they don't add to it. See also Figure 7.13 for a collage of artwork taken from Mage Wars: Arena (2012).

Guidelines for Socioeconomic Accessibility

- *Games to look to for inspiration*:
  - Prisma Arena, Perudo, Legacy of Dragonholt, The Mind, Tsuro, Inhuman Conditions, New York Slice, and Hanamikoji.
- *Games to look to as cautionary tales*:
  - Exit: The Game, Tales of the Arabian Nights, Arkham Horror: The Card Game, and Cards Against Humanity.

Text

Aim for Inclusive Language in the Game, Box, and Title

It's easy to be casually exclusionary in language choice if it is pitched – intentionally or otherwise – to specific audiences, particularly those to whom we will naturally default. Even the order in which you list things sends messages regarding the perceived importance of those things. Avoid the problematic assumption that gendered pronouns or words will be read as inclusive. Similarly, when explaining game mechanisms through worked examples and example players, try to ensure you are drawing from a diverse range and offering gender ambiguity – not 'Bill, Jim, Eric, and Bob' but perhaps 'Sam, Chadi, Aya, and Mohammad'.

Remember too your box will be the first thing people see of your game, and the title is often the most obvious part of the box. Exclusionary titling can set the tone of your game right from the get go.

- Aim for a title that does not skew the audience towards any particular gender assumption.
- Make use of gender-neutral pronouns throughout unless referencing specific characters.
- Use inclusive text through the manual and game components.
- When providing worked examples, use the names of a diverse range of people.

Make Minimal Assumptions Regarding Game Literacy

It is common when writing game instructional material, or developing game content, to make assumptions of knowledge. The use of jargon is common, with certain short-hand terminology serving the job of efficiently communicating recurring concepts. 'Shuffle your discard pile into your deck and draw five cards face-down into your hand' is a clear, unambiguous instruction, provided one knows the difference between a deck, a pile, a hand and understands the concept of a discard and also the distinction between face-down and face-up. It can be stigmatising to admit one doesn't know words or concepts with which everyone else is familiar, so try to limit unintentional gatekeeping.

- Avoid the use of terms and language that presume players have read, watched, or consumed particular media content.
- When making use of common game-related jargon, include a definition and glossary for players less familiar with the vocabulary.

General Aesthetics

Aim for Inclusive Art

Modern board games are beautiful objects, and a lot of that is down to the art and the production values. Since the art is such an important, visual part of a game, it's proportionally important that it reflects the makeup of the kind of people you want to be playing. Avoid relying on 'realism' as an explanation for reflecting homogenous cultural groups unless you truly want your game assessed on the basis of its fidelity to its setting. Even if realism is an accurate reason, consider whether it is important enough to sacrifice an inclusive feel for players and of course whether your understanding of realism reflects the true facts.

- Aim for a diversity of sex, gender, and ethnicity in character art in the game and in the box.
- When representing different ethnicities, sexes, and genders, consider prominence and context of representation.

- If drawing from a particular time period, consider taking the opportunity to boost the profile of marginalised people from diverse groups that history may not have given fair recognition.
- Include representation of people with various categories of disability and impairment.
- Include intersectional representation, such as varied ethnicities with varied sexes and genders and varied represented disabilities.
- Avoid heteronormative or gender-normative game aesthetics and mechanics.
- Avoid sexual objectification of men and women in the artwork. Dress characters for their likely environment or ensure sexualised representations hold true for equal proportions of all represented sexes and genders.

Give Players Options for Representation

While many players will not care either way, there are those who feel uncomfortable in circumstances where they cannot choose a character in game that is similar to them or of a type they feel most comfortable playing. The more your game does to bridge the gap between the character and the player, the more the player will feel the game has been designed with them in mind.

- Consider the use of double-sided player representations showing characters with different genders and ethnicities.
- If sex or gendered character roles are required, ensure a proportional balance for each option.
- Consider too representation of factors such as skin tone, hair style, body shapes, and more.
- If feasible, consider the use of stickers and other ornamentations that allow players to customise miniatures, cards, and player boards.

Be Respectful of Your Subject Matter

A lot of the concepts in this chapter require deep familiarity with complex conditions and how they manifest. Game mechanics can be offensively reductive or simplified to the point of being harmful. When including potentially sensitive subject matter, ensure that you do not accidentally end up with trivialised portrayals. If you don't know enough to recognise it yourself, consult with someone who does.

- Avoid reductive representations of complex conditions, such as mental health.
- Avoid potentially stigmatising or infantilising tropes such as 'insanity gauges' or 'inspirational disability'.
- Avoid cultural cliches about disabilities, ethnicities, sexes, and genders.

Rules

Consider the Subtext of Mechanisms

One of the common things that occurs as part of 'sociological storytelling' is that game mechanisms can end up sending unintended messages. Everything – from the words we use to the colours we ascribe components – conveys meaning. It is important to carefully consider what your game mechanics are saying, even if you didn't intend on them saying anything.

- Avoid explicit or implied racism, homophobia, and transphobia in game systems and surrounding elements unless justified by context.
- Be careful as to which roles within a game are ascribed which representational elements – certain colour choices mapped to certain mechanics for example.
- Be very wary of ascribing evil, uneducated, or malicious intention to game antagonists where physical characteristics are the primary differentiating factor.
- Consider the sociocultural implications of asymmetrical character powers.
- Avoid heteronormative or gender-normative game mechanics.

Support a Wide Range of Player Counts

Few things feel quite as exclusionary as seeing everyone playing a game that you have to sit out due to player count. There's only so much that can be done within the constraints of a design, but if there are opportunities to support alternative player counts, or to allow for easy inclusion of late-arriving players, this can massively reduce the need to exclude individuals during game play.

- Aim for scalable player counts – too few players can make it difficult for family game nights, too many difficult for smaller groups.
- Include variants to allow for solo play or for large group play.
- Consider providing automata to fill in for absent players in larger player-count games.
- If it's possible to add players in mid-game, add some mechanisms to support this.
- Add in, where feasible, 'audience participation' systems or simply ensure the game is entertaining to observe.

Be Careful Where You're Punching

The inclusion of intentionally transgressive material is a valid design choice, whether it is for serious commentary or simple comedy. Making jokes at the expense of others can be absolutely appropriate for the feeling you want people to have coming away from the game. However, such things tend to be more effective when they are mindful where they are throwing punches. Punching down (the powerful making fun of the disempowered) or punching up (the disempowered making fun of the powerful) are fine, provided you know that's what you're doing and are happy to accept the consequences.

- When employing 'edgy' content, consider the degree to which it 'punches up' or 'punches down' and whether that's what you want.
- If aiming to be an equal opportunity offender, you should be sure that you punch everywhere in equal proportion.

Business Models

Consider the Cost to Your Intended Players

While many hobbyists may not care about spending hundreds of pounds on a prestige board game, Monopoly remains the anchor point for most of the potential 'new' market in gaming. For many buyers, value is an important consideration and it comes from perceptions of replayability, flexibility in player counts, and flexibility in social context. In order to make a meaningful determination there, it must also be the case that purchasers are aware in advance of the financial commitment needed to have the promised amount of fun from a game.

- Consider the cost of the game as a 'per player' value and see if there is scope for making the financial burden scale to this.
- Ensure the expected level of buy-in for a 'minimum viable product' is clearly communicated ahead of the first purchase.

Offer Responsible Expandable Content

Expansions are a wonderful way to inject new life into an overly familiar board game. When it is clear that they are designed to offer more from an already complete experience, there is little to which someone can object. However, some expansions make it clear that the 'vanilla' game is an intentionally stripped down version of something designed to be bigger. Expansions too can be problematic when they do not guarantee content (such as in booster packs), compensate for fundamental shortcomings in the original, or duplicate large portions of other content with only a few additional elements.

- If your game is expandable, make sure the base game represents as much diversity as possible. Don't require people to buy expansions for base representation.
- When putting together a game with a collectible or expandable aspect, make sure that the core fun of a game is meaningfully expressed in the base box or starter set.
- When designing a collectible game with random drops, try to avoid rare cards being meaningfully more powerful than less rare cards.
- If the business model works around selling expansions or additional models to inject new novelty, consider the value proposition presented and how many times a game might be played before a new expansion is required.
- If novelty of narrative is a game deliverable, strive to provide regular points of conclusion into the expansion cycles.
- Don't release multiple versions of the same game, with the only difference being box colour and the absence/presence of a rule or component variation.

Minimise Unnecessary Mandatory Expenses

One of the things that heavily influences the cost of a board game is production value. In some cases, such as quality of card stock and clarity of printing, these are clearly appropriate and worthwhile from an accessibility perspective. However, many board games come with large numbers of 'prestige' components that do not substantively add to the game experience for many players. Metal coins, pre-painted miniatures, and more all fall into this category. Where possible, these should be separated out into deluxe editions or luxury upgrades so as to keep the price of the base product as low as possible.

- Avoid 'overproduced' components like moulded plastic miniatures when equally functional, less expensive components like tokens or standees can be used in their place.
- Consider the availability of print and play variations of your game.
- Offload 'bling' into luxury expansions or deluxe editions.

Limit the Environmental Impact of Your Production

Box size, shrink-wrap, and amount of discardable cardboard all of these contribute to the upfront environmental cost of your game. A full accounting of how to minimise your environmental impact is outside the scope of this book and even further outside the author's area of expertise. However, it is clear that less waste leads to less cost and that the design of certain games creates problems that could perhaps be designed out.

- Minimise the size of a game box, conforming as far as is possible to one of the standard form factors.
- Minimise as far as is possible the amount of shrink-wrap in a game.
- Minimise as far as is possible the amount of cardboard that needs to be thrown out after tokens are punched.
- If a game involves annotation of game components, consider offering a 'recharge' kit that allows a game to be returned to its baseline state.
- Minimise or eliminate the need to destroy or deface game components.

Notes

1. https://shrinkthatfootprint.com/how-big-is-a-house/
2. https://www.amazon.com/gp/customer-reviews/R1BNZWP3S6S0LE/ ref=cm_cr_getr_d_rvw_ttl?ie=UTF8&ASIN=B01NBIJZAN
   There is a worthwhile point in here amongst all the weird conspiracy theorising.

BIBLIOGRAPHY

Alexievich, S. (2018). *The unwomanly face of war: An oral history of women in World War II*. Random House Trade Paperbacks.

Bagues, M., & Perez-Villadoniga, M. J. (2013). Why do I like people like me? *Journal of Economic Theory, 148*(3), 1292–1299.

Demby, G. (2013). Taking a magnifying glass to the brown faces in medieval art. Code switch: Frontiers of race, culture, and ethnicity. *NPR*, 13. https://www.npr.org/sections/codeswitch/2013/12/13/250184740/taking-a-magnifying-glass-to-the-brown-faces-in-medieval-art

Erickson, J. (1990). Night witches snipers and laundresses. *History Today, 40*(7), 29–35.

Furnham, A., & Boo, H. C. (2011). A literature review of the anchoring effect. *The Journal of Socio-Economics, 40*(1), 35–42.

Monahan, E., & Neidel-Greenlee, R. (2007). And if I perish: Frontline us army nurses in World War II. United States: Knopf Doubleday Publishing Group.

Niedermeier, K. E. (2009). Predictably irrational: The hidden forces that shape our decisions. *Journal of Pension Economics & Finance, 8*(2), 249–250.

Parkin, S. (2020). *A game of birds and wolves: The ingenious young women whose secret board game helped win World War II.* Hachette UK.

Perez, C. C. (2019). *Invisible women: Data bias in a world designed for men.* Abrams.

Strack, F., & Mussweiler, T. (1997). Explaining the enigmatic anchoring effect: Mechanisms of selective accessibility. *Journal of Personality and Social Psychology, 73*(3), 437.

8

Communicative Accessibility

We're coming to the end now of our main categories of accessibility, and we're going to wrap up here with the one that is perhaps best served already by board games. This is a differentiating factor between board games and video games, in that video games tend to be auditorily complex as a matter of course. Densely layered soundscapes create a challenging environment for deaf players, but the expected standard of accessibility is quite high. Subtitles, closed captioning, and alternatives to voiced communication are either culturally or legally mandated.

Board games on the other hand rarely have sound at all – games have to explicitly decide to include this channel of information, and only a comparative handful really do. The complexity of an accompanying soundscape is entirely in the hands of the players at the table – maybe you have music playing in the background or loud children in another room. Maybe you don't.

Likewise, actually communicating within most board games is a matter of choice rather than a mandatory part of the game. There's some common game etiquette around narrating what you do on your turn, but that's mostly a matter of convention rather than design. If a board game stresses communication between players, it has to be put there intentionally. As per our discussion in Chapter 1 – it's presumably there for a reason.

The only area where we regularly see communication issues in tabletop gaming as a whole is in language – for example, written manuals and text on game components. Even this is only a problem if games are presented in a language that a player does not understand.

The issue is that when communication **does** matter, then it **really** matters.

As usual, before we get into the design discussion, let's talk about what communication impairments mean in the context of this book. We're going to break them into three broad categories:

- *Expression*: This relates to a player's ability to communicate ideas and intention in a way that is clearly understandable to others at the table. Someone with a speech impediment for example may experience inaccessibilities in this area.
- *Reception*: Thisrelates to a player's ability to understand and interpret the expression of other players at a table. Someone who is deaf, or has an auditory processing disorder, may be impacted here.
- *Cultural*: This relates to the ability of a player to turn received expressed information into a comprehensible form. The complexity of language, the specificity of idiom, and exclusionary in-jokes are all relevant here.

DOI: 10.1201/9781003415435-8

These are just internal definitions for our convenience, though. Medical definitions of communication disorders can cut across all of these, and we often see four primary groupings:

1. *Speech disorders*: It impact on how individuals can create or form the sounds of speech.
2. *Language disorders*: This relates to both the expression and reception of language cues.
3. *Hearing disorders*: These are concerned with recognising or understanding auditory information.
4. *Processing disorders*: These relate to how auditory information is interpreted and contextualised.

We're grouping them differently from this because how these conditions manifest in gaming can be complex. For example, in normal everyday life, it's entirely possible that sign language is a 100% effective alternative to speech, provided all participants in a conversation are fluent. This is a translation of communication that does not work equivalently well in the constrained circumstances of games. We'll see why later. We're most concerned about accessibility rather than diagnosis or treatment.

To get a fuller grasp of how these conditions may manifest though, let's spend a little time going over the four primary medical groupings.

Speech disorders are not just related to the ability to vocally form parts of words, although that is a major component of many manifestations. *Articulation disorders* are usually linked to structural differences in the muscles and bones, resulting in speech patterns significantly at variance with the majority of the population. This is often a physiological condition. *Phonological disorders* often manifest similarly, with the key difference being not in the forming of sounds but in the correct application of the **context** of sounds. For these, there may be no obvious corresponding physical source, but others are related to cognitive processing complexities.

These are distinct from *disfluency disorders* such as stuttering and cluttering. These create atypicality in the rhythm of how speech is expressed. Stuttering often manifests as a kind of breakpoint in speech, where particular combinations of sounds are difficult to articulate and result in repetition until the breakpoint can be breached. Cluttering is the opposite, as if the brakes on conversation have been cut – it manifests as rapid speech, words that run together, or parts of words simply never being expressed.

Language disorders relate not to the expression of sound but rather how sound should be constructed and understood. Typically we break language up into several conceptual groupings known as *domains*:

- *Phonology*: This relates to the rules by which distinct units of sound (phonemes) may be combined and applied. This relates to capabilities such as spelling, understanding how the sound of letters associate to their symbols, and the broader phonological awareness required to recognise words as being made of building blocks.
- *Syntax*: This is how words, made up of phonemes, may be combined to create larger groupings such as sentences. Syntax relates to the ability to perceive and replicate sentence structure and to properly associate the composite parts of a sentence with their role.

- *Morphology*: This relates to how phonemes become morphemes, which are the minimal units of meaning within a language. This also plays an important role in spelling, but also in terms of grammar.
- *Semantics*: This relates to the definitions ascribed to morphemes and larger syntactic groupings. The primary impact here is in vocabulary.
- *Pragmatics*: This is the set of rules that govern relevance and appropriateness of words in a cultural context, essentially knowing what to say, how it should be said, and when it should be said.

Someone with *dyslexia* for example may experience difficulties with *phonological awareness* – particularly in writing – as well as in *syntax*. Others with particular kinds of autism may instead find impossible complexity to be found within the *pragmatics* of language such as understanding the need to wait for others to stop speaking or contextualising the tone shift required between a funeral and a wedding.

Hearing disorders relate to the conditions that prevent someone from interpreting audio information at full capacity. This can not only impact on comprehension but also on the ability to replicate sounds that have been experienced in conversation. People who are categorised as deaf will most commonly have experienced nerve damage that results in very little functional hearing. This may be correctible to an extent with accessibility tools such as cochlear implants and hearing aids, but such compensations will rarely serve to return full auditory range and precision. Those with cochlear implants for example may be able to have a perfectly functional conversation but be unable to enjoy music. It may end up resolved into buzzes, and beeps, with the pitch and timbre of the sound being at best a clumsy approximation. Others experience no problems. As with everything, it's a wide spectrum.

Those that are hard of hearing will still be capable of receiving auditory information, but the accuracy and reliability may be compromised. It may manifest only in one ear, for example, or fluctuate in severity in line with external factors. *Sensorineural hearing loss* (damage to the hearing system) often occurs in those with a long history of attending loud concerts; regularly being in the vicinity of loud noises; and naturally occurs as part of the aging process. It can be sudden, occurring immediately or over a few days, or gradual. Sudden loss can sometimes be reversed if the core cause is found and treated immediately. Otherwise, the hearing loss is most often permanent.

Conductive hearing loss relates to obstructions in the outer or middle ear, such as through a build-up of earwax or through the presence of foreign matter in the ear canal. Bone abnormalities, ear canal deformities, and infections may likewise result in conductive hearing loss. It may be correctible through medical intervention, but not always.

Finally, we have the category of *processing disorders* that relate to disruptions in how the brain understands auditory information. It's not hearing loss in the sense we have previously discussed – the information is received by the brain, it's just interpreted atypically. This category includes things such as *hypersensitivity* (being overly sensitive to sounds or being unable to apply auditory filters to background noise), *decoding* (unable to correctly process audio information into its constituent bits), *integration* (a difficulty combining multiple channels of information), *prosody* (difficulty understanding the cues around audio information), and *organisation* (difficulty with multi-tasking, sequences, and impulse control).

Thus, we come back to the way in which we address this topic in this chapter – a medical lens is too complex for our purposes. We just want to make things easier for our players. We don't care so much if a communication impairment comes from permanent hearing loss or is a consequence of hypersensitivity to background noise. We just want to make sure our games work as best they can for those who have difficulty with auditory information. With that in mind, let's move on to some examples of games we can use as benchmarks.

For all of these games, let's work from a set of common assumptions:

- Everyone at the table has already learned the game (so language issues around manuals are out of scope – for now)
- Everyone at the table is able to communicate to a reasonable level in a shared form. They all speak the same language for example.

We hold these to be true because the complexity of the makeup of a group is incredibly important here but primarily as an intensifier. Imagine a group of French speakers, another group of Spanish speakers, and a guy (usually me) who only speaks English. All of the problems we talk about here just get worse, to the point a game may not be playable at all. We however have no control over who plays a game, but only how the game presents itself to its players.

Problematic Communication Contexts

Let's start here with **The Resistance**, which we have already discussed in our chapter on emotional accessibility but has new complexities here. Some of the aspects of this game are already clear. It requires adversarial communication. You need to convince people who have a vested interest in not being convinced. You have to fight to be heard in the hubbub of an argument. You have people acting at cross purposes, attempting to undermine everything you say through obfuscation and outright falsehoods.

Right away we can see something here – the goals of a game that stresses communication are often at odds with the norms in which communication compensations are experienced. In normal everyday conversation, we can usually assume people will be trying to come to a common understanding or at least be prepared to find some common ground. In **The Resistance**, there are parties (the bad guys) who have a game role that requires the deconstruction of common understanding, which they can do through all kinds of techniques:

- Drowning out problematic information by speaking loudly over another person or interjecting to undermine their contribution.
- Intentionally injecting false information, or faulty conclusions, into the miasma of accusation and counter-accusation that forms every round of **The Resistance**.
- Taking advantage of miscommunication or misunderstandings to undermine the reliability of those getting too close to the truth.
- Avoiding giving an opportunity to contribute to someone who has information they'd prefer nobody received.

This is all exactly how the game should go if everyone is on equal footing. Consider though the situation of a player using sign language trying to gain the attention of a whole table full of people. People who are already fully cognitively loaded with conducting the discussion in its current form. In everyday conversation, a group of friends can be assumed in most cases to be willing to make pauses in a discussion so as to allow full contribution by all participants. Here, imagine being a government agent knowing that a player using sign language can prove you're a bad guy – why would you stop everyone's arguing to say 'Listen to the person that will be able to finger me as a traitor'?

Even if you're not struggling to make a point over the protestations of other players, those with reception impairments may find the whole thing impossible to follow. Lip-reading for example requires intense attention to be paid to a small number of people at any one time, and they may not be the ones saying the most valuable things. Voices at a similar level may be difficult to separate out for people with an auditory processing disorder, and the nature of the conversation may be such that it's really several smaller conversations between ever changing groups of people.

This style of 'vibrant arguments over partial information' is common to games of this nature. **One Night Ultimate Werewolf**, **Secret Hitler**, **Spyfall**, **Blood on the Clocktower** (2022), and many others – they all work on this system of giving a piece of the puzzle to different players while also undermining the case for why you should believe any information you get. They're games about forcing new information into the game but only on your own terms. They don't work so great for people with communication impairments when other players are incentivised to diminish the clarity of uncomfortable contributions.

Chinatown (1999) is my single favourite board game despite its often problematic aspects – poor availability, and some unfortunately challenging portrayals of the immigrant Chinese experience. However, it's also a game that shows that issues around communication are not limited to social deduction. They're also prevalent in games where it's necessary for a player to convince another of something more generally. In **Chinatown**, the game is entirely about making deals and making those deals seem like they are great for everyone involved. At the same time, other players are trying to make their own deals – often at cross purposes – and so a lot of the game is a deep, dense mess of proposals and counter-proposals within past, present, and future tenses.

There's a second factor here, which is that those who use sign language may also have access to a translator for general social circumstances. There is a considerable conversation lag that can come in when someone using sign language has to communicate a complex argument, at speed, to someone who then has to try to have it heard over the rest of the table. The more signers at a table, the more conversational lag that is present.

This issue doesn't even need to stem from incompatibilities in communication regimes. It can emerge simply as a result of linguistic confidence. Some games make heavy use of jargon or unconventional vocabulary. Most of the games I play these days are at the university during our game nights, and the group there is intensely multicultural. You have people who are fluent in multiple languages. You also have those that speak only English because one of the downsides of speaking the world's Lingua Franca is that you're never truly incentivised to learn any other language. Yeah, that's me.

All of our students speak English, regardless where they come from. In my experience as a Scottish man, I find the average European university student speaks English better than the average Scot. They are all distressingly articulate in what is their second, third, or even fourth language.

And yet, when we play something like **Time's Up** (1999) or **Telestrations** (2009), it is all but guaranteed that when they draw a card at least some of them will need to load up a dictionary on their phone to work out what they are supposed to explain (**Time's Up**) or draw (**Telestrations**). Native speakers of English likely know between 20,000 and 30,000 words well enough to be able to draw on them regularly in conversation. To speak a language at C1 (proficient) level, the Common European Framework of Reference for Language Learning suggests that around 8000 words of vocabulary are expected. The expectation is 16,000 for the next highest degree, which is to say 'mastered a language to an exceptional level'.

This is before complexities such as cultural references, idioms, and figures of speech are taken into account – especially because those rarely translate cleanly. The English expression 'put your foot in it' has perhaps its closest Swedish parallel in '*trampa i klaveret*' or 'To stamp on the accordion'.

The problem here is largely not to do with the words that are in common circulation in a language but rather the variety and obscurity of words used with a game. However, even common words and common vocabulary can be problematic if tied to a game system that requires them to be used imaginatively. **Snake Oil** (2010) is a conversational game in which players must come up with advertising pitches for ridiculous products. The products themselves are made up from two cards played in combination. One player is the 'customer', who draws a particular profile that indicates they are a protestor, or a cheerleader, or a werewolf, or whatever. Each other player then makes a 30-second-long pitch as to why their particular product is something that the customer should buy. Why should a rock star buy a pair of bread trousers? Why would a life guard need a wax unicorn?

Fun? Definitely … but also inaccessible from a number of perspectives. The performance aspects we discussed in our chapter on emotional accessibility are relevant, mainly though we're not talking about fluency so much as creativity. **Snake Oil** is a game that thrives on cleverness, with the best pitches being those that combine allusion, synonyms, antonyms, and cultural references into a polished performance. We can see a similar mechanism in **Once Upon a Time** (2012, Figure 8.1), a storytelling

FIGURE 8.1 A story being constructed in Once Upon a Time. (Photograph by the author.)

game in which players must convincingly play out all their cards while creating a fairy tale. The trick is if they use a word or concept that reflects a card owned by another player, that player is able to take control of the story and change the direction it goes. The result is a game where you not only need to be able to purpose words in a particular context but you also need to remember how they have been used within a shared, collaborative story and how you might leverage that to shape the story so it reaches the conclusion you require.

Medium (2019) is essentially the folk game 'Mind Meld' packaged up and sold for profit. The premise is simple – players each try to say the same word by finding a happy convergence of two other words. If I say the word 'car' and someone else says the 'robot', we will do a countdown and say together the first word that comes to mind that will bridge the gap. 'Transformer!' we might say, and in doing so win a point. If we don't say the same word, we try to meld the two new words. 'Court' and 'Job' might result in 'Judge' and 'Tennis', which then becomes 'Umpire'. That sort of thing. You might think, as per our chapter on physical accessibility, that synchronising the expression of a word seems like it might be a problem – and you're right.

What this game does is interesting in that it doesn't stress vocabulary so much as it does the semantic orbit of words – as in, what words are associated with which other words? And since it's two people trying to make the connection, 'What is the standard deviation of association that might be at play here'. Figure 8.2 shows an example – in this circumstance I'm almost certainly going to say 'Turtle' because come on – ninja turtles, right? A fan of Lego though might instantly make the connection to Ninjago and say 'Garmadon'. At which point we need to find a bridge between 'Turtle' and 'Garmadon',

FIGURE 8.2   A mind meld in progress in Medium. (Photograph by the author.)

and let me tell you folks I think I'm just going to pass this round because I don't know what a Garmadon is.

Let's not forget **Dobble,** which we have discussed often elsewhere in this book. The simple time pressure associated with playing a game which is basically a souped-up version of Snap can utterly destroy our semantic connections with symbols, to the point that even regular, reliable, basic words become as inaccessible as ancient texts of Mesopotamian grammar.

Games with Good Communication Design

The solution to communication in emotionally inaccessible contexts is also the one that we see best applied to confrontational communication regimes – **Deception: Murder in Hong Kong** (2014) solves this issue by creating distinct spaces in the turn where people get a chance to put forward their evidence mindfully, without the need to constantly fend off allegations of lies. It also accomplishes a secondary goal – it focuses everyone's attention on the current player, which means there's no need for someone who may be using non-verbal communication regimes to be 'heard' over a cacophony of other sounds. We recommend this as a variant for every game in the social deduction category.

We used **Time's Up** as an example of problematic communication design, and here we actually have a rare scenario that we can see another game with exactly the same design that also takes meaningful steps towards solving the problem. **Monikers** (2015) is effectively the same game as **Time's Up.** They are both re-implementations of the same public domain game – **Celebrities.** The difference is largely just in their presentation and the specific cards they give to players. At least, that's what it looks like. The thing is that **Time's Up** provides the subject of its rounds as an unaccompanied word or sentence. **Monikers** provides it along with an explanation. It also explicitly permits 'reading out the explanation' as a solution when someone doesn't know enough about the person, or concept, to effectively communicate it otherwise. It's a tremendously effective solution that bridges not just communication impairments but also generational ones. Kids today, and all that.

One game that definitely deserves some attention here is **The Mind** (2018, Figure 8.3) which plays like a weird spooky séance conducted during poker night. What's fascinating is how it creates accessibility for people with communication impairments through making communication inaccessible to everyone else. The game is centred around the silent playing out of face-down cards, with the job of the players to collaboratively put their in-hand cards into a shared order in the centre of the table. No information about the cards may be provided other than through implication. If I am quick to play out a card, it sends the message 'I am very confident none of you have a card nearer our current one'. If I'm hesitant, it suggests that my card **might** be the nearest but there's a good chance someone else may have a better one. Through the offering, and retraction, of prospective cards, the group can build up a sense of who is best placed to reveal the next in sequence.

The gradual accumulation of understanding is something that will be dependant on the group. It's a fascinating case study in communicating at right angles to other people and definitely worth your attention if you wanted to explore the ways in which games can innovate within accessibility while being undeniably an original experience on the table.

FIGURE 8.3   A hand of cards in The Mind. (Photograph by the author.)

Games with Interesting Communication Design

We might also in this chapter profitably consider the idea of the *locus of attention*, which is the location that someone is currently devoting their mental energy towards interpreting and manipulating or, in less academic terms, 'Where you're currently thinking about'. An interesting example of this is to be found in **Escape: The Curse of the Temple** (2012). The music track which sets the pace of the game can be substituted for an egg-timer – or perhaps, supplemented. This seems on the surface like a perfect solution because it meets all the criteria we have used throughout this book – it's non-stigmatising and it is a translation of one channel of information into another. The problem is that not all translations are lossless, and the use of an egg-timer requires people to split their attention in a way that an audio signal does not. It's also a more ambiguous way to communicate when someone's time is up because it relies on people seeing the sand has run out at the exact same moment it does. As such, while this definitely **does** provide an alternate channel of information, it does it in a way that changes the texture of play.

Wavelength (2019) is a game where cultural conventions, definitions, and semantic orbiting are all explicitly part of the experience. I consider it basically a flavour of existential dread in a box – a repeated reminder of how all experience is personal and fundamentally we can only ever know ourselves. Our friends are unfathomable, their minds alien and alarming. In the end, we are all hopelessly and irrevocably alone in an unfeeling and uncaring universe.

Others just see it as a fun game.

The premise is this – players are in teams, and in each round one of the team members will draw a card that outlines a spectrum: hot to cold, poorly made to well made, and easy to difficult. They will spin a dial (Figure 8.4) and then privately look to find the range they want the other players on their team to hit.

FIGURE 8.4 Wavelength – the clue given by the current player must direct their group to move the dial to the correct location. (Photograph by the author.)

They will cover up the dial (Figure 8.5) and turn it to face their teammates. They then give a clue which is supposed to guide them to place the indicator in the correct region. So, maybe you say ….

What? What do you say? That's a big question because it resolves around what your team mates know of you, what you know of them, what you think they know of you, and what you put at the extremes of this scale. Literally my first thought here was 'Prisoner: Cell Block H' because it was a TV show that I really enjoyed but was infamous for its wobbly sets. There are maybe five people in the world I'd know and would trust to make that same connection. What about 'fast fashion'? What is the lower bound of 'poorly made', and is fast fashion proportionately in the right vicinity for that[1]?

In **Wavelength** we find that words, what they mean, and the intensity to which they are viewed in relation to other words are a complex mix of culture, vocabulary, social context, and personal knowledge. It requires a lot of pragmatic interpretation of the game too – am I saying it intentionally, ironically, or comically? It's inaccessible, perhaps, but intentionally so and like a lot of games of this type it's also fun to get wrong. It's been said elsewhere in this book that good games are fun when you're winning, but great games are also fun when you're losing. **Wavelength** is fun when you see it collapse into baffled argumentation.

Finally in this chapter, I want to talk about **Magic Maze** (2017), which shares a lot of the features we have discussed in **The Mind**. Specifically, a lot of the game is about

FIGURE 8.5 Wavelength, as seen by those trying to make the guess from the clue given. (Photograph by the author).

intentionally limiting the ability of players to communicate. Everyone is in control of a certain instruction that can be applied to pieces on the board – in other words, you don't play the role of characters but rather limited activities that any pawn can perform. Perhaps you are the embodiment of the direction 'right'. Only you can move pieces in that direction. Your job as a group is to get the pawns from their starting location to their destinations, avoiding obstacles and problems along the way. It sounds trivial, but the bulk of **Magic Maze** is played in absolute silence – the only way anyone can communicate to anyone else is by passive-aggressively thumping a 'DO SOMETHING!' token in front of the person who has no idea what to do.

That's obviously funny, and it makes for a game that seems like it would be almost perfect from the perspective of this chapter. The thing is though that the game in reality operates under a feast or famine model – there's a sand-timer that can be flipped, at which point everyone can speak and strategise for as long as there is sand left to run. In other words, you go from blissful silence to frantic conversation where nobody has time to set common parameters for the discussion because there isn't enough time to do so. People with reception impairments may find a conversation carried out frantically at speed to be difficult to follow. Those with articulation impairments will find it difficult to make what may be nuanced points in the time available. In short, it's the most stressful possible model of communication that I can imagine, embedded in some of the most communicably accessible gameplay that I have ever seen.

Guidelines for Communicative Accessibility

- *Games to look to for inspiration*:
  - Assembly, Suburbia, and Love Letter.
- *Games to look to as cautionary tales*:
  - The Resistance, Chinatown, Dobble, and Decrypto.

Text

Maximise the Clarity of Text

Communication issues can be as much about language as they are about impairments. Clear, common-sense language can be useful but it's not enough in and of itself. Domain-specific knowledge or jargon can be problematic, but so too can idioms and slang. Remember too that the text which is part of your game may not just be on the cards and in the manual. 'How to Play' videos and other external resources should be subtitled and close captioned for maximum clarity.

- If providing non-standard text to describe components, ensure that there is a secondary channel of information such as size, colour, or silhouette.
- Minimise the use of idioms, colloquialisms, and other forms of figurative and/ or context-dependent language.
- Define acronyms clearly and provide a suitable lookup table in the manual.
- Provide a lookup table for all game-specific and hobby-specific jargon employed.
- When making instructional videos, include close captioning and subtitles. Make the transcripts available for download.

Icons

Use Culture Independent Iconography

Some symbols have particular meaning that is linked to their cultural context. This is similar to the issue often seen with colours – that cultural association in other countries may not reflect the norm as understood by the designer. Symbols can greatly reduce the communication burdens on players, to the point that a game can be made functionally language independent through effective iconography. Be mindful of what those symbols may mean worldwide.

- Limit the need for reading during the game through the use of clear icons and symbols.
- Ensure that cultural connotations of symbols are taken into account.
- Ensure that cultural connotation of symbol colouration is taken into account.

General Aesthetics

Provide Alternatives for Sound-based Gameplay Mechanisms

Sound is something that is usually explicitly designed into tabletop games – it's rare that it is relevant unless it is part of the game's mechanisms. As such, it may not be possible to make a 'sound-enabled' game accessible by removing the sound. If possible, though, providing alternate modes and variants can be an excellent compromise.

- Provide additional visual identifiers for games where sound time cues are a key feature.
- Consider the locus of attention associated with any alternative component that should replace sound.
- When time limits are a factor in play, document their duration and spacing so as to permit someone to use an accessible alternative.

Rules

Minimise Complex Communication Scenarios

The largest thing that games can do to ensure that they are accessible from a communication perspective is to ensure the accessibility of the mechanisms within which communication is undertaken. High pressured, adversarial discussion will undermine the culture of mutual support which is critical to accessibility compensation at the game table. However, if designed properly, even adversarial conversation can be accessible.

- Reduce the amount of lying or bluffing in a game, or permit those players unable to do this a secondary role within the game where it is not required.
- Where complex communication of strategy may be required, limit the amount of game-specific or thematic jargon required to understand. Try to rely on common terms from a real-world context.
- If players are required to talk or discuss the game, make sure that players are not disadvantaged by having to express themselves with sign language or a restricted vocabulary. Provide gaps in the game where only a single player is permitted to communicate.
- Limit the speed at which communication is necessary.
- Limit the need for stridency or eloquence to be a key method of interacting with player.

Design for Interpreters

When designing for maximal accessibility here, it's important to remember that it's not just players who may be involved. Translators may be present, or there may be intermediaries who can translate between groups. Particularly in mixed-generation immigrant households, where second- and third-generation children will be more familiar with the country's language than first generation, it is important to remember people may be receiving information second hand.

- Limit the range of necessary vocabulary and cultural knowledge as much as is possible.
- Minimise the number of distinct incidents through which a player may have to turn to another player for communication support. Favour sequential over interleaved communication, as an example.

Note

1. I polled our game night group for their answers, and got IKEA (from Johnny Hamnesjö), 'mass market clothes' from Katya Voloshina (I definitely need to recruit her to my team next time we play), and Deutsche Bahn from her friend Anya Melnik. I had to look that last one up, which is pretty good evidence of the larger point being made here.

BIBLIOGRAPHY

Anderson, J. M. (2011). *The substance of language volume i: The domain of syntax* (Vol. 1). Oxford University Press.

Brysbaert, M., Stevens, M., Mandera, P., & Keuleers, E. (2016). How many words do we know? Practical estimates of vocabulary size dependent on word definition, the degree of language input and the participant's age. *Frontiers in Psychology*, 7, 1116.

Council for Cultural Co-operation. Education Committee. Modern Languages Division, C (2001). *Common European framework of reference for languages: Learning, teaching, assessment*. Cambridge University Press.

Crabb, M., & Heron, M. (2023). Communication challenges in social board games. *Simulation & Gaming*, 54(5), 10468781231183908.

Culatta, R., & Leeper, L. (1989). The differential diagnosis of disfluency. *NSSLHA Journal*, (17), 59–64.

Dawes, P., & Bishop, D. (2009). Auditory processing disorder in relation to developmental disorders of language, communication and attention: A review and critique. *International Journal of Language & Communication Disorders*, 44(4), 440–465.

Noble, K., & Crabb, M. (2016). Projection mapping as a method to improve board game accessibility. *ACM SIGACCESS Accessibility and Computing*, (116), 3–9.

Schilder, A. G., Su, M. P., Blackshaw, H., Lustig, L., Staecker, H., Lenarz, T., Safieddine, S., Gomes-Santos, C. S., Holme, R., & Warnecke, A. (2019). Hearing protection, restoration, and regeneration: An overview of emerging therapeutics for inner ear and central hearing disorders. *Otology & Neurotology*, 40(5), 559–570.

Toppelberg, C. O., & Shapiro, T. (2000). Language disorders: A 10-year research update review. *Journal of the American Academy of Child & Adolescent Psychiatry*, 39(2), 143–152.

Zhao, F., Manchaiah, V. K., French, D., & Price, S. M. (2010). Music exposure and hearing disorders: An overview. *International Journal of Audiology*, 49(1), 54–64.

9

Applying the Tabletop Accessibility Guidelines

This has been quite the journey through the world of tabletop games, and as part of our discussion, we've talked about a lot of issues and a lot of solutions. And now it's down to you as to how you make your own games more accessible. It's perfectly understandable if the task seems overwhelming – there is so much advice, much of it seems contradictory, and it's hard to even know where to start.

Let's finish up our discussion then with some pointers about how you might apply these guidelines to a game – either as an intellectual exercise or in a sincere attempt to improve the accessibility of a game you are designing or producing.

The Golden Rule

Here's the first and most important rule about building accessibility into your game – **talk to people with disabilities.** I may have written an entire book about this topic, but I did that on the basis of the unearned confidence of middle-aged white academics everywhere. You shouldn't listen to me – I'm basically an idiot. I have explicitly outlined within this text why we need to consider impairment more broadly than in the frame of disability, but none of that is to diminish the vital, peerless guidance that comes with embodied experience.

Include disabled players in your brainstorming, include them in your playtesting, and include them in Kickstarter planning. If you're in the position of being able to make some advanced review copies available – make them available to people reviewing games on the basis of their accessibility. Sometimes the value to be gained from a review is in insight, not outreach. Sometimes it's spend that comes from your design, rather than marketing, budget.

The most important recommendation I have for you when it comes to engaging with accessibility is to make it obvious that you see its value. Include a contact address for accessibility feedback in all your public facing resources – website, game manuals, and your socials. Make it known that you react positively to feedback in this area, and you will find it comes your way.

Sometimes you can't adjust a design to make the game more generally accessible – that's no great failing. All of this stuff is complicated. But you can go a long way towards helping by including accessibility **advice** in your game material. You already know where that comes from – talking to people with disabilities. And, when you're looking at broader issues of socioeconomics, it comes from talking to people who are most impacted by a lack of representation or economic consideration. But be mindful here of a common theme. There is as much, if not more, intra-conditional variation than there is inter-conditional variation. Avoid tokenism and endorse breadth of viewpoints.

DOI: 10.1201/9781003415435-9

One worthwhile approach too is to consider accessibility as a first-order category of evaluation. Direct your playtesters to answer specific and open-ended questions about the accessibility issues you want to take into account. For this to be feasible, you'll also need to be mindful of the fidelity of your prototyping versus the accessibility feedback you need. The closer the prototype components are to the final components, the more accurate the analysis.

One thing I will say here is that you should consider the embodied experience that comes with disability as an **expert-level skill** and budget for it properly. You wouldn't expect an artist to work for free (people die from exposure and all that) – their skill and insight are financially valuable. So too is the work that people put in to help your game be more accessible. You'll be opening up new market segments, and that's worth paying for.

In this though, we also have to come back an earlier point – no one player can speak for all players, and no one disabled person is a proxy for all disabled people. The more people with disabilities you include, the more of their perspectives you will capture. The more diverse viewpoints you solicit, the more inclusive your work will be.

The Accessibility Teardown

For years, the technique I have used to arrive at accessibility evaluations is what I have termed the **accessibility teardown**. It is the examination of a game through a series of evaluative lenses. We go stepwise, category from category, examining the game specifically within a frame of reference. We don't worry about permanent, temporary, or situational aspects here – we just collect all the observations that come to mind by practising informed empathy. Make a note of everything of which you can think, drawing on our discussions about how impairments may manifest. Consider other games that do similar things to yours, and check to see if anyone has written about their accessibility.

Make copious notes, and **repeat the exercise with diverse voices.** If possible, draw in the perspectives of people with disabilities. Repeat it with different people and combine insights. Note here you are not trying to work out if someone can play a game. You're working out what a game asks of a player in each of these categories. 'It needs players to be okay with being bullied', or 'it needs players to perceive colour information', or 'it needs players to shuffle cards a lot'.

The end goal is to have a categorised list of potential accessibility considerations. Remember, some of these will be critical to the game design. Others may not be possible to deal with without making things worse. We'll get to that.

It's not possible to give a fully exhaustive breakdown of how to do this, but we can take a look at some of the major things that should be taken into account.

Visual Accessibility

The lenses in this category relate to issues of colour blindness, visual impairment, and total blindness. For visual accessibility, here's what I traditionally look at below table (Table 9.1).

TABLE 9.1

Some of the Things to Consider when It Comes to Visual Accessibility

Lens	Description
Colour blindness	Here we look at how colour works in a game, where there are palette problems, and whether colour is accompanied by secondary channels of information.
Contrast	We check the contrast between text and background and between information bearing elements of the game state and the way they are presented in the game.
Font choice	Here we look at ornamentation and size of fonts and whether these are readable.
Tactility of tokens	We look at tokens to see whether they can be differentiated by touch and if that actually makes a game more playable. Consistency of tactility and ease with which that can be assessed and manipulated are also important.
Binocularity	Here we check to see if judgement of distance and perspective are going to be important in accomplishing game goals.
Paper money	Paper money is an inaccessibility wall to wall, but especially so in a game where the economy is likely to move too quickly for standard real-world visual impairment compensations to work. Generally, just – 'are we using paper money and can we use something else?'
Non-standard dice	Dice are important randomisers, but players with visual impairments will usually have their own accessible variant – oversized dice, braille dice, app-based rollers, or other digital tools. Here we assess whether players can make use of these if necessary and how difficult it would be to make them work.

Cognitive Accessibility

These lenses relate to *fluid intelligence* and *crystalised intelligence* as we saw in our chapter on cognitive accessibility. These are conflated in a teardown because I've found trying to extract the often subtle interrelationships between them makes the task otherwise impossible (Table 9.2).

TABLE 9.2

Some of the Things to Consider when It comes to Both Fluid and Crystalised Intelligence

Lens	Description
Required literacy	How much reading is needed, and how sophisticated is that reading? Here we assume there's no need for a player to read the manual – the game will be explained to them somehow or they'll make use of one of the many fine 'learn to play' videos out there.
Game state complexity	How many 'moving parts' are there in the game and how dependent is one part of the game state on another? If you change one part of the game state how much does it affect other parts?
Memory requirements	What do you need to remember in order to play at all? What do you need to remember to play effectively? What do you need to memorise to play **well**?
Game flow	How different will one round be from the one that preceded it? How different is your current round to the next one? How consistent is turn order, and how reliable is the flow of play agency?
Number of token combinations	How many different tokens do people need to track, and how consistent is their meaning?
Synergy of rules	To what extent do players need to leverage subtle (or not so subtle) card interactions to attain core game effects?

(Continued)

TABLE 9.2　(Continued)

Some of the Things to Consider when It comes to Both Fluid and Crystalised Intelligence

Lens	Description
Scoring	What skills are needed to work out how well you're doing, and how much of the scoring is going to be based on implicit understanding of concepts like risk and probability?
General knowledge	What information do people need to know that comes from outside the game? Do they need to know history or geography or social context? If they don't **need** to know, does a well of general knowledge help or give an advantage? Does its absence impose a penalty?
Multitasking	How many interrelated game systems will a player need to simultaneously track in order to execute upon a plan? How tightly bound are those systems?

Emotional Accessibility

The emotional accessibility category relates to issues of anger, behavioural control, and occasionally simple 'bad winners' and 'bad losers'. Here are some of the things we take into account for that (Table 9.3).

TABLE 9.3

Some Things that Introduce Emotional Accessibility Considerations

Lens	Description
Challenge	Here we assess how the challenge of a game manifests and how likely that is to be fulfilling or frustrating.
Despair	Some games work on the assumption you are going to fail and do everything to make that happen. This requires players to find enjoyment in their failure, and it can be a powerful trigger point for upset if that's not possible.
Arbitrary fates	The extent to which an outcome is controllable is a predictor for how suitable it will be for a player. Some players like to be able to take comfort in losing through randomness. Others hate losing because of something that they couldn't control.
Bluffing or lying	If games involve misleading players, it requires a certain amount of emotional intelligence, and this can be a heavy ask.
Need for closure or symmetry	Certain emotional and behavioural conditions include a strong compulsive aspect, and games that involve pattern creation without permitting pattern completion can be problematic.
'Take that' mechanics	The ability of a player to countermand the intentions of another can be an important aspect of emotional inaccessibility if not managed well. This is essentially frustration with a proximal cause that is associated with a particular player at the table – it binds intention into the frustration which can be a significant problem.
Upsetting themes	Mature themes and 'edgy' content can run the risk of bringing a game into dangerous emotional territory. Some people do not like to engage with violent themes. Others may have a history or experience of trauma that can be triggered with careless game content.
Player elimination	If players can be removed from play at any point, this can create an intense feeling of exclusion that becomes worse the longer a game goes on. A related concern is about elimination of competitiveness – it's not much better to be in a game you have no hope at all of winning.
The ability of players to gang up	Some games incentivise players to gang up on a runaway leader, which can be frustrating. It can be worse when games incentivise players to pick on the losing player.

TABLE 9.4

Aspects of Physical Accessibility that Should Be Considered

Lens	Description
Size of cards	Unconventional card sizes can be a problem, whether it be over large or over small.
Token shapes	The smoother the tokens are and the lighter they are, the more they will tend to be difficult to manipulate.
Regularity of piece manipulation	How often do players need to manipulate pieces on the board or in their player areas? Do they need to stretch over a board? How much of the board do they need to take into account?
Ease of verbalisation	How easily can a player issue verbal instructions in a game to indicate what they'd like to happen? How much of the game's fun is bound up in the tactility of the experience? How much judgement must another player exert in the interpretation of instructions?
Physical acting	Does the game require any physical acting such as raising hands, acting out instructions, standing up, or sitting down? If so, these will often have an impact on the accessibility of play.
Paper money	Paper money tends to clump, is hard to manipulate, and is often susceptible to environmental elements such as wind. Basically, avoid paper money if you can.
Number of tokens	How many tokens will a player need to control, and how much physical movement is required to handle them?
Size of game board elements	The tighter the constraints of a target zone, and the more densely knotted the pieces are around it, the harder it is for people to manipulate game state.

Physical Accessibility

It's rare that games ask nothing in terms of physical interactions from their players, but the extent to which physicality is **required** is what is most important here (Table 9.4).

Communication

We work on the assumption that communication within a group is largely a solved problem – some combination of techniques ensures that all players can be conversational. In this category, we mostly focus on the communication requirements within the game itself (Table 9.5).

TABLE 9.5

Some Considerations Pertaining to Communication

Lens	Description
Expected reading level	Complex text on cards and components can create a problem, partially due to the need for literacy and partly due to the context of that literacy. The issue might be due to the sophistication or nuance of language or the use of metaphor, antonyms, or the like. This also includes jargon and unusual wording since these may have no immediate and direct analogue in alternative modes of communication.
Audibility	Are there external audio cues in the game, and are there alternatives provided for those who are hard of hearing? How effective are those alternatives, and do they change the nature of the game in any way?

(Continued)

TABLE 9.5 (*Continued*)

Some Considerations Pertaining to Communication

Lens	Description
Lying/Bluffing	Lying and bluffing are based on confidence, verbal fluency, and body language. Communication impairments can make it difficult for a player to fully engage with these gameplay systems.
Communication of strategy	If it's a co-operative game, how much communication of strategy is required and how contentious will that communication be? What are the risks that go along with mistakes in communication or interpretation? How much do you need to convince people, and how much freedom are you going to have to express your view without someone being incentivised to talk over you?
Need for audible communication	Does a game mandate the making of some kind of non-trivial sounds during the course of play? What is lost if these are translated into written text or a visual communication language? For example, if communication must be secret, then sign language would not be an appropriate compensation even if it's otherwise a perfectly reasonable ask.

Socioeconomic Accessibility

One of the more controversial aspects of this work is the emphasis I place on socioeconomic aspects of gaming. I consider barriers of exclusion or representation to be inaccessibilities even if the barrier is primarily perceptual. Several lenses are used in this analysis (Table 9.6).

TABLE 9.6

Some Socioeconomic Complexities

Lens	Description
Inclusivity in artwork	We look to see if the artwork for a game is inclusive in terms of sex, gender, and ethnic balance. We want to make sure that everyone can see 'people like them' reflected in the artwork.
Sexism in art and instruction	Here we look at the extent to which a game is objectifying in its art or assumptive in its descriptions. This comes through in terms of art choice, wording in a manual, assignment of colours to roles, and the defaulting to masculinity for pronouns in instructions. We also assess games for the extent to which they make use of gendered or heteronormative assumptions.
Theme	Some games have themes that are inherently problematic and come with a risk of alienating players simply as a result of how the theme is pitched. Our focus is on ensuring that there is appropriate guidance so others can consider whether the game is suitable for their groups.
Player counts	The number of players a game supports, cross-referenced against its cost, gives a rough measure of 'cost per player'. Those on a budget looking for games that support large or complex family environments will often need to take this into account.
Cost	Board gaming is largely a luxury hobby, but value for money is important for many. More important though is the expectation that goes along with the business model for the game. Consider a 'one and done' purchase versus the longer investment of money required for a collectible card game or miniatures game. In this case, we ask 'How much fun can you have with just the base box?' and 'How much will you have to spend to get the game everyone is raving about?'

Intersectional Accessibility

There are many issues that emerge primarily through a combination of impairments. These may not manifest in isolation. It's impossible to be proscriptive here because it is highly dependent on individual, game, and social context. However, there are some common lenses we use (Table 9.7).

TABLE 9.7

Intersectionality Makes Everything More Complex – It's a Book in and of Itself. Here Are Some Factors to Consider though

Lens	Description
Physical/Cognitive	
Size of cards/Hands	The number of cards, and the size of the cards, will determine whether or not a game is physically accessible but also cognitively and visually accessible. The number of options a player must concern themselves with at any one time is a factor here, as is the complexity of consequence associated with each option.
Dice	Randomness can create compounding problems because it leads to unpredictable game states. When impairments intersect, the tractability of randomness goes down because it becomes more difficult to ascertain cause, effect, and outcome.
Hidden hands	Hidden hands of cards usually have gameplay information that must be obscured, and this prevents players seeking assistance from others at the table if they have queries.
Agency	The extent to which a supported player is still in charge of their own role in the game is important – physical and cognitive impairments that intersect can often result in games where someone is participating but not actually playing.
Emotional/Cognitive	
Downtime	Downtime can make it difficult to keep someone's attention focused. It also creates a cognitive burden as players try to constantly re-evaluate their coming turn in light of another player's actions. That in turn can create an anxiety as players suspect something horrible is heading their way yet being unable to prevent or perhaps understand it.
Competition	Competition is a common part of games, but here it depends on just how pointed the competition will end up being. Many games rely on players being able to mislead someone away from their real objective. Accessibility support from the table relies on people perhaps pointing out things someone else might have missed. Aggressive competition undermines the collegiality that is often at the core of respectful, supportive game experiences. It leads to situations where someone may not have understood what was happening. Then perhaps losing because of someone's active choice not to inform them of something they reasonably should have known.
Cognitive/Visual	
Aesthetics	There is a cognitive cost that comes along with trying to read things that are artistically presented – even if they can be visually perceived they take more mental processing to comprehend. The more visually impaired a player may be, the harder it will be to read, which in turn makes it harder to understand.

(Continued)

TABLE 9.7 *(Continued)*

Intersectionality Makes Everything More Complex – It's a Book in and of Itself. Here Are Some Factors to Consider though

Lens	Description
Symbolism	Symbols on game components are an effective way of encoding lots of complex information in a visually compact way, and this **can** be great. It can also be very problematic because it adds a memory burden to play – there's a translation process between symbol and its meaning that must be navigated.
Physical/Communicative	
Verbalisation	The solution for many players with physical impairments is verbalisation. If this intersects with a communication impairment, then it might not be appropriate. Not always though – sometimes games are playable with some agreed upon way to indicate assent along with an exhaustive exploration of a player's options.
All	
Time constraints	Accessibility compensations take time – whenever there is a time constraint on an action, the accessibility of a game takes a major nose-dive. The impact of time constraints in an accessibility context is often intensely asymmetrical.
Ability to drop in and out	All impairments exist on a spectrum, and players may have symptoms that modulate in severity on a day-by-day, hour-by-hour, or minute-by-minute basis. Games that are resilient to players who find it necessary to drop out of play tend to be a better prospect than those that aren't. Those that support 'saving' of a game in progress – or allow subbing in another player – also allow dropping back in.
Length of game sessions	The longer a game is, the more likely it is to bring about discomfort. This might manifest as physical symptoms or emotional and cognitive distress. The longer a game lasts too, the larger the consequences tend to be for inaccessibilities, and the greater the perceived cost for players who feel the need to drop out of play. It's less psychologically costly to drop out of a ten-minute game than it is a game that you've been playing for three hours.
Board complexity	When there is an intersection of physical, visual, or cognitive impairments, players may lack one of the compensatory regimes they could use to understand game state. For example, a visually impaired player might be able to inspect a board closely and remember board state. That wouldn't be true if there was also a physical accessibility consideration or a memory impairment.

The Report Card

Once you have that list of identified problems, give yourself a grade for each category. I use typical letter grades, with a plus or minus to deal with subtleties. Essentially this becomes a rough description of how much I would broadly recommend the game to someone who had to take into account impairments linked to the category in question. Table 9.8 for how this breaks down.

TABLE 9.8

You Don't Need to Use These Grading Bands. They Work for Me, but You May Have Other Preferences

Grade	Meaning
A	I can perceive no significant problems that would prevent someone from playing this game.
B	There are some problems, but they can be resolved with house rules, adaptations, or with the use of alternative aides.
C	It's a mixed bag – it really depends on the specific way an impairment manifests.
D	I suspect what this game asks of its players is too much for it to be enjoyably playable. Enough effort will probably overcome whatever barriers are there.
E	If this game is playable at all by someone impacted by accessibility issues in this category, it is only at great personal cost and with significant detrimental impact.
F	I never say a game is completely unplayable in any given category – people are too clever and creative for that – but insofar as it is ever true, this game is probably completely unplayable.

You don't need to use this grading scheme – I often advise people to completely ignore the grades I give other than as rough indicators of the shape of an accessibility profile. It's only in the accompanying discussion about why the grade was awarded that any real insight is to be found in any Meeple Like Us teardown. It's usually fair to say though that if there's an A in a category, there is good reason to believe a game is playable, and an F is usually a good indicator that it's not worth the effort to make it so. The combination of grades and categories is essentially your report card, as seen in the example which is for **Game of Thrones: The Card Game** (second edition, 2015, Figure 9.1).

It has been noted, several times by several commentators, that it is ironic that the report card used by Meeple Like Us employs red and green despite red-green colour blindness being the most common category. To that I point out that this is actually a **double-coded** report card since it also comes with letter grades (triple coded, if you include the radar chart which shows the same information in a different form), and it uses the cognitively accessible colour coding of 'green is good' and 'red is bad'. Still, it's a reasonable point and just goes to show how accessibility considerations come up everywhere!

The important thing here is to nail your colours to the mast as to where you believe your game lies. You can then chart it. I use a radar chart (also known as a spider chart) to give an at-a-glance fingerprint of how a game's accessibility shakes out. See Figure 9.2 for the radar chart associated with **Skull** (2011).

Radar charts are imperfect guides, but in general, the amount of area covered by a radar graph gives a reasonable overview of the game's accessibility. Figure 9.3 is for the second edition of **the Game of Thrones Card Game** (2015) as a counter-example.

The idea here is not to mourn your failures but to identify your accessibility pain points so they can be dealt with. The first step in making anything more accessible is a triage, and this is step one **of** step one.

Category	Grade
Colour Blindness	A
Visual Accessibility	E
Fluid Intelligence	F
Memory	F
Physical Accessibility	B
Emotional Accessibility	E
Socioeconomic Accessibility	C+
Communication	B

Game of Thrones: the Card Game, Meeple Like Us, [CC-BY 4.0]

FIGURE 9.1 A game report card as published on Meeple Like Us. (Screenshot [and report card] by the author.)

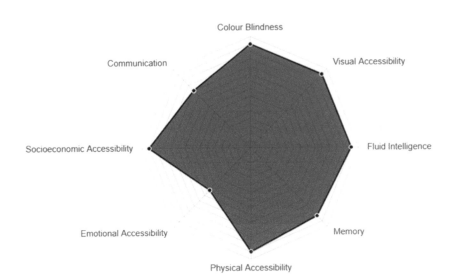

FIGURE 9.2 The radar chart for the game Skull, as published on Meeple Like Us. (Screenshot (and data) by the author.)

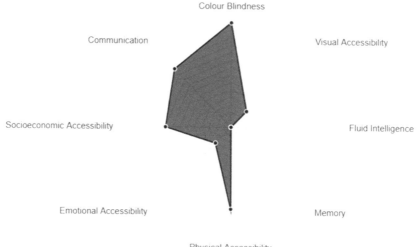

FIGURE 9.3 Another radar chart, this one for the Game of Thrones Card Game. Published on Meeple Like Us. (Screenshot (and data) by the author.)

Dump Stats

What I am going to write here is going to be controversial because it involves making the conscious choice to exclude certain people from your design. I do believe there are games that can be broadly accessible to everyone – you can see from Figure 9.2 that Skull would likely fall into that category. However, of all the games I have looked at in my time exploring board game accessibility, I would put the number at perhaps 1% or 2% of the games I have examined. It is a very laudable goal – but it has to be seen as **aspirational** and that aspiration puts some very severe restrictions on how complex a game can be.

In roleplaying games, there is a concept known as the **dump stat** – it's the aspect of your character you are going to sacrifice in order to improve capability in other areas. A wizard probably doesn't need a lot of strength, and a fighter probably doesn't need a lot of charisma. Maybe your priest sacrifices a few points of dexterity so they can get a few more points of wisdom. The idea is that for certain character builds, some stats just don't matter.

It's not the case here that categories don't matter. The nature of intentional inaccessibility though may result in some categories offering very few opportunities for improvement without a fundamental change in what a game is supposed to be. Imagine **Scrabble** without the cognitive processing of letter positioning, combined with the need to apply vocabulary in complex ways. I don't know what the game you're imagining looks like, but I guarantee it's no longer **Scrabble**. You can certainly make improvements in the cognitive accessibility profile of **Scrabble**, but you're never going to drag its grade up to, or past, a C minus while keeping the bits of it that matter. For **Scrabble** perhaps cognitive accessibility and communication become dump stats. It's not that you don't care about them – rather it's that if a game must have inaccessibilities, it is more beneficial for everyone else if they cluster there. Those with cognitive impairments probably aren't going to find any version of **Scrabble** enjoyable anyway.

If you can't even get out of the doldrums of a D grade in a category, you can consider this book's advice in that light. A lot of these guidelines involve trade-offs – making things better in one category while making them worse in another. Icons for example can result in information dense representation that is ideal for a player with visual impairments. The cost is that icons put an increased cognitive burden on players who need to remember and recognise them. You have to choose which group you are trying to advantage in that case, and if you have either visual accessibility or cognitive accessibility as your dump stat … well, it becomes a lot easier to make those decisions.

This is step two of your triage – identify your dump stats and prioritise your accessibility fixes in light of what you can do without compromising on design.

Solutions

Having identified and prioritised the issues, you can now move on to what you can realistically fix.

It's here that the dump stat concept starts to break down because if you **can** address inaccessibilities in these categories you should still do it. The only permissible inaccessibilities in the frame of our discussion are those that are fundamental to the fun.

Our job here is simple – get our report card to the point we could show it to our hypothetical parents in the confidence it represents our best possible effort in the subject. This is about more than just a sense of satisfaction regarding a job well done – every accessibility fix opens up a game to more players. Remember, every person occupies a point on a complex spectrum of impairments, and the difference between 'playable' and 'unplayable' for any given person may be nothing more significant than slightly increased spaces between words. The potential financial value of any fix you make is literally incalculable – we have no way to calculate it – but rest assured someone new has been brought into the fold of potential players with every improvement you implement.

However, these guidelines are provided without reference to industrial context or the pragmatics of time and cost. It's easy for me to say 'Provide 3D models of accessible player aids', but it's not like those can be conjured out of thin air. They require someone to do the work that makes them available. That might be fine if you have the resources of Hasbro behind you. Probably not if you're designing games in the hour you are free after the kids go to bed. As such, many of these guidelines might not be feasible for a given individual game. As with our general approach to accessibility teardowns, we are not placed to say what you **should** do. We can only outline what you **could** do. When a could becomes a should is a decision that must be taken at your end.

Within each individual context, the list of identified issues can be mapped on to the guidelines as we have presented them. Then, this dyad of problem and solution can be assessed for its feasibility. Don't feel bad if something can't be done – any improvement **at all** is a net gain. There is some genuine low hanging fruit – double coding, foreground/background contrast, word choice, and such are all almost always feasible. Others may require more time than can be justified for the perceived benefit or fall foul of manufacturing limitations.

For a triage, you want to map out the highest impact and lowest cost changes you can make. A scatter plot is a good way to do this – map the cost of a change against predicted impact and then you can use that as the basis of a simple MoSCoW analysis – those things you **must** do, the things you **should** do, the things you **could** do, and the things you **won't** do. In the style of project management everywhere, consider this in the frame of a budget. Decide the time and money you are prepared to invest in your accessibility efforts, and choose where those resources are best spent.

It's always the case that accessibility is cheapest to consider at the start of a project, but there's a certain familiarity with the topic needed before you can know what you **should** have considered at the start. Taking advantage of the services of an accessibility consultant is an additional expense. If you're serious about accessibility though, it's good to think of it as another specialist aspect of game design that warrants the price tag of an expert. It's the difference between drawing the art in a game yourself or hiring someone who knows what perspective is.

Going Further

If you are going to take accessibility seriously in your game design, then you're going to be at the vanguard of what I hope will become an increasingly important movement. The conversation regarding accessibility in tabletop is many years behind where it is for video games, and there is an opportunity here for you to help shape how this movement progresses. You will have insights into the process that nobody else has by virtue of the unique circumstances of your evaluation. You should weave your interest in accessibility into every part of the game – make it prominent in your Kickstarter campaign and in your storefronts. If you're doing design blogs or such, talk about how you're addressing the topic. That's a great way to get additional feedback too! Put accessibility notes in your manual – if your testers have suggestions for variants, document them.

A lot of this work is pragmatic, but there's a philosophical aspect to it too. If you're reading this book, you are presumably interested in changing this hobby. It's vital to do the actual work and not just talk about it. It is though equally vital to talk about the work you do. We can all inspire each other to ever greater accomplishments. See how Blood on the Clocktower comes with a specific page of accessibility guidance[1] and how Wren Games documented their design strategy for inclusion in a blog entry[2]. This is the belt and braces work of activism – deciding that a thing is important, doing the work, and then talking about it so as to inspire others that the thing is important!

There are also websites that have specific focus on providing accessibility guidance with regards to tabletop games, and it would be wonderful if you supported those by providing your own analyses of the games you have developed. The Family Gaming Database for example welcomes all submission of accessibility features for video and tabletop games, and my own site Meeple Like Us would certainly be interested in seeing and publishing your own internal accessibility teardowns of games. If you have proposals for guidelines, or suggestions for revisions, consider me always interested in hearing your thoughts.

Intersectional Accessibility Guidelines

Our last order of business in this book is to include our last few guidelines, which relate to broader considerations than those that are linked to any one specific category. These are intersectional considerations.

General Aesthetics: Avoid Stigmatising Language

Stigma is an important issue in accessibility. I avoided getting glasses for many years as a child because I was afraid the other kids would call me 'speccy' or 'four eyes'. They did, too – fear of the stigma of being 'different' is rooted in reality. Do what you can to avoid players feeling as if they are 'lesser' for requiring accessibility support.

- Don't present game modifications as 'accessibility fixes'. Emphasise they are variants, although noting their effectiveness for accessibility can be valuable.
- When providing scaffolded rules, or difficulty modes, avoid describing the simplest levels as 'easy' or 'basic' or 'simple'. Begin with 'standard' and make each more complex mode sound increasingly impressive.

Rules

Encourage Collegial Accessibility Support

Much of what makes a game accessible emerges as a product of how people at the table behave – players moving pieces on the behalf of other people, narrating their turns, or helping someone shuffle a deck. Some game designs though are based on someone identifying opportunities ahead of others, and this can disincentivise them from offering all the help they can.

- Try to minimise the amount of 'secret information' or 'secret opportunities' in a game.
- Avoid game states that require players to identify actions that require a supporting player to disclose their own vulnerability.

Be Mindful of Conditions with Modulating Severity

All through this book we have discussed how the assumptions that people have about disability are often at odds with the lived experience. Just because someone has a particular impairment, it doesn't mean it is at a steady, reliable level of severity. Sometimes people have good days, sometimes they have bad days, and one kind can segue into another without warning. That is to say, just because someone feels okay at the start of a game it doesn't mean they'll feel the same way in the middle.

- If your game is long, give some thought to how players might 'save' the game state so as to be able to pause and restart at a later date.
- Offer short game variants for games with long play times. Long sessions may exacerbate issues of discomfort or distress in players. If possible, permit a long game to be shortened mid-game if necessary.
- Support if possible a solo mode that permits players to learn the game in a relaxed environment, or play it in scenarios where social circles are limited.
- Avoid game rules that potentially greatly increase the length of the game or make those rules optional and easy to remove.

Let People Choose the Level of Challenge

Difficulty modes are a good broad tool for letting players match their current level of comfort against the challenge they want. The more granular this can be though, the better – especially if difficulty can be adjusted during the course of play.

- Layer in opportunities for choosing difficulty levels to allow people to set the scale of their own challenge.
- Consider offering opportunities to scale or change the difficulty of a game while playing.
- If possible, choose a form of randomness in your game that permits weighting the odds – token draws, and card draws as opposed to rolling dice.

Allow Players to Choose Their Desired Level of Emotional Involvement

A player may wish to play a game but not at the same level of emotional investment as others. Low impact, low-cost roles that can be chosen are a great way of accomplishing this – not every player has to be as important as every other. Similarly, real-time games require considerable investment on the part of each player, and turn-based alternatives can be much more accessible.

- If your game is primarily real-time, consider a turn-based variant or roles within the game that do not require a player to participate at the same speed as others.
- Offering a range of different roles in your game can allow people with different abilities to take part. For example, a game that generally requires dexterity that has a role that does not require it.
- When a game offers different player roles of different intensity, allow players to select these rather than have them randomly assigned.

Permit Open Information Variations

Closed information games (for example, where a player has a secret hand of cards) put considerable burdens on those with memory impairments or those with difficulties in deciding strategy. Offering a variant where people can play with open information can help with this. In collaborative games, it does encourage quarterbacking (one player directing everyone else), but quarterbacking can also be a tremendously useful cognitive accessibility feature.

- Consider the provision of a 'fully visible information' variation for closed information games.
- If a game must involve hidden hands, consider whether some secret elements can be offloaded to an open, visible space.

Game Layout and Experience

Mindfully Consider How Downtime Manifests in Your Game

Downtime is a common feature of most board games, but there are good and bad ways to do it. The bad way is when you need to wait for every player to consider and make a move, and it has no impact on you until your turn comes around again. Interleaving actions within a turn or having player turns include reactive phases can help. However, downtime is also a way to build natural breaks into activity, and it can be helpful from a comfort perspective. The model of downtime you build into a game is impactful, and it's worth making sure its implications are intentional.

- Try to reduce downtime so as to support players with attention or emotional control concerns.
- Consider building mindful downtime into play so that players can take a short break or receive support from the table.
- Build natural breaks into games with highly threaded player turns.
- Try to minimise the amount of time that everyone has to be paying attention to everything.

Permit People to Drop In and Out of Play

As with our section on modulating severity, we must also be mindful that there are other considerations that may require someone to be added into a game, or removed from play, outside of the normal setup and endgame. Relying on the vagaries of public transport (a socioeconomic consideration) and having to tend to suddenly ill children are all factors that may require someone to be removed as a player while others continue on or may impact on their availability at the start of a game.

- Permit as far as is possible for players to drop out of a game in session without disrupting the experience for everyone else.
- Formally permit resetting, redistribution, or reallocation of resources that a departing player may have gathered.
- Consider the use of automata that can be put in place for a player who may need some time away from a game but intends to come back.
- Include a mid-game 'quick start' option for players who arrive late to play.
- Limit the amount of contextual information within play that cannot be easily transferred between players, and formally allow within the rules for another player to 'sub in'.

Box and Insert Design

Aim for Consistency of Dimensions

Non-standard box sizes lead to non-standard storage solutions, and these can create inaccessibilities. My copy of **Gloomhaven**, for example, is in a cupboard behind some other stuff. **Kemet: Blood and Sand** is on top of a set of bookcases and needs a step-ladder to bring down. Both of these are physical inaccessibilities even if they are self-inflicted. For those with obsessive compulsive disorder (OCD) and other conditions, irregular box-sizes can trigger the compulsion to find an arrangement in which perfect order can be achieved and maintained, even when no such configuration exists.

- Consider the size of your boxes and aim for one of the 'standard' dimension forms.

- Try to ensure box text can be oriented in a way where symbols and text align consistently with other game boxes.
- When external standards for form factor, dimensions, or scale exist, try to conform to these as much as is possible.

Use Every Part of the Box

The box that a game comes in is an often neglected accessibility resource. Most are bare cardboard, and when an inlay is provided, it is often recessed to hold components rather than to aid in playability. A well-designed inlay can optimise table space, minimise setup and teardown time, and offer cognitive affordances that can help increase learnability. The humble board game box should take more of a starring role in game design.

- Your box is part of your user interface. Consider creative designs for the inlay to allow it to serve double duty – game storage **and** gameplay convenience.
- Ensure sufficient flex in a game insert so as to ensure tokens can be easily removed and returned.

Notes

1. https://bloodontheclocktower.com/accessibility
2. http://wrengames.co.uk/main/designing-to-be-inclusive/

10

Conclusion

I hope you have found this book to be useful, and it has inspired you to look for opportunities to make your games more accessible than they might have been before. Suffice to say, a book of this size and focus can only scratch the surface – we are all at the start of a long journey, and the path ahead has many obstacles. It also has many forks and twisty little passages, all alike. This topic remains largely unexplored – I do not intend for this to be the end of the conversation but rather the start of it. This is such a rich, interesting, and varied problem domain for accessibility that we may never get to the end of the trail. On the one hand, that's a sad realisation. On the other, it's profoundly exciting.

There's never been a better time to go exploring.

There are hundreds of topics I might have liked to have talked about in this book, but there just wasn't room. I would have liked to have spoken about how game manuals are the common shared inaccessibility in board gaming. I would have liked to have talked about the wider inaccessibility of the culture of hobbyist consumption. I would have liked to have written a bit about the public response to this work and the role of social advocacy that goes along with what was a largely academic research project. I would have loved to have spent a bit of time digging into board games as a tool for addressing social isolation and the controversy associated with my focus on the socioeconomic inaccessibility in the hobby. Much of this I have discussed a little bit on my blog, Meeple Like Us, but there's always more. So much to talk about, and we have so few words in which to do it.

That all feels like a problem for a vainglorious bloviating academic like me, but really what this absence marks out is opportunity – a space I hope many others will start to occupy with their own thoughts and insights. This book is a capstone on eight years of research in a topic that for a long time received virtually no attention from players, publishers, and the wider hobby. No attention that is, except from those excluded by the absence of its consideration. There are positive signs that this is changing. I'm having conversations with people in the industry who were literally unthinkable as recently as 2020. This is a topic that is in the process of **becoming** – becoming something people care about, and importantly becoming something people are working towards improving.

One of my favourite sections to write in any paper is the further work section. There you get to theorycraft, outlining all the exciting ways the work could go if only one had the luxury of infinite time. It always occupies a paper as the brightest spot of the purest enthusiasm – the 'what if' of possibility.

Within the topic of board game accessibility, there is much future work to do. More than that though, there is future work needed to uncover the shape of what that future work should be, and that's something we get to do together. There is more ahead of us than behind. More to do than has been done. Miles to go before we sleep. It is my fondest hope that this book will encourage some of you to begin the journey and send back your observations to the rest of us. I hope to see you there on the trail. Please do say 'hi' if you see me passing.

DOI: 10.1201/9781003415435-10

Index

Note: Locators in *italics* represent figures and **bold** indicate tables in the text.